CARS OF THE ROOTES GROUP

CARS OF THE ROOTES GROUP

GRAHAM ROBSON

MOTOR RACING PUBLICATIONS

MOTOR RACING PUBLICATIONS LTD
Unit 6, The Pilton Estate, 46 Pitlake, Croydon, CR0 3RY, England

First published 1990

ISBN 978 1 903088 29 6

Reprinted 2007
Mercian Manuals Ltd
353 Kenilworth Road
Balsall Common
Coventry
CV7 7DL

With the permission of the copyright holders
Graham Robson and Motor Racing Publications Ltd

Jacket Illustration: 1967 Humber Imperial.
Photograph courtesy of *Classic Cars* magazine

Photoset by Ryburn Typesetting Ltd, Halifax, West Yorkshire
Printed in Great Britain by The Amadeus Press Ltd
Huddersfield, West Yorkshire

Contents

Introduction

This is the first book to be written about the long and turbulent history of the Rootes Group – and I now know why! Other authors have set out on the same road, but have given up, daunted by the complications. Because the Group no longer exists, and there have been several changes of ownership and emphasis during the last 20 years, the continuity and sense of history has been lost.

Yet this was a story simply aching to be told. In the years before the 'classic' movement was founded, vintage-car enthusiasts dismissed every Rootes achievement with a sneer. The Family were branded as charlatans. How could *anyone*, they asked, convert honourable old companies like Hillman, Humber, Sunbeam and Talbot into assemblers of mass-produced machines and be proud of it?

Thank goodness the pendulum swung sharply in the other direction in the 1970s, when the classic car movement grew so rapidly. Most people now see Rootes as the saviour of several marques which would otherwise have died, and as the generator of thousands of jobs. Not only that, but 'Billy' and Reginald Rootes built up an astonishingly virile organization, one which produced many exciting and interesting cars and trucks, and was the pioneer in many product-planning, badge-engineering and marketing techniques.

Ever since the 1950s, when I began my working life in Coventry, I have been fascinated by the history, heritage and products of the Rootes Group, a dynasty which, following its birth, prospered and expanded mightily, then crashed into financial ruin, all within the space of 50 years.

For a few years, I maintained a tenuous connection with the Group as a co-driver in the Rootes works rally team, and after Chrysler had established total control of Rootes I worked for a time in the design and development areas of the business.

There are other Rootes-Robson connections, too. In the late 1950s and early 1960s, I rallied in Rapiers and Imps on many occasions, and for a period in 1960–61 I had business connections with a Rootes dealership in the Midlands. When I worked with *Autocar* magazine in Coventry in the 1960s, I must have spent hundreds of hours in and around the Rootes factories in order to describe new cars and test the finished products. I have owned several Rootes cars, ranging from Singer Vogue Estates to Humber Sceptres, Sunbeam Rapiers and a Hillman Avenger GLS, while my wife has owned a Hillman Super Imp and a Sunbeam Stiletto.

Soon after I started to write books, I vowed that eventually I would produce a history of the Group. For a while my chosen publishers (John Blunsden and Motor Racing Publications) were concerned by the complexity of the project, but fortunately the success of *The Cars of BMC* convinced us that this was the correct way to present the story.

Here, then, is my personal view of the life and times of a concern the foundations of which were laid in the 1920s, but which was finally squeezed out of business in 1970. As with my book on BMC, I hope that it is also a complete buyers' guide, or directory, of an interlinked series of cars built over a 40-year period.

Because the great car-making Group did not spring, ready-formed, into existence in the early 1930s, and because there was a long drawn out period in the 1960s when both Rootes *and* Chrysler could be said to have been in charge, I have had to make my own rules as to the cars which qualify as true Rootes products.

To give the story coherence, I have mentioned the products taken over by the Rootes family when they gained control of various companies, as well as those latterly built by Chrysler United Kingdom, but designed by Rootes. In general, however, the story of Rootes cars begins with the launch of the Hillman Wizard in 1931 and ends with the design of the Hillman Avenger in the mid-1960s.

As with BMC, it was clear that Rootes always had a Grand Design, so I have also thought it important to probe into the way that it sourced its bodies, laid down a series of engines, and cross-pollinated bodies, engines, marque badges and marketing images.

Summer 1989 GRAHAM ROBSON

Acknowledgements

Although the obvious way to begin the preparation of a book of this nature was to use my own records, then check a mountain of manufacturers' publicity material – and cross-check it against descriptions of new models published in those two magnificent magazines of record, *Autocar* and *Motor* – I needed a lot of extra help to get a complete Rootes picture.

In the beginning, it was *Classic Cars* and its stylish treatment of my four-part Rootes Group history which encouraged me to expand it into a full-scale book. W.E. 'Bill' Hancock's recollections, sent to me later, also spurred me on.

Peter Wilson, for whom I worked at Rootes over a three-year period, and Roy Axe, chief stylist at the same time, have both dug deep into their memories over the years.

Jon Pressnell, of *Classic & Sportscar*, read carefully through the manuscript, corrected my mistakes and made many helpful suggestions.

Leon Gibbs allowed me to consult his extensive Rootes records and to cross-check my own findings.

John Rowe (a long-time Rootes PR chief) provided valuable financial and production records.

Stephen Lewis and David Clark, of the Post-Vintage Humber Car Club, provided many facts and figures regarding Humber and checked over the appropriate manuscript.

Simon Worland and David Freeth, of the Singer Owners' Club, provided production figures and read the appropriate manuscript.

Chris Barker, of the Sunbeam-Talbot Alpine Register, not only provided pictures, but read through the section on Sunbeams; the Rolls-Royce public relations departments in London and Bristol pointed me in his direction to find those fascinating Bristol-Siddeley photographs.

Keith Draper and the *Coventry Evening Telegraph* Reference Library allowed me to dig back into the local news of the 1940s–70s period.

Anders Clausager, of the BMIHT, helped me with Rootes facts related to the Pressed Steel Co Ltd.

Anthony Blight's magnificent book about the Talbot marque helped me to sort out fact from fiction as far as the early 1930s is concerned, while the reference section of the Coventry Library has many maps, books and other records in its possession which proved invaluable.

On the other hand, I regret that for personal reasons the second Lord Rootes and his distinguished public relations director John Bullock both declined to see me or to provide me with information. Similarly, although company records covering the postwar years of the Rootes Group are known to have been preserved by Peugeot-Talbot, they were not made available to me.

The 'typical performance' figures quoted in the data tables are all based on road test information published over many years in *Autocar* and *Motor,* magazines which have now been merged into the authoritative *Autocar & Motor*. I am happy to acknowledge that without their testers' magnificent dedication it would have been impossible to provide such accurate information.

As to all the illustrations – including the 'record' pictures which accompany each of the model descriptions – I started with my own collection, added that of my publisher, plundered the records of Richard Langworth (my personal 'American connection'), and then started to fill in the gaps.

I would like to thank the following specialists for helping me to build up a complete record: Michael Allen; Jon Pressnell, of the Haymarket Photo Library; Anders Clausager, of the British Motor Industry Heritage Trust (for Pressed Steel archive shots); Dave Turner; Stephen Lewis, of the Post-Vintage Humber Car Club; Mirco Decet; Roy Axe; Talbot expert Anthony Blight; Peter Henshaw (the Imp expert); Chris Barker, Malcolm Hepple and my friends at the *Coventry Evening Telegraph*; Vernon Cox, Simon Worland and the Singer Owners' Club; David Burgess-Wise; the Hillman Register; and the National Motor Museum.

Thank you, one and all.

GRAHAM ROBSON

Chapter 1

Rootes

A powerful motoring family

Our story begins at Station Road, Hawkhurst, in Kent, a village 15 miles north of Hastings, where William Rootes (senior) had a cycle shop. Two sons were born to the Rootes family – William Edward in 1894, and Reginald Claud in 1896. Although it was only 50 miles from London, Hawkhurst was in truly rural surroundings – no place, one would think, for future captains of industry to be born.

William Rootes, however, wanted his sons to have a good start in life, so he sent them off to be educated at Cranbrook school, just a few miles away. Meanwhile, as his business prospered, he became interested in the new-fangled motor car trade and he set up a motor agency business in Hawkhurst. By 1914, this one company held agencies for a multitude of motor cars, including Ford, Morris, Wolseley, Itala, Delaunay Belleville, Briton, FN and Metallurgique, as well as Darracq, Humber, Singer and Sunbeam.

When they left school, neither son showed any interest in going straight into the family business, so young William – 'Billy' as he was always known to his friends – was sent off to Coventry by his father to become a penny-an-hour pupil at Singer Motors. He joined Singer in 1909, just a few years after the first car to carry that name had appeared, and soon he became enthralled by the whole motoring business – building, selling and running the cars. In 1913, he returned south to Maidstone to run a new branch of his father's business.

During the First World War, however, Billy joined the navy, became a lieutenant in the RNVR, then was demobilized in 1917 to begin working in an aero-engine repair facility in Maidstone, which was not far from his home. Along the way he found time to marry Nora in 1916; his eldest son, Geoffrey (who would later become the Chairman of Rootes in succession to his famous father and his uncle), was born in 1917.

After he had left school, Reginald trained as an accountant and started out on a civil servant's career with the Admiralty. However, the two brothers got together immediately after the war, when Billy persuaded Reginald to join forces with him. Each was presented with a cheque for £1,200 from his father; they then set out to develop a new company, Rootes Ltd, from a base in Maidstone. It was the first of several different companies to carry the Rootes name, most of which seemed to trade with each other from time to time.

Each brother soon developed his strengths – William as the salesman, the ideas man, and Reginald as the calm administrator, who made sure that the business followed on logically after William's bright ideas had taken shape.

As his 1930s PR chief Dudley Noble once wrote when comparing their characters, they were: 'a perfect pair in the business sense – Billy seeing the visions on the horizon and striding towards them in, so to speak, seven league boots; Reggie surveying the intervening ground with his keen and calculating eye and making sure that no loose ends in whatever project was afoot were left untied.'

In 1958, another observer wrote that Billy was: 'short, stocky and walks with an eager, bouncy stride that is almost a gallop', while Reginald: 'is taller, slimmer and has a tread that is softly firm and discreet. They are the Hobbs and Sutcliffe [a one-time famous opening partnership for the England cricket team] of the motor industry.'

Or, as Billy himself once remarked: 'I am the engine and Reginald is the steering and brakes of the business.'

The Rootes brothers – particularly Billy – had great ideas, and after weathering the early 1920s slump in

The first Lord Rootes, the powerhouse behind the Rootes Group from the 1920s until his death in 1964. After he had gone, the Group rapidly lost its impetus.

British car sales they formed Rootes Distributors, moved into London and picked up the important business of distributing Austin cars in London and the Home Counties. At first, their showrooms were located in Long Acre and Bond Street.

Even in the early 1920s Rootes was expanding rapidly. In 1924, it took a stake in the Birmingham-based garage chain of George Heath, then followed it by a stake in Warwick Wright, of London. The first significant *industrial* move, however, which signalled a widening of Billy's interests, came in 1925 when Rootes took control of the prestigious and long-established London coachbuilding business of Thrupp & Maberly.

Billy, in the meantime, having made his first visit to the USA in 1919, had become a regular voyager on the great transatlantic liners and a real expert on North American manufacturing and distribution methods.

Even at this stage, it seems, Billy had begun to formulate his master plan – he wanted eventually to control companies making several different makes of car, as well as companies making the car bodies and companies which distributed the finished products. He did not want to set up new businesses for this purpose, but to take over established concerns with respected names, perhaps those which were no longer as prosperous as they might be – in other words, those which *might* be amenable to takeover or rescue at an appropriate price. But that was in the mid-1920s. The jigsaw did not truly take shape until the 1950s, when Rootes' final purchase – that of Singer – took place.

In the meantime, the Rootes head office was moved into truly palatial premises in Piccadilly, just across the road from the famous Ritz Hotel. This was Devonshire House, the building from which the Rootes Group would be directed for the next four decades.

Since 1666, an elegant Jacobean town house (originally named Berkeley House, but renamed Devonshire House in 1698), stood on the corner of Berkeley Street and Piccadilly, but after the First World War it lay empty for some years. The Duke of

Devonshire soon sold out, demolition of the gracious old house began in 1925, and in its place came an impressive new office building.

When Rootes moved into a major part of the new building in September 1926, the rest of the motor trade was astonished, and it wondered if the brash Billy had finally over-stepped himself. As *The Motor* columnist wrote: 'this rather staggered the retail trade'. At this time, after all, Billy was still only 32 years old, and Reginald was 30.

Before the opening, however, *The Autocar* was more impressed and commented:

'What are claimed to be Europe's finest motor showrooms are to be opened on 22 September at Devonshire House, Piccadilly, W1, by Rootes Ltd. Apart from the spaciousness of these showrooms, which occupy the corner of the basement, ground and first floors of the huge new building, the general scheme of decoration is superb.'

A week later, *The Autocar* came back with a longer comment:

'The Society of Motor Manufacturers & Traders will have to look to their laurels if the present epidemic of building palatial new showrooms becomes chronic! The latest example is that part – two huge floors and an equally immense basement, to be exact – of the new Devonshire House, Piccadilly, W1, which was opened last Tuesday as the showrooms and offices of Rootes Ltd and Thrupp & Maberly, famous respectively for motor cars and carriage work. To walk through these magnificent showrooms and to have there a chance of examining at leisure the latest things in Rolls-Royce, Daimler, Austin, Fiat and Clyno cars, to mention but a selection with standard bodies or with Thrupp & Maberly special 'creations', is almost as instructive as, and far more agreeable than, to fight one's way foot by foot around Olympia! Unquestionably, no good American and no conscientious visitor from the provinces will consider he has 'done' London properly unless he has strolled round the Rootes – Thrupp & Maberly section of Devonshire House.'

By this time, for sure, Billy was consumed with the urge to build up the manufacturing side of Rootes Ltd. He had started the 1920s by acquiring a stake in Standard, but this came to nothing and was eventually sold off. In the beginning, he could not raise enough capital, and even with the help of a powerful, cash-rich ally in the form of the Prudential Assurance Company (which was to remain associated with Rootes until the 1960s), he was unable to complete either the projected takeover of the Wolverhampton-based Clyno concern in 1927, or a second assault on the Coventry-based Standard concern. Rootes Ltd was the largest distributor and exporter of Clyno cars at the time, but when the company turned to other more vital projects, its interest in Clyno waned and that famous name soon disappeared.

Sir Reginald Rootes (left) and Sir William Rootes (right), together, as on so many occasions, in Devonshire House, in London's Piccadilly.

Billy's real chance – it must have been fate – came in the late 1920s when two neighbouring Coventry car makers – Humber and Hillman – both struck trouble and decided that a merger was the only solution to their problems. Even before the merger was made public, Rootes (and 'The Pru') had taken an interest, but it was the merger itself which launched Rootes Ltd on the way to becoming one of Britain's Big Six car makers.

Hillman and Humber before the merger

Both Hillman and Humber had been set up in Victorian times, when the cycling boom inspired Coventry to transform its industrial base. William Hillman, a young engineer from Greenwich, had joined John Kemp Starley in producing pedal cycles in the 1870s, but later he drifted off to found his own concern, Auto Machinery, to build his own pedal cycles. This company expanded mightily, such that by the end of the 1890s William Hillman was a millionaire.

Having bought a home in what were then the eastern outskirts of Coventry – Abingdon House, in Stoke Aldermoor – he laid plans to build a car factory in the grounds which fronted on to what we now know as Humber Road, but was then called Folly Lane. The very first Hillman car, actually a Hillman-Coatalen (because

Devonshire House, in Piccadilly, West London, built in the mid-1920s, and serving as the Rootes headquarters for more than 40 years. The showrooms were on the ground floor, the executive offices immediately above them. This was a mid-1960s picture in a strangely deserted London!

of the identity of its designer), was launched in 1907, but production was very limited before the First World War.

In the 1920s, Hillman developed slowly and cautiously, with a new building added alongside the original to increase the company's manufacturing space. The 11hp model of 1915 was gradually improved, but not significantly modernized, throughout the vintage period and became the 14hp model for 1926. Ten years after the Armistice, Hillman was still building the same type of chassis. It was still a company entirely controlled by the Hillman family.

By the late 1920s, William Hillman had withdrawn from day-to-day management and his joint managing directors were Captain John Black and Spencer B. Wilks, both of whom would become even more famous in later years. Each, incidentally, had married one of William Hillman's daughters! Surprisingly, for its next new car, Hillman chose to introduce a much larger, more complex and costly eight-cylinder model called the Straight Eight. Naturally enough, this was new from end to end – new engine, gearbox, axle, suspension and body styles. Previewed in 1928, but not to go on sale until 1929, just at the time when Britain's motor industry output was starting to decline, it was a *very* brave project to conceive.

Thomas Humber had started up a general workshop in Sheffield in the 1860s, but by the 1870s he was building pedal cycles in Nottingham and Beeston and would soon have a third plant in Wolverhampton. A fourth plant in Whitefriars Lane, Coventry, followed in 1889. The first motorcycles were built in 1895, but in 1896 the company rather precariously set out to make Bollee tri-cars in Lower Ford Street, Coventry.

The first Humber car (built in 1899) was produced at Beeston, but the first Louis Coatalen-designed 'Coventry-Humber' followed early in the 1900s. A new factory was built in Folly Lane, a little further north (and up the hill) from the new Hillman plant, and by 1908 it was not only producing cars, but Coatalen had defected to Hillman, and the road had been renamed Humber Road.

An important personality, Lt Col J.A. Cole, joined the Humber board in 1912. After the First World War, he became chairman and saw the publicly-owned company expanding and joining the takeover trail. In 1926, in fact, Humber Ltd bought up the commercial vehicle manufacturers Commer, based in Luton.

The urge to merge – Rootes move in

By 1927, neither Hillman nor Humber was in a very comfortable financial position. Each was making less than 5,000 cars a year, and neither seemed to be willing (or apparently able) to invest in modernization. Humber, in fact, was making losses by 1928.

Published accounts of what happened next are sparse and variable, for the Rootes family has always declined to provide full details.

The original Hillmans were built under William Hillman's control, and designed by Louis Coatalen, here seen at the wheel of a 1907 model.

Before the First World War, Humber had designed twin-ohc racing cars to take part in the Tourist Trophy race, but there were to be no such flights of fancy under Rootes direction – and anyway the marque was better known for more staid products like this 1923 8/18 model, below. By the end of the 1920s Humber was controlled by Rootes, but was still making a few graceful tourers like this example, below right, pictured at Angmering-by-Sea in the 1950s.

A Rootes publicity leaflet published in 1950 states that Rootes Securities Ltd: 'acquired, in 1928, an interest in Humber Ltd, which already had control of Commer Cars Ltd....These two companies were then merged with the Hillman Motor Co Ltd....'

On the other hand, a Chrysler United Kingdom Ltd leaflet, published in 1977, states that: 'In 1927, the Rootes brothers acquired an interest in the Hillman Car Company, and this was quickly followed by a similar interest in Humber Ltd....'

According to that doyen of British motoring journalism, Maurice Platt, Rootes had secretly secured control of Humber before turning their attention to

Geoffrey Rootes, son of 'Billy' Rootes, became managing director of Humber Ltd in the 1950s and 1960s, and eventually succeeded to the title, as the second Lord Rootes, in 1964.

Hillman, the marriage being suggested to them by A.C. Armstrong, who was at that time editor of *The Motor* and Platt's boss. Yet more sources suggest that the first injection of Rootes/Prudential capital did not take place until 1929, which was *after* the merger. Confusing!

One fact, however, is clear – Hillman and Humber merged at the end of 1928, and it now seems that Rootes Ltd (aided by 'The Pru') were already intriguing for influence, a merger and ultimate control. It seems to be agreed, however, that Rootes had complete control and that Humber Ltd was a wholly-owned manufacturing subsidiary from 1932.

Since everyone concerned seemed to have very strong characters, no-one should be surprised that William Hillman retired (he died two years later), while Capt Black and Spencer Wilks left the combine soon after it was formed; John Black soon joined Standard, Spencer Wilks joined Rover, and both achieved remarkable things with their new companies. The only truly 'top' personality to survive was Lt Col Cole. When Humber Ltd became the manufacturing subsidiary for *all* Rootes cars, he remained as chairman, and did not retire until 1943, at the ripe old age of 75.

Under the headline 'Humber and Hillman combine', this is how *The Autocar* reported the merger announcement:

'A merger of two leading Coventry works, which has as its object economies of purchase, general administration and production methods, was announced this week....The fact that the Hillman and Humber works are in juxtaposition has long given rise to rumours of amalgamation, and now, subject to the approval of Humber shareholders, the amalgamation is an accomplished fact....The factory facilities of this new group extend to approximately 80 acres....*The Autocar* is informed that the Humber and Hillman cars will continue to bear their separate identities, the manufacturing resources of the companies will be pooled for their general good......An important decision announced simultaneously with the merger...is that the export activities in their entirety will be undertaken by Rootes Ltd, whose world-wide organization is responsible for the growing popularity of Hillman cars in overseas markets.'

Note, incidentally, that at merger time there was still no public word about Rootes having a stake, or even an interest, in this merger! Nevertheless, as soon as the new combine started operations, the Rootes brothers began to call all the shots.

Making sense of the merger – 1929 to 1931

Perhaps this part of the Rootes story has never properly been told before. Billy Rootes, having made several visits to the USA, and being impressed with what Alfred Sloan was doing at General Motors, knew exactly what he wanted to achieve. Now, with the backing of Prudential Assurance and the huge selling network of UK and overseas-based businesses which Rootes had established, he could put it into effect.

All in all, Rootes had to make sense of a real mish-mash of models, factories and old tooling. In the beginning, Billy had to grit his teeth and carry on building the cars which Hillman and Humber had already launched, or were about to produce, but these would be cast aside as soon as practicable. In the beginning, of course, he was not able to promote the sale of true 'Rootes-Hillmans' or 'Rootes-Humbers'.

From the autumn of 1929, therefore, the Olympia stands showed off the established Hillman 14 and Straight Eight, the Humber 9-28, 16-50 and 20-65 models and the new 25-70 Snipe, which had an enlarged version of the 20-65hp model's engine. In the spring of 1930, to stimulate demand and counter some of the effects of depression, price cuts were announced.

Rationalization and expansion, however, was already under way. Billy, it seems, wanted to see a new range of cars produced, but was not at all impressed by the design talent which he had inherited. Accordingly, he went out and head-hunted his new chiefs.

The first appointment was a real surprise. Capt Jack Irving had made his name in the design of three successful Land Speed Record cars – the 1926 Sunbeam, the twin-engined 1,000hp Sunbeam of 1927 and the Irving-Napier (more familiarly known as *Golden Arrow*) of 1929. The last car had been bodied by Thrupp & Maberly, who also paid for the job, and presumably this is how Billy met Irving.

After *Golden Arrow* had successfully raised the record, Capt Irving was persuaded to join Humber-Hillman at the

This early 1960s study of the five members of the Rootes family who controlled the fortunes of the Group throughout the 1950s and early 1960s brings together (left to right) Sir Reginald, Geoffrey, Lord Rootes (then Sir William), Timothy, and Brian.

end of 1929 to act as technical chief of the new combine.

The poaching of Alfred Wilde from Standard was more logical. Wilde had been chief designer for Morris Engines in Coventry until 1927, when he moved to Standard to produce the very successful and ultra-reliable Standard Nine. At the end of 1930, however, Rootes announced: 'the Humber-Hillman combine are about to embark on the production of a small car at a popular price....', and that Wilde was moving across to Rootes to collaborate with Jack Irving.

Reputedly, too, he was delighted to do this in order to get away from John Black (the ruthless and egotistical Black seemed to have that effect on a lot of people....). Unhappily, he died suddenly at the end of 1931, just as his influence on future Rootes cars was becoming obvious. He was only 41 years old.

By this time, Billy Rootes had established his master plan. He wanted to see three new model families developed as soon as possible to take over from almost all the old-fashioned Hillmans and Humbers. Each of the new types was intended to sell in large numbers, and each had to be simpler, less costly and more ruggedly reliable than the cars they would replace.

These three cars, of course, were to be the small Minx, the medium-sized Humber 12hp and the large Hillman Wizard, though they were not launched in that order. They were all to have simple side-valve engines, a choice of bodies (but in each case based on standard steel saloon styles from Pressed Steel and special coachwork from Thrupp & Maberly), and they were meant to be attractive to export (which really meant Empire) customers. Reginald Rootes was installed as managing director, and Harold Heath became works director.

By the spring of 1930, the spending on new facilities at Humber Road was becoming obvious. *The Autocar* visited Humber in April to find that production was reputedly at an all-time peak – 200 cars a week were being planned for the near future – the magazine noting that 3,000 people were employed on site, that the machine shop measured 280ft by 210ft (almost football field size) and that many new machine tools had recently been installed.

A few weeks later, Rootes let it be known that the two factories were to be unified. New machine tools, worth £700,000, were being installed, and by March 1931 the Rootes brothers were expecting capacity to be up to 100 cars a day, 25,000 cars a year.

The first of the new-generation Humber-Hillman cars, the Hillman Wizard, made its bow in May 1931. The Rootes Group was on its way.

Chapter 2

Rootes Group – the early years

Hillman, Humber, Sunbeam and Talbot before the Second World War

If the Rootes Group was conceived and born in the 1920s, it grew up in the 1930s. It came to manhood and established a fine reputation in World War Two, but full maturity was delayed until the 1950s and 1960s.

In the first decade, annual car sales rose from 8,762 in 1930 to nearly 50,000 in 1938. The financial turnaround was achieved painfully at first, but once the depression eased and the massive initial investment in new models had been made it became more rapid.

For the year ending August 31, 1928, Humber had announced a trading loss of £36,806 (Hillman's performance at this time was not revealed as it was a privately owned company). In the next financial year (11 months actually, for the cut-off was brought forward to July 31 to commonize with other company accounts) the recently enlarged Humber Ltd lost £67,158.

A year later (year ending July 31, 1930), Humber Ltd reported a trading profit of £42,275, but in 1930–31, as Britain slumped into the worst of its trade depression, a loss of no less than £96,156 had to be reported.

Rootes Ltd was the official majority shareholder by 1931 (but had already been masterminding the recovery plan for two years), and a capital reorganization proposed in June 1932 completed the changeover. At this point, the board of directors comprised Col Cole as chairman, Billy Rootes as deputy chairman, Reginald Rootes as managing director and Viscount Ratendone and W.H. Johnson as non-executive directors.

In the year ending July 31, 1932, Humber Ltd reported a loss of £107,840, but by this time the depression was lifting, car sales were recovering – and the Hillman Minx had gone on sale. From this point on, Humber Ltd began to make regular and increasing profits and within four years it was to report an annual surplus of £241,886.

As far as the press and the public were concerned, Rootes could do no wrong during the next 30 years. Traditional-minded motoring enthusiasts might not always have liked the changes which Billy Rootes made to the marques which he bought up, and the labour unions sometimes fought hard against the working conditions imposed on them, but in general the Group prospered and continued to grow. Wealth and jobs were created, whereas it seems certain the constituent companies, had they been left independent, would have died within a very short time.

The modern Rootes Group, as opposed to Hillman-Humber, was effectively launched in a flourish on April 27, 1931, when a thousand VIPs in London's Albert Hall saw the symbolic export packing cases lifted off seven new Hillman Wizards. Rootes hoped that this 'Car for the Moderns' was to be the first of many successes for its new car-building operation.

There was a long way to go, yet Billy and Reginald – one the visionary, the other patiently making sure that the visions could be turned into practical achievements – were always pushing ahead towards the limits of the master plan. This was to produce a vertically integrated set of businesses, with Rootes factories building a range of cars and trucks, bodying them from Rootes-owned coachbuilding concerns, exporting them through Rootes-controlled networks, and finally selling them through Rootes-owned garage businesses.

Except for the acquisition of Tilling Stevens (in 1951) and Singer (1955–56) the shape of the Rootes Group was effectively settled in the 1930s. These were the main events: Karrier (the Huddersfield-based commercial vehicle business) was bought in 1934; Sunbeam and Talbot were bought in 1935; Rootes became involved in the government Shadow Factory scheme in 1936; British Light Steel Pressings was bought in 1937; the second, extremely large, Shadow Factory at Ryton-on-Dunsmore was built in 1939–40.

Nowadays, of course, everyone realizes that it takes up to five years to bring an all-new car to market. There is, however, a fiction that in the 1930s new cars could be produced very quickly indeed, and certainly between one Olympia Motor Show and the next. It simply wasn't ever that simple.

All the evidence suggests that Rootes conceived its three-model master plan in 1929, but there was neither time, manpower, nor space to develop all three new models at once. Work began on the first of these, the Hillman Wizard, in 1929, on the original Hillman Minx in 1930, and on the Humber Twelve in 1931. The Wizard went on sale in 1931, the Minx in March 1932 and the Humber Twelve in the spring of 1933.

There were very few high-tech aids to designing and developing new cars at this time so, by any standards, here was a massive and ambitious undertaking. In the end, Rootes only achieved its goal by farming-out much of the tooling work to specialists.

In the space of three years, the Humber Road site in Coventry was rejigged, expanded and rationalized. New buildings were erected on the south side of the orginal Humber site so that machinery to make three completely new cast-iron side-valve engines – a small 1,185cc 'four' for the Minx, a medium-sized 1,669cc 'four' for the Humber Twelve and a 2,110/2,810cc 'six' for the Wizard – could be installed and new 'corporate' gearboxes and axles could be built.

The importance of these mechanical building blocks was not for what they could do immediately in the new cars, but because they enabled Rootes to relax the pressure for some years and turn to other more pressing matters. These engines, in fact, were Rootes' front-line passenger car units for the next 22 years (Minx), 34 years (Humber Twelve) and 22 years (Wizard)! In many cases they were the most successful, if not the most technically exciting, part of the cars which they powered. All served with great distinction in a number of models, not least in the machines churned out in their tens of thousands during the Second World War.

Of the specialist suppliers, Pressed Steel obtained the major contracts to build saloon bodies, Thrupp & Maberly and other smaller coachbuilders were to produce the higher-priced speciality shells (limousines, drop-head coupes, tourers and the like), while Rubery Owen was contracted to produce the range of chassis frames.

Each model family broke new ground. The Minx was the first truly small Hillman; the Wizard was the first six-cylinder-engined Hillman of the post-Great War period; and the Humber Twelve was the first new four-cylinder Humber engine for a decade.

One suspects that Billy (if not Reginald) Rootes firmly expected all his company's new designs to be successful, so it must have been something of a shock to discover that the public really did not like the Wizard very much. Even before the Minx was put on sale it was clear that the six-cylinder Wizard (like similar uninspired cars being produced by Austin and Morris) fell between too many stools.

It did not sell in the UK – maybe because of the way it was hyped. The sales catalogue gushed: 'The voice of the modern world can be heard on all sides calling out for still finer achievements at the hands of man – the striving of the modern world towards still greater beauty, towards still greater comfort and luxury in living – can be seen in all these great works of iron and steel.' It was not an attractive car with a known pedigree, it was too costly to licence every year (the horsepower tax was levied on a measure of piston area, which meant that small-engined cars always fared better than large-engined models) and it was slow and had a depressingly ordinary specification.

In export markets, even when fitted with the large engine, it had to fight very hard for sales against competition from American cars which, frankly, were often faster, just as strong, cheaper and better suited to local conditions. To quote that doyen of motoring historians, Michael Sedgwick: 'They offered nothing that a Chevrolet did not have except leather upholstery (unnecessary in the outback) and sliding roofs, which let in dust.'

The master plan, therefore, began to go wrong even before all three cars had been revealed, and the Wizard was only built as such for a couple of years. Reborn in September 1933 as the 16hp and 20-70 models, it struggled on until 1935, after which it was gently killed off and forgotten.

Except that the Hillman Minx was not immediately available for sale when launched in October 1931, there was never any doubt about its success. The first 10,000 were sold before the end of the 1932 model-year, and it trebled Humber-Hillman sales at a stroke. Here was the car which Rootes had always needed, and which neither Hillman nor Humber was previously able to sell. More for the home market than for export, it was a light, simple, economical and – above all – cheap 'Ten'. Even the car's name ('pert or mischievous', according to the dictionaries) was exciting in the rather prim, nudge nudge atmosphere of the stiff-necked 1930s. Thank goodness a proposal to call it the Witch (an alliterative relation to Wizard) was turned down.

It was typical of the sort of car which appealed to the ever-growing middle-class market in the UK. In almost

The original Hillman Minx of 1931 was a ruggedly simple car which opened up the British 10hp market and underpinned Rootes profitability for the next decade. This Saloon De Luxe version sold at £175.

every way, the original Minx was the Escort of the early 1930s, the type and size of car which depression-hit British buyers were buying in ever larger quantities. SMM&T statistics prove just how timely was the Minx's arrival. In 1930, only 9% of UK sales had been in the 9hp/10hp category, but a year later it had moved up to 14%. With the aid of the Minx, this leapt to 24% in 1932, to 34% a year later, and stayed at that level until the outbreak of war. One in three of those Tens, year on year, was a Minx.

Even by the standards of the day, the Minx was technically uninspired – separate chassis, leaf-spring suspension, cable-operated brakes, side-valve engine, non-synchromesh gearbox, upright styling – but above all, it offered very good value. When sales began in the spring of 1932, prices started at a mere £159 for the Family saloon, and there were five other slightly more costly models. Bumpers cost £2 10s (£2.50) extra, and a sliding roof just £4! Within two years, there was a four-speed gearbox option, a freewheel for the transmission and a facelift for 1934 models, followed by a new all-synchromesh gearbox for 1935 models.

Even though the new Minx faced serious competition from other models – the new Austin Ten at £155, the well-established Morris Ten at £165 – and from well regarded cars like the Standard Big Nine at £205, it never had any problem in establishing its reputation. In 1932, as in 1942, 1952 and 1962, a Minx was a standard-setter against which most competing cars were to be measured.

The third car in the master plan was the Humber Twelve (12hp), which made a surprisingly discreet entry on to the scene at the Olympia Motor Show in 1932. Rootes, by the way, were already well in to the 'model cocktail' business, for the new Humber had a Wizard-type gearbox and back axle at first, though later in life it was to lean on the Hillman Minx for its transmission. It did not go on sale until the spring of 1933, and even though it offered excellent value in its own sector (£265 for the Pressed Steel-bodied four-door saloon), it never seemed to make many headlines.

The Autocar, as you would expect from what was then a very reserved, middle-class and conservative magazine, reported favourably on the new car in its test, calling it a 'True De Luxe Model Among Smaller Saloons' and writing: 'It gets under way with a zest....in fact it is quite an exhilarating car to handle on the open road...' All this, mind you, with a top speed of a mere 65mph and a 0–50mph 'sprint' of 26sec.

It was going to take time, however, for Rootes to be

'Billy' Rootes had a flair for combining style with simplicity – the Talbot Ten of the late 1930s, after all, was little more than a Hillman Minx in sporting attire.

able to sweep the old models away and completely change the face of the Group. At the end of 1930, the unsuccessful Hillman Straight Eight became the Vortic – but it was still an awful and unreliable car. However, the ancient Humber 9-28 and 20-65 models were dropped.

A year later, at an Olympia Motor Show where the Minx was one of the stars, the Vortic still lingered on at reduced prices, while there were no important changes to the existing Humber 16-50 and 25-70 Snipe models. However, in 1932, four years after the Humber-Hillman-Rootes merger had taken place, there were more important developments to be seen at Olympia. With the Minx family car now established, Rootes added the rather dashing Aero Minx coupe and gave the Wizard a new chassis frame and engine modifications. There was also a new Humber 16-60 to replace the 16-50 (with a Wizard-family engine instead of the old overhead-inlet/side-exhaust Humber engine as well as a Wizard-style chassis frame).

Over the next two years, Rootes became confident that it had established and stabilized itself. It was time to produce varieties of the bread-and-butter cars, to indulge itself a little, and to use a few famous names and publicity stunts to hammer home the Rootes message.

This explains why the sleek but essentially under-powered Aero Minx came along for 1933 – a car which had not only a new short-wheelbase underslung chassis (where the back axle sat above, rather than underneath, the chassis side-members) and wire-spoke wheels, but also Thrupp & Maberly coachwork. Perhaps it was a touch impractical, but at £245 no-one was complaining.

Not only that, but in the spring of 1934 Rootes also revealed the Melody Minx, a de luxe saloon model which, according to *The Autocar*: '...embodies special refinement, and has been designed from the start as a radio-equipped model, at a price of £195'. This was probably the first car in the world to be sold with radio equipment as standard, actually supplied by Philco.

The RAC tested a Minx in April 1933 to see how far it could be driven for £5 5s (guineas!). Heavily laden with crew and luggage, the answer was from London to Land's End, to John O'Groats, to Edinburgh and beyond; the car completed 2,364.5 miles in 11 days at 36.5mpg. When it repeated the '5 guineas' test in 1934, the RAC chose a 20-70 seven-seater limousine, in which it covered 1,727 miles and reported a 21.4mpg fuel consumption figure.

Not only did HRH The Duke of York (who was to become King George VI in December 1936) buy a Humber Pullman limousine, so did the Queen of Norway and the Emir of Transjordan, while the show-business star Gracie Fields bought a Snipe limousine.

In corporate terms, however, there was something of a lull until 1934, when the Rootes brothers, backed as

This sort of elegance – from Talbot in the mid-1930s, pre-merger – could not be maintained by Rootes, who wanted to bring down prices and jack up sales.

Georges Roesch, B.B. Winter and Norman Garrad (left to right) examine the supercharged six-cylinder twin-ohc two-litre engine of the 1924 Grand Prix Sunbeam. While Rootes, as this picture indicates, were not averse to basking in the reflected glory of the past achievements of companies they absorbed, this kind of complex, specialized and expensive engineering had no place in their own plans, as Roesch, for one, discovered when technically advanced cars of the sort he had designed for Talbot were very quickly abandoned after the take-over. Under Winter's technical direction the Group stuck to much more prosaic designs, though Garrad, in his role as competition manager, helped to bring new glory to the Sunbeam name in the postwar years.

usual by the Prudential, once again set out to build up their empire. First of all, in 1934, they completed the purchase of Karrier, the commercial vehicle manufacturing concern from Huddersfield. That company's managing director, R.F. Clayton, promptly resigned and went off to run Tilling-Stevens of Maidstone. To invoke the 'isn't it a small world?' syndrome, Rootes would take over Tilling-Stevens in 1951....

Then, in 1935, Billy Rootes finally saw his chance of creating the 'British General Motors' concern. To do this, he pulled off the greatest *coup* of all by taking over the financially troubled British components of the STD (Sunbeam-Talbot-Darracq) combine! This French-based group was incompetently managed, had made no attempt to rationalize its various businesses and – worse, having borrowed heavily in 1924 to finance Louis Coatalen's motor racing ambitions – found itself in financial trouble in the early 1930s as the repayment period for the loans drew nearer. By the spring of 1933, Rootes, along with Prudential Assurance, had advanced STD a great deal of money to keep the businesses afloat, taking in exchange a Second Debenture against all the English assets. And there, with STD still floundering, they sat.

STD was a very unbalanced business. To quote Anthony Blight, from his monumental study of Talbot (*Georges Roesch and the Invincible Talbot*): 'The ground covered by Roesch in [his] inventions must have assured Clement Talbot Ltd an almost limitless future, but for one vital factor: their lack of self-determination. They were not their own masters in control of their destiny but were inextricably bound up with STD, whose fortunes by this time were near to total collapse.

A display mounted by Rootes dealers Heath & Wiltshire in the early 1930s, with potted palms and celebratory flags all but hiding various Minxes and Humbers of the period. The Rootes family brought a flair for salesmanship – some called it fun – into the business of marketing cars.

Nowhere else within the combine was there a hint of any activity to match the outburst of creation at Barlby Road....'

Although Talbot (under Georges Roesch), who built cars at Barlby Road, in Kensington, West London, was producing fine cars and making good profits, Sunbeam of Wolverhampton was losing a great deal of money, while Darracq was only a supplier of bodyshells and would stand or fall by what happened to Talbot.

Blight, once again, sums up admirably: 'Under these circumstances the creditors could no longer withhold action, and by the end of June [1934] STD was under final attack. The main assailants were the holders of the Ten Year Notes, due for repayment on September 30. They were doubly aggrieved, for even the borrowing from Rootes had been insufficient to allow their previous year's interest to be paid; and they now took steps to appoint a receiver of STD and its English assets secured under the notes. Through all the manoeuvrings which followed, Rootes Securities Ltd kept discreetly silent; they were content to rest on their Second Debenture, aware that events were moving swiftly in their favour and confident that the assets would be theirs before very long.'

Blight, who is a great and knowledgeable Talbot enthusiast, has always maintained that the very profitable Talbot concern should have been cut loose to secure its own future in 1935, but the Receiver would have none of this. Abruptly, in January 1935, it was announced that the Clement Talbot Ltd business had been sold to the Rootes Group. Within weeks, a magazine advertisement for Talbot proclaimed:

'A New Chapter....Rootes Securities Ltd has now undertaken control of the old established firm of Clement Talbot Ltd....Maintaining the same characteristics, but backed by new and energetic direction, Talbot will continue to occupy the pre-eminent position which it so richly deserves....'

Blight, on the other hand, succinctly described the process as 'Rape', and insisted that: 'Rootes....had absorbed Talbots for an unconstructive reason – simply to enable their Humbers to regain the market which they had been unable to hold on merit', and suggests that everything which Rootes did to Barlby Road was unjustified and should never have happened. I agree with this *and* disagree with it. What happened to Talbot's heritage, and the splendid Roesch-engined cars themselves, was a tragedy. What happened to the Talbot marque, in Sunbeam-Talbot, was one of the most obvious badge-engineering success stories in the British motor industry.

Rootes, for sure, wanted Talbot as an extra marque to add to its collection along the way to fulfilling Billy's British General Motors dream, and it did not want to persevere with the Roesch-designed cars for long. Talbot staff (and particularly the proud Roesch himself) soon discovered that Rootes would not authorize major new capital programmes. Existing models were to be continued as long as parts were available and then, where possible, these were to be replaced by cheaper Hillman or Humber parts.

Roesch was taken over by Rootes as part of Talbot's assets and was soon asked to glamorize certain Rootes models. His first effort was to turn the Aero Minx into

The Talbot stand at the Olympia Motor Show in 1936, with old-style Talbots and Rootesified Talbots nestling rather uneasily together. The change in the marque's identity under its new owners was to culminate in the coining of a new title, Sunbeam-Talbot, in 1938.

Cause for celebration: the 10,000th 'Minx Magnificent' rolling off the assembly line at Humber Road early in 1936, less than six months after the model had been launched. The chairman of Humber Ltd, Col J.A. Cole (grey hair and large moustache) looks on.

the Talbot 10 and his second was to create a magnificent new 4.5-litre eight-cylinder engine to power a new Sunbeam Thirty flagship.

The sale of STD's Sunbeam business, on the other hand, caused a great deal more public controversy. Late in 1934, the Receiver had already sold off the trolley-bus business to Rootes, which renamed it Sunbeam Commercial Vehicles almost at once. When the cars side of the business was put on the market by the Receiver, the first important suitor to make a bid was the Coventry-based machine-tool company of Alfred Herbert Ltd. This company soon agreed that if the deal went through, it would then sell the car assets to William Lyons at SS Cars Ltd, also of Coventry. One contemporary press statement was that: 'SS Cars will take over the name, goodwill and patents of the Sunbeam Motor Company Ltd, and will produce a range of Sunbeam cars at their modern factory in Coventry.'

Then, at the beginning of July 1935, everyone was cast into confusion. The *Birmingham Post*'s story read: 'Enquiries in Coventry yesterday failed to clarify the position regarding the reported sale of the assets of the Sunbeam Motor Car Company Ltd....'

Almost overnight, it seemed, the Rootes Group, backed by its powerful financial interests, had moved in and swept up Sunbeam from under the noses of Alfred Herbert and Jaguar. William Lyons, it is said, never forgave the Rootes Group for that. Rootes, in fact, had no intention of building any more existing-design Sunbeam cars, was already merging the trolley bus business with Commer, and in the 1940s this Wolverhampton factory would eventually be acquired by Guy. Rootes, in fact, was initially only interested in keeping the Sunbeam trademark to use in the future.

The calendar year 1935 was one of the most active which Rootes ever faced. To take over Talbot, then Sunbeam, and then to begin the integration of the businesses, one would have thought, was quite enough activity for one year. However, Billy Rootes obviously didn't think so because the same year the company's

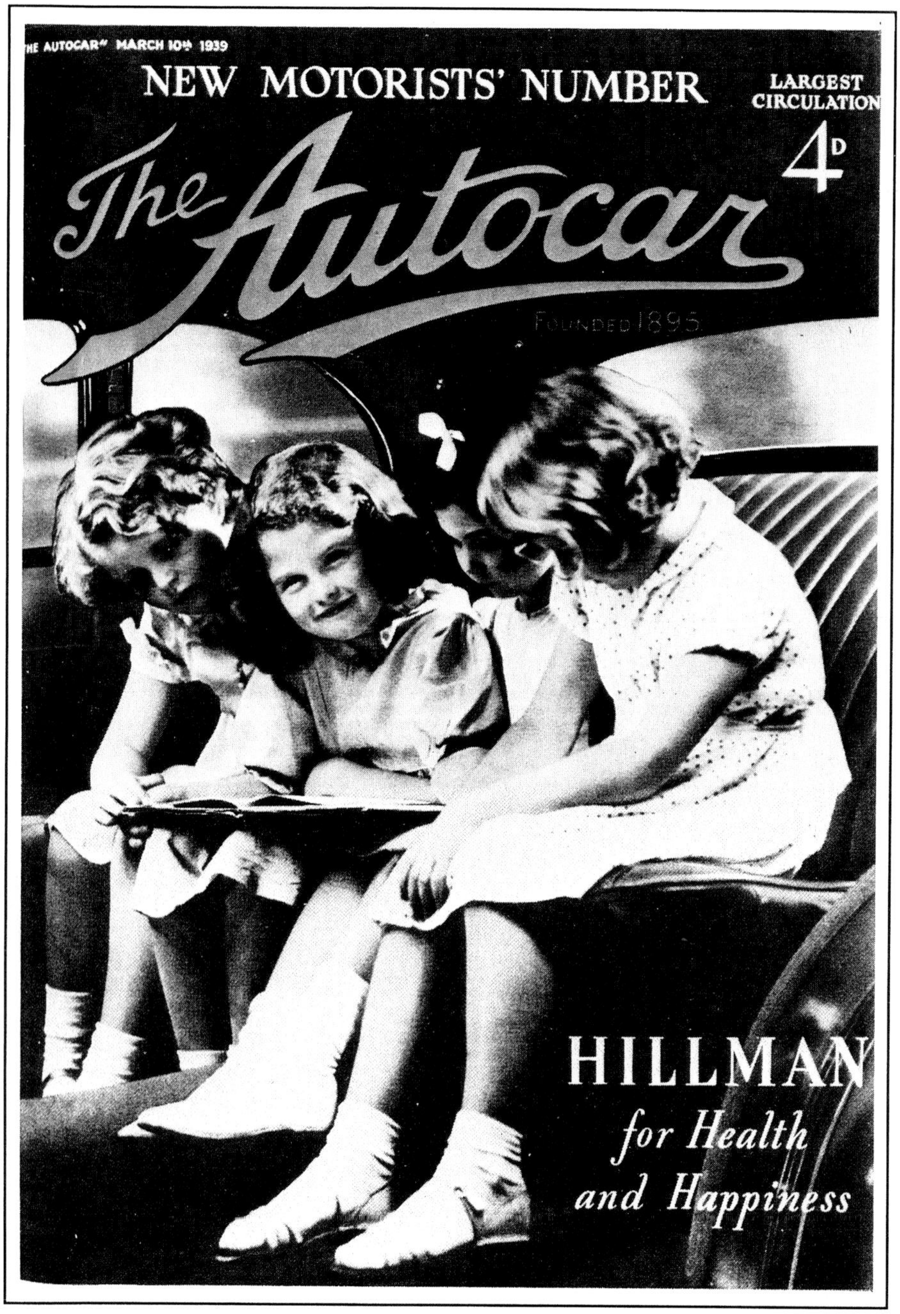

Were they serious? This is how Rootes were advertising the Hillman range on the front cover of *The Autocar* in March 1939. The car, presumably, is a Hillman 14hp model.

share capital was increased by the issuing of 600,000 new 5% Preference shares and two entirely new model families were launched!

Technically, 1935 was a watershed year for Rootes. Until then, the cars had been extremely conventional, and even the series-production body styling had been bought in from Pressed Steel without much influence from Rootes itself. At the Olympia Motor Show in 1935, though, there was not only a new, smoother-shaped and completely individual second-generation Minx (the 'Magnificent' variety), but a whole new family of medium and large-sized Hillmans and Humbers, all with a chassis featuring Evenkeel independent front suspension, also with new Pressed Steel saloon styles.

Of Evenkeel, one wag later suggested it was: 'more independent than suspension', so approximate was the geometry provided. This, mark you, was despite the attentions of bright young engineers like William Heynes (who moved from Humber to SS in the spring of

1935) and Alec Issigonis, who also moved away, later to join Morris Motors with altogether more spectacular results.

Not only that, but Roesch had duly waved his wand to turn the Aero Minx into the Talbot 10, while the first 'Rootesification' of large Talbots (which now shared some panels with the larger Humbers) was also evident.

Nor was there any pause for breath, for after celebrating the building of 10,000 new Minx Magnificent cars in four months, and 20,000 by May 1936, the company also opened a small tarmac test track in the grounds of the Humber Road factory and set Georges Roesch to designing the magnificent Sunbeam Thirty, which was exhibited, but never put into production.

By this time, Adolf Hitler had come to power in Germany, the war clouds were already beginning to gather on the horizon, and the British government finally decided to re-arm. One of its major moves was to expand production of aircraft and aero engines, and to do this it set up the shadow factory scheme. This did not mean that factories would be camouflaged, but that a replica of existing production facilities would be set up – the aim being to create a second image, or shadow, of the original.

In 1936, a number of the motor industry's leading concerns – Rootes, Austin, Daimler, Rover and Standard – got together to shadow the production, first of Bristol Mercury and later of Bristol Pegasus aero engines. It was to be a complex deal, with some businesses building components and Austin assembling the complete engines. Each would build a new factory close to its existing car plants, for which the government would provide funds, the financial reward being an annual fee of £50,000 and £75 for each completed engine. Lord Austin became chairman of the Shadow Factories Committee.

Billy Rootes thought this was a marvellous idea, and immediately agreed to join the scheme. In 1937, a new factory block, the Stoke Aldermoor complex, was erected on the Humber Road site and the first aero engines were completed in December 1938.

By this time, Phase 2 of the shadow factory scheme was also under way, with the motor industry now being invited to build complete aircraft. Rootes' part in this is described in the next chapter.

Between 1937 and 1939, Rootes took several other well-planned steps to complete its integrated business. In 1937, a little known pressings company, British Light Steel Pressings, was taken over. As this company was next door to the old ex-STD Darracq bodybuilding business, it meant that more space and expertise could be allocated to building bodyshells. At first for a new

Bernard ('B.B.') Winter, who was technical director of Rootes from the late 1930s to the end of the 1950s: his conservative approach to engineering loyally reflected Rootes family policy.

generation of Sunbeam-Talbots, but in later years for other Rootes Group car and commercial vehicle bodies, BLSP was a valuable addition to the conglomerate.

1937, too, was the year in which the 100,000th Minx was built (there was a suitable publicity-generating celebration cake to be cut when the facelifted 1938 model was announced), and it was also time for the arrival of the Evenkeel-suspended Hillman 14hp model. Not only was the new 14hp car significant in itself, it was also the founding member of a Humber model family which was lastingly successful in postwar years.

By this time, Captain Jack Irving was long gone (he joined Bendix, Lucas' brake-manufacturing subsidiary, in 1932), while Bernard Winter (always known as 'B.B.') had become director of engineering of the Rootes

Group (he joined the Rootes Securities board in 1947). It was a job which he was to occupy with distinction, but no great fame, until the end of the 1950s. 'B.B.' was a loyal Rootes man who always reflected what the family wanted rather than encouraged his engineers to stretch themselves. Originally he had worked for Ford in India, he joined Rootes as chief service executive in 1923, later became service manager in Coventry, and did not move to engineering until 1935. He was not a born, nor an intuitive designer. Perhaps this explains why several accomplished designers left Rootes before they were suffocated by the limited aspirations of the Winter regime.

For a whole generation, Rootes tended to make conservatively engineered cars with good looks, which confirmed the way that Billy in particular wanted to see them. To him the style of a car was much more important than what was under the attractive skin. Perhaps this explains why the Minx lost its first-gear synchromesh in 1938 – you couldn't see it, you couldn't attract customers into a showroom with it, and by the way, none of Rootes' rivals had such a feature....

It also explains how Rootes, with Billy the long-time expert after his multitude of trips across the Atlantic, had become adept about producing great variety from a very restricted range of major components. One oft-quoted statistic is that Rootes reduced an early-1930s line-up of dozens of engines and chassis and more than 50 body styles to an integrated range, for 1940, of two Hillmans, five Humbers and four Sunbeam-Talbots by using only three different engine families, two gearbox/axle families, three basic chassis and three mass-production body styles. Even Henry Ford would have been impressed....

There was no advance warning of the announcement of the new Sunbeam-Talbot marque in August 1938, for

World War Two 1939–1945

When World War Two began in September 1939, the Rootes Group was already involved in the expanding war effort. When it ended, nearly six years later, Rootes contribution was seen to be truly massive. Yet, as Billy Rootes later stated: 'At the time we had not the slightest knowledge of the aircraft industry, and no small sacrifice was involved. We diverted some of our best executives and most skilled craftsmen just when competition in the car industry was at its fiercest....'

Rootes publicists summed this up in no uncertain manner – in 1940, Rootes built 30% of all bomber aircraft, the Group produced one in seven of all the British bombers used during the war, built 50,000 aero-engines (including 10,000 parts sets of Merlins for Rolls-Royce to assemble) and repaired 21,000 of all types. It had built 60% of all the armoured cars and 35% of all the scout cars, plus 3,500 other armoured reconnaissance vehicles. It assembled 20,000 vehicles imported from the USA in knocked-down form and repaired 12,000 others. It made 300,000 bombs, 5 million bomb fuses and 3 million ammunition boxes. It was also chosen to build tens of thousands of Hillman Minxes and large numbers of Humber Snipes, which were produced in quite bewildering variety – this was 11% of the total UK output of wartime wheeled vehicles. It was a staggering effort.

By the spring of 1939, the Munich crisis had come and gone, Czechoslovakia had been overrun by Germany, and it was clear that a war was inevitable. The RAF realized that it needed far more aero-engines and aircraft than current factories could provide, and so the second-generation shadow scheme was born.

A series of massive factories, much larger than the original buildings, was planned. These factories, still allocated for management to the major companies in the motor industry, were to be remote from the parent concerns, rather than next to them, so as to minimize the risk of enemy bombing.

The Rootes No 2 factory was one of the last to be planned, and was positioned on a 60-acre greenfield site close to Ryton-on-Dunsmore, in the fork of the A45 and A423 main roads, just 4 miles south-east of the centre of Coventry. It was in operation by the end of 1940.

That, though, was just a start, for Rootes also added more new buildings at Stoke and was to become responsible for a huge new airframe factory at Speke, near Liverpool (initially to build Blenheims and later heavy four-engined bombers), factories at Pontefract in Yorkshire and other buildings in the Potteries.

During the war, Rootes was incredibly lucky in that none of its major factories was heavily damaged by bombing, though none escaped completely unscathed. Photo-files, held on behalf of Peugeot by the Museum of British Road Transport in Coventy (unhappily, these were not made available to me for use in this book), graphically record the damage inflicted to various plants, though this never caused production to be halted completely.

Coventry itself, of course, did not escape, particularly on the night of November 14, 1940, when the centre of industry watchers had become used to the 'Rootesification' of Talbot and to the fact that the Sunbeam marque was dormant. It was a real surprise to learn that all future products from Barlby Road, Kensington, were to be called Sunbeam-Talbot (and even more so to discover that there was very little Talbot and no Sunbeam heritage in the new cars!

At that time, in fact, the last of the much degraded Roesch Talbots was dropped; in 1938, the range had comprised the Talbot 10 (alias 'Minx in a party frock'), the New 3-Litre (effectively a badge-engineered Humber Snipe with a different nose) and the 3½-Litre, which was a much Rootes-rationalized version of the 3,377cc Talbot 110. The new Sunbeam-Talbots, announced in waves from September to October, were Hillman and Humber-based cars.

By this time, Rootes was producing cars at the rate of 50,000 a year, which meant that it was now a solid paid-up member of the British Big Six, with at least 15% of the market. This level, moreover, might have been pushed up still more if it had not been for the outbreak of war in September 1939. The 1940 models were partly stifled – a new monocoque Minx, inspired by what Opel/Vauxhall and Morris had already put on sale, was ready to go and was actually launched a few days *after* Britain had declared war on Germany, as were a facelifted Hillman 14hp model, a new Sunbeam-Talbot 2-Litre and revised large-engined Humbers. What had been intended for civilian consumption found great favour as military transport – though a few thousand monocoque Minxes had also found their way into private hands by the early 1940s.

For Rootes, the next six years would bring vast changes, not merely to its factories, but to the markets which it served, and the type of cars it planned to build. In the meantime, there was a war to be won.

---

the historic city was plastered by enemy bombing, 554 people were killed and several thousand were made homeless. Within 24 hours, Lord Beaverbrook, the Minister of Aircraft Production, set up the Coventry Industrial Reconstruction and Co-ordinating Committee, to be chaired by Billy Rootes. As anyone in the motor industry expected, he threw his prodigious energies into the project and into becoming chairman of the Supply Council, Ministry of Supply, so successfully that his efforts were recognized by a knighthood in the New Year Honours List of January 1942. From that moment on, Billy officially became Sir William Rootes, KBE, though his friends and close associates continued to call him Billy until the day he died.

After supplying several thousand Phase 1 (monocoque) Hillman Minxes to civilian customers in the early years of the war, Rootes concentrated on building military versions of this rugged design. The Humber Super Snipe, complete with its near-unburstable side-valve 4.1-litre engine, was built in many varieties, most famously as the staff cars used by senior officers, not least Field Marshal Montgomery on his victorious campaigns across North Africa, Sicily, Italy and Northern Europe.

Drawing on its extensive chassis experience in the Commer-Karrier commercial vehicle division, Rootes also produced four-wheel-drive utility vehicles using Super Snipe engines and at the same time scout car and armoured car chassis were produced in large numbers. One famous name, drafted into Rootes after Triumph had gone into liquidation and after his watching brief at Claudel Hobson had ended, was Donald Healey. It was while working on weapons of war for Rootes that Healey found the time to refine his thoughts on a new postwar car. The rest, as they say, is history....

In mid-1945, therefore, Rootes was the landlord, if not the owner, of a series of factories spread all over the UK. The Humber Road complex, now built over to its practical limits, covered 66 acres, while the Ryton plant covered no less than 80 acres, with virtually no space left for external expansion. In addition, of course, there was the modern Commer-Karrier plant at Dunstable, Thrupp & Maberly in Cricklewood, British Light Steel Presssings in Acton, the Talbot factory at Barlby Road, Kensington, and several other, smaller, satellite businesses, not to mention the splendid and palatial Devonshire House premises. A prewar workforce of 17,000 was more than doubled when the war was at its height; Sir William, though, was still proud to recall that: 'When we entered the manufacturing field the total number of workers employed was 673'.

Right away, the Group decided that it wanted to pull out of the aircraft manufacturing business as soon as possible. Rumours of the development of civil aircraft projects were rapidly killed off. Like other motor industry concerns, however, in 1945 and 1946 it contracted readily back to its industrial base, the West Midlands, and made haste to lease the shadow factory premises from the government in order to fuel its hoped-for postwar expansion.

Chapter 3

The Empire at its peak

1945 to 1964

Rootes emerged from the Second World War in extremely good shape. Despite the attentions of the Luftwaffe, its factories were virtually intact, financially it was well balanced (it recorded a £1.5 million profit in 1945), and commercially it was well placed to face the future. For his part in maintaining Rootes' war production, Reginald Rootes became Sir Reginald in 1946, four years after brother Billy had become Sir William for his part in the industry's war effort.

'Great Britain Ltd', on the other hand, was not in such good shape. As a result of the war, the country's overseas reserves had been exhausted and borrowings (particularly of US dollars) were extremely high. To make any dent on this situation it was essential for industry to export most of its products for years to come.

For the British motor industry, this amounted to a complete revolution. In the late 1930s, car makers had been used to exporting no more than 20% of their output. Now, in the late 1940s, the government was telling them to export no less than 60 to 70%! Furthermore, sheet steel supplies were only to be made available to those companies who could meet such a target.

For Rootes, as for every other major car maker, this meant a complete reorganization of methods – not only of organization, but of marketing and planning for future models. The old Empire countries – Australia, New Zealand, South Africa, Canada and India, for instance – could not possibly absorb so many cars, so it was necessary to assault the enormous United States market as well as many small territories previously ignored by the Group.

To Sir William Rootes, whose reputation as an achiever was even greater by the end of the war than it had been at the start of it, this was an enormous challenge which he faced with relish. Although he would have to sell 1930s-style products for the first two or three years, he believed that Rootes held one distinct advantage over its rivals – his styling consultant was the renowned Loewy organization in the USA.

Raymond Loewy, already a distinguished industrial designer before Sir William approached him, had signed an agreement with Studebaker in 1937. The following year he joined forces with Rootes to advise on vehicle styling and he opened a London office, which was run by Clare E. Hodgman. Prior to the war, there was insufficient time to develop new Rootes shapes for 1939 and 1940, but all the postwar cars were influenced by the ideas put forward by the Loewy offices.

First, however, the factories had to be converted back to civilian production, and provision had to be made for further expansion. For the time being, Humber Road was slated to produce Hillman and Humber cars, with Sunbeam-Talbot assembly still being concentrated at Barlby Road, Kensington.

Sir William wanted to see more than 100,000 Rootes cars built every year, but this could not possibly be achieved at Humber Road. Accordingly, although Rootes soon disposed of its wartime interest in aircraft assembly, it secured space for expansion by leasing the vast modern Ryton-on-Dunsmore shadow factory for its own use. In January 1946, it announced that final assembly of all Rootes cars was to be concentrated on Ryton 'when new assembly lines are made ready'. The last London-built Sunbeam-Talbots were produced in May 1946, after which Barlby Road was reworked to become the London export and engineering headquarters of the group.

Once Ryton had been established as the Group's final assembly centre, Humber Road concentrated on the casting and forging of hardware, the machining and assembly of engines, gearboxes and back axles, paint and trim work on Pressed Steel bodyshells and all the design and development of new models.

[At the same time, the original shadow factory at Stoke Aldermoor, part of the Humber Road complex, was converted to civilian use for the assembly of some Commer commercial vehicles; the existing Commer-Karrier plant at Dunstable was retained. An extension of the Dunstable plant followed in 1953, and the ex-shadow factory reverted to private car manufacture soon afterwards. In fact this was where all the tooling for the new-generation overhead-valve Hillman Minx engine was installed, assembly beginning in 1954.]

It was at about this time that Sir William Rootes (and the British motor industry in general) missed a unique opportunity. Immediately after the war, a government commission headed by Sir William visited the ruins of the VW plant at Wolfsburg to assess the merit of the new-fangled air-cooled 'Beetle'.

Not only did the Rootes Commission recommend that Wolfsburg should be razed to the ground, 'or it will collapse of its own inertia within two years', it also stated: '....the vehicle does not meet the fundamental technical requirements of a motor car. As regards performance and design it is quite unattractive to the average motor car buyer. It is too ugly and too noisy....To build the car commercially would be a completely uneconomic enterprise....' How wrong can you be? At the time of writing, more than 40 years later, the VW Beetle has passed the 20 million production mark and is *still* being produced in Mexico....

During the next few years, there were material shortages, queues for every sort of facility and a number of serious labour problems to be overcome. Accordingly, it was not until 1949–50 that annual production rose to 66,262 to finally exceed the previous record levels set in the late 1930s. Along the way the Group went public in 1949, with Rootes Securities Ltd becoming Rootes Motors Ltd and new shares replacing the debentures which had been held by Prudential Assurance since the early 1930s. Yet more capital was raised in October 1950 when 1.25 million ordinary shares were offered to the public at £1 1s (£1.05) each; they were quickly snapped up, though the Rootes family continued to retain the majority shareholding. Almost immediately afterwards, the Group (which was searching for a specialist diesel engine manufacturer) took control of Tilling Stevens, of Maidstone, which soon began to supply engines to the rationalized truck operation.

Normally, for a company the size of Rootes, it made the most sense if new models were phased-in at well-spaced intervals because there was a limit to the financial and personnel resources which could be deployed. In the late 1940s, however, there was really no time for such refinements. Immediately after the war, all Britain's car manufacturers made haste to produce genuine postwar models, which explains why the new Hillman Minx (Phase 3), the new Humber Hawk *and* the new Sunbeam-Talbot 80 and 90 models were all revealed during 1948. A new overhead-valve six-cylinder engine (for trucks and, eventually, the Humber Super Snipe) was launched in 1949.

After that, the pace eased off a bit. In the next decade Rootes usually seemed to have something new to boast about every year, as this launch summary demonstrates:

1950	New IFS chassis for Sunbeam-Talbot
1952	New bodyshell and OHV engine for Humber Super Snipe
1953	New Sunbeam (Talbot) Alpine
1954	New OHV engine for Minx-size range
1955	New Sunbeam Rapier Takeover of Singer
1956	New Minx range plus new Singer Gazelle
1957	New Humber Hawk range
1958	New six-cylinder engine for new Humber Super Snipe
1959	New Sunbeam Alpine
1960	Public start to new small car project
1961	New Hillman Super Minx/Singer Vogue
1963	New medium-range Humber Sceptre New Sunbeam Venezia
1963	New rear-engined Hillman Imp
1964	New Sunbeam Tiger New Singer Chamois New all-synchromesh gearbox for Minx/Rapier/Alpine/Sceptre/Hawk
1966	New Hillman Hunter 'Arrow' range New Sport-engined Imp-family cars
1967	New-generation Humber Sceptre and fastback Sunbeam Rapier

Rootes, nevertheless, was never exactly flush with profits, or its coffers overflowing with cash. Throughout the 1950s, after-tax profits always seemed to hover around the £3.5 million mark (which was certainly not enough to finance the investment in an all-new body style or engine every year). Full details are given in **Appendix F.**

As the British economy burgeoned and most mass-production car makers prospered, Rootes car production soared, as **Appendix E** makes clear. The 100,000 cars per year target was first achieved in 1954–55 (when the postwar Minx was almost ready to be pensioned-off), and after the nationwide recession of 1956–57 had been shaken off, Rootes production surged again and reached nearly 150,000 in 1960. The government target of 70% exports was regularly beaten until the early 1950s, when a change of government policy released more cars for the home market. Even so, Rootes pushed up its exports from 40,000 to around 70,000 cars a year during the 1950s.

Many of the Hillmans, Humbers and Sunbeam-Talbots exported at this time were shipped in CKD (completely knocked down) form, final assembly taking place in the modern factories Rootes had established in Australia, New Zealand and South Africa. Exports to Canada and the USA, however, were always in fully-assembled form.

This, as in the late 1930s, was the time when Hillman Minxes were rebadged as Humber Tens when delivered to customers in New Zealand....

Throughout this period, Rootes was still on the acquisition trail. In 1955, it purchased Hills Precision, a Coventry-based concern which specialized in zinc castings (used for door handles, badges and other brightwork). But that was just a mid-year skirmish before the main event of the autumn – the purchase of Singer.

Singer, the firm with which Sir William had started his motor industry career, was the last major company to be taken over by the Rootes Group. The origins of Singer were in Coventry, where the company started by building pedal cycles. In 1901, it moved into the motor industry by building motorcycles and tricars, and the first Singer car was produced in 1905. In the beginning, the company used proprietary engines, but began building its own units before the First World War. The motorcycle business was abandoned in 1915.

Singer began to expand from 1920, not only with more models, but with extra factory space and heavier financial commitments. That year it bought the Coventry Premier Company, in 1922 the Coventry Repetition Company, in 1925 the Sparkbrook Manufacturing Company and, finally, in 1927 it absorbed Calcott. The first of a long line of overhead-camshaft engines was launched in 1926.

Sales boomed and to find space to build more cars Singer bought a massive six-storey factory in Coventry Road, Birmingham, which had 34 acres of floor space; this had originally been built by BSA during the First World War for small arms manufacture. The famous Singer Junior was built there, but until the end of the 1930s some Singers were built in Birmingham and some in the original Coventry premises.

Before Britain was hit by the depression, Singer was Britain's third largest car-making concern (behind Austin and Morris); in 1929 it built 27,000 cars, which was three times the output of Humber and Hillman combined. During the 1930s, however, there was a steady slide from grace. While the family cars were well received, the radically styled (and ugly) Airstream model, which aped the bulbous lines of the Chrysler Airflow, was a failure. An ambitious motorsport programme was partially successful, but short-lived.

By 1935, Singer saw that it needed a partner to survive and offered itself as a merger candidate to companies such as Rover, but there were no takers. Singer survived the 1930s only by producing the little Bantam (which was a Morris Eight lookalike, introduced a year after the Morris) and a series of appealing sports cars and tourers, but the future was always in doubt.

However, like many other car makers, Singer prospered during the Second World War, its factories were never badly knocked about, and in 1945 the directors felt bold enough to invest in an important new

One of Rootes's most glamorous products in the early 1950s was the Sunbeam-Talbot 90. Here is Ronnie Adams's 'works' team car tackling a driving test in the RAC Rally of 1951.

Rootes always hoped to carve out a large market in the USA in the 1950s. The smart Sunbeam Alpine sports car was almost, but not quite, the car for this job.

model, the SM1500 saloon. Car assembly was concentrated on the Birmingham factory, an amazingly unsuitable building where chassis assembly was located on the fourth floor, body trim and paint on another and final assembly on yet another level!

From 1947 (when the SM1500 was previewed) until 1955 (when Rootes stepped in), Singer built the same two basic models, the four-door saloon and the Roadster, although model names were changed from time to time – the SM1500 later became the Hunter, for instance. All cars eventually used the same 1.5-litre overhead-camshaft engine and four-speed gearbox.

By 1954, the company was already in trouble, for it badly needed new models, but could not afford to invest in them. The SMX roadster was shown, but never put into production, and sales of engines to H.R.G. were tiny. H.R.G.'s Stuart Proctor designed a twin-cam conversion of the engine, which Singer then modified, productionized and offered for sale, but this was to be in the ageing Hunter saloon, not in a sports car.

At this time, sales were low and Singer production was often down to less than 40 saloons and five Roadsters per week. Sub-contract work for the aircraft industry helped to keep the company afloat, but the chance to assemble West German Champion cars was discarded.

An overdraft of £206,000 was noted in 1954, and despite the directors resolving: '....only one course is possible to improve the company's position, namely to expand and sell our turnover, be it motor cars or other work....', this did not happen in the months which followed.

The company announced a loss of £89,379 for the year ending July 31, 1954, a four-day week was introduced for a time during the winter of 1954–55, and by February 1955 the bank overdraft had risen to £317,000. The company brushed off a suggestion that it should take over manufacture of the new tubular-chassis twin-cam H.R.G. sports car, allowed itself to speculate privately on the new cars it would *like* to make, but then saw the overdraft exceed £500,000 by mid-summer 1955.

By the autumn, Singer was in desperate trouble, especially as Standard-Triumph's tentative proposal to

Monte Carlo Rally 1962; Peter Procter's Sunbeam Rapier IIIA leaving the start in Paris, with Norman and Lewis Garrad seeing off 'their' team. Successful competition in international motor sport was an important marketing tool for Rootes.

have its bodies built in the Birmingham plant was withdrawn. The loss for the year ending July 31, 1955 was £140,117, and the reserves were almost exhausted.

What followed at Singer between September and December 1955, when the shareholders agreed to merge the company with the Rootes Group, split the directors, caused the premature resignation of director/general manager Maurice Curtis, and saw a battle for control between Rootes and representatives of the George Cohen 600 Group, which was only resolved by a shareholders' vote.

At the end of November 1955, Singer's directors accepted a complex offer from Rootes. This provided Singer with £235,000 in cash and a quantity of new Rootes shares, but Rootes also took over all existing liabilities. Singer, it was said, had gross assets of more than £2 million, much of which was in property and land.

The first meeting of the Rootes-owned Singer board took place on December 29, 1955, and in January 1956 (when Rootes officially took over the shares) the transfer of ownership was complete. Sir William Rootes became chairman of Singer Motors, A.E. Hunt (Singer's old chairman) became his deputy, and three other members of the Rootes family – Sir Reginald, Geoffrey and Brian – also joined the board.

Within a year there were further upheavals. With Singer's future firmly locked into that of Rootes, A.E. Hunt retired, as did the 71-year-old Leo Shorter, who had been Singer's technical director since the 1930s. Along the way, Rootes accountants threw in as many losses as they could allocate into the same pot and wrote off as much as they could on cancelled projects and contracts – effectively clearing the decks for the future – and for the year ending July 31, 1956 a huge loss of £604,522 was announced.

By the end of the 1950s, Sir William's long-term strategy for Singer had become apparent. Profits were once again being made by October 1956, and in the following year a modest £21,617 was made. A year later that figure had risen to £93,554, and 1958/59 produced no less than £446,451. What did the 'we-must-stay-independent' diehards make of that?

There had never been any sentiment involved in this takeover, which had been made purely on logical grounds. Not only was the Singer marque name speedily integrated into the Rootes family – placed above the Hillmans but below the Humbers in prestige and price with the aid of suitable badge engineering and decorative and trim enhancements – but the big six-storey building in Birmingham provided an ideal base for Rootes' expanding spare parts operation. This was officially opened in May 1959, by which time the old parts operation had vacated its premises in Humber Road, leaving space for expansion on the original Humber site.

In the meantime, merger talks had been going on over a considerable period with Alick Dick, managing director of Standard-Triumph, another Coventry-based car-making concern. In absolute terms, both groups were too small and under-capitalized. Here was the classic case of two medium-sized manufacturers trying to get together to secure their joint future.

The first moves came early in 1955, but after 18 months they were abandoned. Both suffered financially in Britain's mid-1950s recession, and a proposal to set

Rootes's biggest financial gamble was to design a revolutionary new small car, the Imp, then have it built at a brand new factory in Scotland, with a novice workforce. The gamble failed, and Rootes had to merge with Chrysler of Detroit.

up a joint company called R & S Holdings found no favour. Rootes offered to take over Standard-Triumph, but this was also rejected. Even so, by the end of 1956, Standard's 2-litre diesel engine (which was mainly produced for use in the Ferguson tractor) had become optional in some Commer-Karrier vehicles, and rumours of pending amalgamation had appeared in the *Coventry Evening Telegraph* (though emphatically denied by Rootes....).

Rootes were determined to hold all the advantages, for Sir William eventually insisted on becoming chairman of the parent board, with Geoffrey Rootes as managing director and Alick Dick less senior than either of them. Further negotiations in Nassau, which dragged in the proposed status of Standard's chairman, Lord Tedder, the probable unscrambling of Standard's tractor-production deal with Massey Ferguson, and a host of less critical matters, produced an impasse. Merger talks were abandoned.

By this time, Sir William (who was long past his 60th birthday), had begun to draw back from day-to-day management of 'his' Group, though he made sure that he never lost ultimate control of everything which went on. His brother, Sir Reginald, took over as chairman of Humber Ltd (the manufacturing subsidiary) in 1956, and in the same year Brian took over as managing director of the sales and service divisions. Geoffrey (Sir William's son) was also on his way up – in 1949 he had been appointed managing director of Humber Ltd (when his director/general manager was W.E. 'Bill' Hancock), he became deputy chairman in 1955, and in 1962 he went on to become chairman and managing director of Humber Ltd.

Sir William had always seemed to be tireless, not only in running his own Group, but also serving as chairman of the government's Dollar Export Council. For this work, and many other services, he became a Baron on January 1, 1959. Having established his home at Stype Grange, at Ramsbury, near Hungerford (from which palatial house he was habitually chauffeur-driven to all his appointments), he took the title of Lord Rootes of Ramsbury. As this was to be an hereditary title, his eldest son now became the Honourable Geoffrey Rootes.

One-time senior employees of Rootes have told me that once Lord Rootes took a back seat, the main driving force seemed to fade away and the Group never felt as vital after that. Contemporary descriptions of the brothers make fascinating reading:

'To talk business with him [Sir William] in his incredibly tidy – he refused to use a desk with drawers – and sparsely furnished office overlooking Green Park is quite an experience. Breezy, enthusiastic, mercurial, never at a loss for an idea, Sir William's mind and conversation races away with propositions and possibilities. He dazzles his visitors with a flashing stream of conjectures, carrying everyone along with him by sheer weight of personality.

'Through a cream-painted door in an office of identical size sits Sir Reginald. At 63, two years younger than his brother, Sir Reginald is deputy chairman of the Group, and he is the production expert who retains the analytical brain and all the keenness of mind which once marked him out as a civil servant of great promise.' It was quite typical of the impression always given by the founding members of the Group.

By this time, however, Rootes was becoming very anxious to expand its car-building operations, for Ryton and Humber Road were full to overflowing. Not only did Rootes want to build more cars, but more *types* of cars.

It was at this time that Rootes came to an agreement with Armstrong Siddeley which covered not only the development and manufacture of the new-generation Sunbeam Alpine sports car, but also the production of a new generation of six-cylinder engines for the next Humber Super Snipe.

Rootes also wanted to start building small cars. The

The Sunbeam Tiger was a brave attempt to produce a 'civilized Cobra'. If only Chrysler had not taken a stake in Rootes, this Ford-engined car might have been more successfully developed.

Group had never had a direct competitor to the Morris Minor, Austin A30, Standard Ten and Ford Anglia models and their dealers were always vocal about the potential business they were lacking. Accordingly, and after a very tentative beginning, the 'Apex', or Hillman Imp, project got under way.

Right from the start (and certainly towards the end), this long-drawn-out affair was a financially costly one. Begun in the late 1950s in a small way, the official start to Apex coincided with the appointment of Peter Ware (chief executive engineer) as B.B. Winter's successor. Ware (and his deputy, Peter Wilson) was much more of a motoring enthusiast than 'B.B.' had ever been – without Ware, the Apex project would probably never have been put to the board for approval. The first prototype, which featured an air-cooled engine, was turned down flat by the Rootes family, Sir William refusing even to ride in it!

By the 1950s, Rootes had purchased a great deal of land close to its Ryton plant, on the other side of the A423 (Coventry to Banbury) road. Although it applied repeatedly for planning permission to develop that land for a new factory, consent was always refused. In June 1960, Rootes was told that the entire area (which was partially covered by unsightly gravel workings!) was now to be preserved as Green Belt. The fact was that the government wanted to force large companies to build satellite factories in other parts of Britain, where old industries were dying out and unemployment was high.

Rootes, therefore, was forced to look around the country and in the end was persuaded to establish a new factory at Linwood, near Paisley, in Scotland. This was about 8 miles due west of the centre of Glasgow, the factory site most conveniently being next door to the modern Pressed Steel Company factory (which was already producing Rover 3-litre and Volvo P1800 bodies and BMC commercial vehicle cabs).

In the autumn of 1960, Rootes made its momentous announcement. It was to build a new baby car at Linwood (although construction of the factory had not even started....), would take its bodies from Pressed Steel 'across the road', and was aiming to produce 150,000 cars a year from a new workforce of 5,500. At least 50% of this production, it was said, would be exported and the whole project had been costed at £22 million.

£3.5 million of extra debenture capital had already been raised in 1959 (the first increase since 1954), but this was clearly not enough to fund the Apex project. In 1962, the Board of Trade advanced an assistance package totalling £10 million, which was to be paid back over a period of 15 years at the rate of £376,000 per annum, starting in 1964.

Rootes was also trying to expand overseas. In 1953, an agreement had been concluded with Isuzu of Japan for that company to build the Hillman Minx under licence. In 1960, that agreement was extended, and it continued until the end of 1964, by which time 60,000 cars had been produced.

In October 1961, however, something altogether more exciting was announced. Carrozzeria Touring Superleggera, of Italy, revealed that during 1962 it was to start building Sunbeam Alpine sports cars and Hillman Super Minx saloons at a new 30,000sq ft factory at Nova Milanese. The first cars would be UK-supplied kits, but local content would increase thereafter.

This, however, was only the tip of this iceberg, for in 1963 Touring also revealed the short-lived Sunbeam Venezia coupe, based on a Humber Sceptre floorpan and running gear. However, as *Automobile Quarterly* later commented:

'It was a mistake. This expansion weakened rather than reinforced Touring....No-one in Italy wanted the

When Lord Rootes, the co-founder of the Rootes Group, died in 1964, the Hon. Geoffrey Rootes succeeded to the title. He became chairman of Rootes, and later of Chrysler United Kingdom Ltd, after his uncle (Sir Reginald) retired in 1967.

already outdated Hillman Minx....As for the Sunbeam Venezia, it won none of the international acceptance of the convertible from which it was derived. It was an ignoble failure, too.' Touring went into the Italian version of receivership in March 1964 and closed down completely in 1966.

On reflection, 1960 and 1961 was the period during which Rootes began its decline, several events having made this almost inevitable. The cause has often been identified by historians as the disastrous 13-week strike which broke out at the BLSP body pressings factory in London in 1961, but the nationwide slump in car sales which affected British car makers in 1960 and 1961 was another, as was the decision to go ahead with the Imp/Linwood project, while a fourth reason was undoubtedly the launch of the Super Minx/Vogue range without getting rid of any old models.

Hindsight is a wonderful thing, so it is now easy to suggest that the Imp/Linwood project was ill-starred from the very beginning. It was one of those rare and risky projects – new from end to end, in a new factory, with a new workforce – which stood every chance of causing trouble. Rootes dealers, who had never been asked to sell small cars, were now to be offered such a machine four years after the already-famous Mini had gone on sale, which was rear-engined instead of front-wheel drive and complex instead of simple.

If the Imp had been reliable and well-built, right from the start, it might have succeeded. If it had been cheaper, it might have succeeded. If it had had front-wheel drive, it might have been a true head-to-head competitor to the Mini. If Rootes had not been forced to settle in Scotland, instead of expanding in Warwickshire, it might have worked. If Rootes had not had to borrow and invest so much to finance this, it might have worked. If, if, if....

Unhappily, though, the car which should have been on sale in late 1962 did not actually come on stream until mid-1963. Rootes never even approached the target of building 150,000 Imp-type cars in a year, their best achievement being about 50,000 in 1964. Running at 33% capacity was no way to make profits, and until the end of the 1960s (when more work was allocated to Linwood) the plant was a horrendous loss-maker.

No wonder, therefore, that the second of the rear-engined, technically advanced new models, the Minx-sized 'Swallow' project, was cancelled in 1963 just as the first prototype was about to start its road trials. In its place, in haste but with a great deal of careful attention to cost control (and with a firm eye on Ford's new lightweight Cortina), the conventional front-engine/rear-drive 'Arrow' project got under way. Its project engineer was a dour Liverpudlian, Harry Sheron, whose own reputation was so enhanced by this car that he went

Gilbert Hunt (right) became chief executive of Rootes in 1967, and succeeded the second Lord Rootes (centre) as chairman of Chrysler United Kingdom Ltd in 1973.

on to become technical director of the Group before the end of the 1960s.

Then there was the episode of the Super Minx/Vogue/Sceptre family of cars, which began at the time when technical chief B.B. Winter was about to retire and Peter Ware was about to take over. The new cars were intended at that time to be a straight replacement for the ageing Minx/Gazelle/Rapier range and would be bigger, heavier and probably less economical. As time passed, it also became clear that they would have to be more expensive, too.

Someone, somewhere (and the final decision must surely have been taken by the Rootes family) then decided to keep the old cars going and run the new cars alongside them. The result, by 1963, was that Rootes was overburdened with medium-sized cars – Minx, Gazelle, Rapier, Super Minx, Vogue and Sceptre – all being assembled at Ryton and sold through the same dealer chain. On the other hand, the new small car (the Imp) had yet to find its feet, while the large cars (Hawk/Super Snipe) were struggling to keep abreast of rivals from Ford, Vauxhall and BMC. The imminent arrival of the Triumph 2000 and Rover 2000 models was soon to make the Humber marque's problem quite desperate.

In any case, there was something of a recession in UK car sales as the 1960s began, one created by the government's tighter money policy, which affected hire-purchase credit deals and interest rates. Market leaders BMC slid from 585,000 to 510,000 cars produced in a year, then crept back to 526,000 in 1962. One of Rootes' natural rivals, Standard-Triumph, slipped so much that it had to be taken over by Leyland to ensure its survival. Rootes, likewise, was also faced with a declining market.

The Group had sometimes suffered from rather volatile labour relations, and this came to a head in September 1961. The most important cause of Rootes' decline, then, erupted at BLSP in Acton, where a disgruntled workforce walked out in a dispute which was nominally about possible redundancies, but had in fact been brewing for some time. Shop stewards refused to discuss future production schedules, demanded a 'no redundancy' agreement and called out its members. Even though the national union leaders instructed the workers to return to their jobs, they ignored this and 1,000 people walked out, and remained out for 13 weeks.

The problem was not only that BLSP built body structures for Hawk/Super Snipe models, but it also supplied pressings and sub-assemblies to Thrupp & Maberly, commercial vehicle cabs to Dunstable and materials to several other locations. In the tense atmosphere of the day, with parts readily being blacked by other workers, this quickly crippled Rootes.

Lord Rootes speedily sacked the entire band of strikers, then opened a recruiting office at Acton to replace these men! In a statement issued on November 24, he said:

'Your directors have long given a large amount of their time to the important factor of labour relations. Generally we can claim that these are good throughout the Group, with the exception, however, of one manufacturing unit in the London area. Unfortunately, during the past financial year we suffered a great number of unauthorized stoppages at BLSP Ltd, and on September 4 a major strike occurred, involving the greater part of the hourly paid employees.

The challenge to industrial law and order was such that your directors had no alternative but to oppose it.

Group production was completely paralyzed and many thousands of employees of our own and of our suppliers have been thrown out of work. At the time of making this statement a partial resumption of work has taken place, but the position is still far from satisfactory....'

It was, in fact, a disastrous strike which achieved nothing for the strikers or the shop stewards (many of whom were permanently dismissed), and cost Rootes dearly. Other car makers were delighted to see a colleague standing up to rampant anarchy, but could do more than offer verbal encouragement.

This, in summary, was the result:

In 1960, Rootes had built 149,290 cars, but in strike-hit 1961 the total fell to 100,337. This rocketed up to 147,535 units in 1962, then 177,646 as the Imp production lines started up.

In the year to July 31, 1961, Rootes made a pre-tax profit of £0.9 million (while spending heavily at Linwood), but in the year to July 31, 1962, this slumped to a loss of £2 million and there was a further small loss of £200,000 in 1962/63.

All in all, the BLSP stoppage cost about £3 million in lost profits at a time when Rootes could least afford it.

After this, there was nothing that Rootes, or its backers, could do to get the Group back on course. Without more backing, or a link-up with another concern, the future looked bleak. Before the end of 1963, therefore, the approach from Lynn Townsend of Chrysler must have seemed like a miracle.

Chapter 4

HILLMAN

Without a strong Hillman marque in the 1930s, it would never have been possible for the Family to develop the Rootes Group at all. Humber was solidly middle-class, Talbot was sporting and definitely up-market and Sunbeam was a useful marque to have ready for use at any time, but none of these could deliver the volume and cash flow which the company needed to survive. Hillman was the lynchpin in the master plan.

At merger time, in 1928, Hillman did not have a very healthy range of cars. The 14hp model had been around for some years, while the company had just announced the new Straight-Eight model, which had an awful engine and stodgy engineering and, even though it would be renamed Vortic in 1931, was doomed to be an utter failure.

Even so, William Rootes looked to the Hillman marque to bring prosperity to his new grouping, and he promoted a stream of new models in the 1930s which did the trick. The six-cylinder Wizard family of 1931-35 was really a false start, but the Hillman Minx, which went on sale in 1932, was an immediate and lasting success. In the late 1930s, the 14, 16, 18 and Hawk were all limited successes and all leaned on current or planned Humber models for their engineering.

After the Second World War, however, Rootes made no further mistakes. Until 1961, the company concentrated on the Minx in a succession of guises (including Commer LCV and Husky estate cars), and the Super Minx which followed was really designed to be a true Minx replacement rather than an additional model. The Minx and Super Minx were also used as the basis of several other Singer, Sunbeam and Humber models of the period.

The marketing tragedy of the 1960s, which really caused Rootes to run for cover under the protection of Chrysler, was the Imp project, this rear-engined small Hillman also forming the basis of numerous Singers and Sunbeams along the way.

From 1966, the Arrow generation of Hunters and Minxes took over, and in 1970 (well after Chrysler took complete control of the Rootes Group), this range was joined by the smaller, all-new, Avenger.

As far as the UK was concerned, the Hillman name was killed off in favour of Chrysler in 1977, but the last of the Hunter types was actually built (in kit form for export to Iran) in the mid-1980s.

Rootes could take no credit (nor did they try!) for the Straight-Eight/Vortic models, and the first true Rootes Hillman was the Wizard, which was launched in May 1931.

Hillman Wizard 65 and 75 (1931 to 1933)

The Wizard was one of three series-production cars projected by Rootes immediately after it had masterminded the merger of Hillman with Humber; the other two were the Hillman Minx and the Humber 12hp model. Even in those simpler times, it took more than two years to bring the Wizard from the 'idea' stage to the modernized production lines at Humber Road.

In engineering terms, the Wizard was a strictly conventional car, having a chassis-frame with channel-section side members, a 9ft 3in wheelbase, leaf-spring and beam-axle suspension front and rear, cable brakes and a new type of side-valve six-cylinder engine, the Wizard 65 having a 2,110cc and the 75 a 2,810cc unit. The four-speed gearbox (as also used in the Vortic) had constant-mesh top and third and a centre-floor lever, and there was a new type of spiral-bevel rear axle.

No fewer than six different body styles were eventually offered, the cheapest and most numerous being an all-steel four-door saloon by Pressed Steel, which had a boot 'bustle' for novelty. In May 1931,

The Hillman Wizard of 1931 was the first genuine 'Rootes Hillman'.

Hillman Wizard 65 and 75 specification

Produced: Humber Road, 1931–33, 7,000 cars built.
General layout: Separate steel chassis-frame, 6-cylinder engine and wide choice of saloon, tourer, DHC and limousine bodies. Front-mounted engine driving rear wheels.
Engine and transmission: Hillman engine, 6-cylinder, sv, in-line. (65) 2,110cc, 65 x 106mm, approx 50bhp; torque not revealed; (75) 2,810cc, 75 x 106mm, approx 65bhp; torque not revealed; 4-speed gearbox, no synchromesh; centre-floor gear-change; live (beam) rear axle with spiral-bevel final drive.
Chassis: Beam-axle front suspension, half-elliptic leaf springs. Worm-and-nut steering. Live (beam) rear axle, half-elliptic leaf springs. Front and rear drum brakes. 5.00-19in tyres.
Dimensions: Wheelbase 9ft 3in; front track 4ft 8in; rear track 4ft 8in; length 13ft 11in; width 5ft 8in; height 6ft 0in. Unladen weight (saloon) approx 3,165lb.
Distinguishing features from previous models: Completely different type of Hillman compared with previous models; fitted mainly with standard Pressed Steel bodyshell, having family resemblance to original Minx of 1931 period.
Typical performance: (75 model) Maximum speed 64mph; typical fuel consumption 19mpg.
Derivatives: 1933 16hp and 20-70 models used same basic chassis and all running gear.
Fate: Discontinued in 1933 in favour of 16hp and 20-70.

prices started at £270. The limousine, when launched, was on a lengthened wheelbase.

For 1933, a different type of chassis-frame was fitted, but the basic running gear and bodies were not changed. A year later, the Wizard disappeared, but the 16hp and 20-70 models which took over used the same chassis and running gear.

Hillman 16hp and 20-70 (1933 to 1935)

The names were new and a good deal of high-powered publicity was applied to these cars, but under the skin they were merely updated Wizards, still with the familiar choice of 2,110cc or 2,810cc side-valve engine.

Mechanically, the big improvement was a synchromesh gearbox (synchro being on top and third gears, with a constant-mesh second gear), plus a freewheel. The subsequently notorious Startix automatic starting feature was optional.

As with the Wizard, a wide choice of body styles was available, the Pressed Steel-built saloon being a slightly more graceful version of the original Wizard type, with a swept forward grille. Prices started at £269 in September 1933.

As with the Wizard, these were stodgy cars which sold much less readily than the Minx, and after only two years they were dropped in favour of the new 16hp and Hawk types, which had different styling and independent front suspension.

This was how Rootes advertised the 16hp and 20-70 models in 1933 – note the distinct family likeness to the current Minx model.

A familiar, but nonetheless important shot – 'Billy' Rootes (right), along with George Vallet, out testing a prototype Minx in May 1931, pre-launch.

Hillman 16hp and 20-70 specification

Produced: Humber Road, 1933–35, 4,092 cars built.
General layout: Separate steel chassis-frame, 6-cylinder engine and wide choice of saloon, tourer, DHC and limousine bodies. Front-mounted engine driving rear wheels.
Engine and transmission: Hillman engine, 6-cylinder, sv, in-line. (16hp) 2,110cc, 65 x 106mm, approx 50bhp; torque not revealed; (20-70) 2,810cc, 75 x 106mm, approx 65bhp; torque not revealed; 4-speed gearbox, synchromesh on top and 3rd gears, freewheel; centre-floor gear-change; live (beam) rear axle with spiral-bevel final drive.
Chassis: Beam-axle front suspension, half-elliptic leaf springs. Worm-and-nut steering. Live (beam) rear axle, half-elliptic leaf springs. Front and rear drum brakes. 5.50-19in tyres.
Dimensions: Wheelbase 9ft 3in; front track 4ft 8in; rear track 4ft 8in; length 14ft 8in; width 5ft 8in; height 6ft 0in. Unladen weight (saloon) approx 3,300lb.
Distinguishing features from previous models: Modernized type of Hillman bodies compared with Wizard models; fitted mainly with standard Pressed Steel bodyshell having family resemblance to Minx of 1933-35 period.
Typical performance: (20-70 model) Maximum speed 70 mph; 0–60mph 24.0sec; typical fuel consumption 18mpg.
Derivatives: None.
Fate: Discontinued in 1935 in favour of new independently-suspended 16hp and Hawk.

Hillman Minx (1931 to 1935)

This was the car which set Rootes on the way to a secure place in Britain's big league of car makers. The first example, launched in 1931 but going on sale in 1932, was new from end to end and smaller and cheaper than any previous Hillman. Once the Minx name became established, it would always be commercially the most important model in the Rootes range.

The original type was conceived in 1929 by Capt Irving and A.H. Wilde (Wilde was thought to be the most capable small-car designer in the UK, for he had been responsible for the 1928 Standard 9) as the smallest of the three-car programme set in motion by William Rootes (the others being the Wizard and the forthcoming Humber 12hp).

It was an extremely simple design, with a channel-section frame, half-elliptic springs front and rear, a rugged little cast-iron side-valve engine (which was to be built, in one form or another, for the next quarter-century!), Bendix cable brakes and, at first, a non-synchromesh three-speed gearbox. Even though it was meant to be a car for 'Everyman', with prices starting at a mere £159, there was a wide choice of bodywork. The most popular was a Pressed Steel four-door saloon using that company's standard cabin, which was used on several other British cars of the day.

An artist's impression (rather stretched!) of the first-generation Minx, as put on sale in 1932.

Hillman Minx specification

Produced: Humber Road, 1931–35, 43,306 cars built.
General layout: Separate steel chassis-frame, 4-cylinder engine and wide choice of saloon, tourer and DHC bodies. Front-mounted engine driving rear wheels.
Engine and transmission: Hillman engine, 4-cylinder, sv, in-line. 1,185cc, 63 x 95mm, approx 30bhp; torque not revealed; 3-speed gearbox, no synchromesh, at first; optional 4-speed gearbox with freewheel from 1933; 4-speed all-synchromesh gearbox, no freewheel, from late 1934; centre-floor gear-change; live (beam) rear axle with spiral-bevel final drive.
Chassis: Beam-axle front suspension, half-elliptic leaf springs. Worm-and-nut steering. Live (beam) rear axle, half-elliptic leaf springs. Front and rear drum brakes. 4.50-18in tyres.
Dimensions: Wheelbase 7ft 8in; front track 4ft 0in; rear track 4ft 0in; length 11ft 2in; width 4ft 10in; height 5ft 9in. Unladen weight (saloon) approx 1,680lb.
Distinguishing features from previous models: Completely different type of Hillman compared with previous models, fitted mainly with standard Pressed Steel bodyshell having family resemblance to original Wizard of 1931 period.
Typical performance: Maximum speed 59mph; typical fuel consumption 35mpg.
Derivatives: 1932 Aero Minx used same basic running gear, but sleek sporty bodies. 1935 Minx Magnificent used same running gear, but new chassis and body styles.
Fate: Discontinued in 1935 in favour of next-generation Minx Magnificent.

From May 1933, a four-speed (still non-synchromesh) gearbox became optional for an extra £2 10s (£2.50), but from August that year this gearbox was standardized, as was a freewheel on all but the basic model.

The 1934 model was given a facelifted style, with a grille swept forward at its base and the tail reprofiled, while semaphore indicators were fitted.

From September 1934, a new all-synchromesh gearbox was fitted, though there were no major style changes; the second-generation Minx (the Magnificent series) then took over for the 1936 model-year.

Hillman Minx Magnificent (1935 to 1939)

The original Minx had underpinned the fortunes of the Rootes Group in the early 1930s, and the second-generation Magnificent range (so called because of its badging) was to do even more.

After four years, Rootes could afford to indulge in a substantial redesign and reinvestment programme. The new type of Minx, of which 10,000 would be built by January 1936, was a somewhat larger and heavier car, with a new box-section chassis-frame and completely new styling with more accommodation; there was still a choice of bodies, but most cars were ordered with a new type of Pressed Steel saloon shell, which had rounded, up-to-the-minute lines closely similar to those of the brand new Evenkeel-suspended six-cylinder Humbers. The engine, transmission and suspension were much as before, as were the prices, which still started at £159.

The Minx was a reliable and trustworthy car rather than an exciting one, but it made tens of thousands of friends before being replaced by the Phase 1 monocoque Minx in late 1939.

From July 1937, the basic design was freshened-up with a new-style grille and an opening boot lid. By this time, 100,000 Minxes had been built since the car was launched in 1932. From September 1938, there was a retrograde step when the gearbox was changed to be given a non-synchronized first ratio.

This model lasted until the eve of the war because the Phase 1 monocoque car introduced in 1939 did not go on full civilian sale until 1945.

The Minx was completely rebodied in the autumn of 1935, becoming the 'Minx Magnificent'. This was the original version.

Hillman Minx Magnificent specification

Produced: Humber Road, 1935–39, 92,095 cars built.
General layout: Separate steel chassis-frame, 4-cylinder engine and wide choice of saloon, tourer and DHC bodies. Front-mounted engine driving rear wheels.
Engine and transmission: Hillman engine, 4-cylinder, sv, in-line. 1,185cc, 63 x 95mm, 30bhp at 4,100rpm; torque not revealed; 4-speed gearbox, all-synchromesh; no 1st-gear synchromesh from autumn 1938; centre-floor gear-change; live (beam) rear axle with spiral-bevel final drive.
Chassis: Beam-axle front suspension, half-elliptic leaf springs. Worm-and-nut steering. Live (beam) rear axle, half-elliptic leaf springs. Front and rear drum brakes. 5.25-16in tyres.
Dimensions: Wheelbase 7ft 8in; front track 4ft 0in; rear track 4ft 0in; length 12ft 9in; width 5ft 0in; height 5ft 1.5in. Unladen weight (saloon) approx 2,130lb.
Distinguishing features from previous models: Completely new style compared with previous Minx models, fitted mainly with standard Pressed Steel bodyshell having family resemblance to 1936-model Humbers.
Typical performance: Maximum speed 59mph; 0-50mph 31 sec; typical fuel consumption 34mpg.
Derivatives: Talbot 10, later Sunbeam-Talbot 10, models used same basic chassis and all running gear.
Fate: Discontinued in 1939 in favour of monocoque Phase 1 Minx.

Hillman Aero Minx specification

Produced: Humber Road, 1932–35, 649 cars built.
General layout: Separate steel chassis-frame, 4-cylinder engine and wide choice of coupe, saloon, tourer and DHC bodies. Front-mounted engine driving rear wheels.
Engine and transmission: Hillman engine, 4-cylinder, sv, in-line. 1,185cc, 63 x 95mm, approx 35bhp; torque not revealed; 3-speed, later 4-speed, gearbox, no synchromesh at first; all-synchromesh 4-speed box from late 1934; centre-floor gear-change; live (beam) rear axle with spiral-bevel final drive.
Chassis: Beam-axle front suspension, half-elliptic leaf springs. Worm-and-nut steering. Live (beam) rear axle, half-elliptic leaf springs. Front and rear drum brakes. 4.50-18in tyres.
Dimensions: Wheelbase 7ft 4in; front track 4ft 0in; rear track 4ft 0in; (typical overall dimensions) length 11ft 7in; width 4ft 8.5in; height 4ft 5in. Unladen weight (typical) 1,960lb.
Distinguishing features from previous models: Completely different type of Hillman compared with previous models, fitted mainly with variety of rakish sporty bodies.
Typical performance: Maximum speed 72mph; 0-50mph 22.2sec; typical fuel consumption 30mpg.
Derivatives: 1936 Talbot 10 used same basic chassis, updated bodies and all running gear.
Fate: Discontinued in 1935 in favour of Talbot 10.

Hillman Aero Minx (1932 to 1935)

Only six months after the Minx family car had gone into production, Rootes revealed the Aero Minx, which was a smart, sporty, but still mechanically simple car. Once described as a 'Minx in a party frock', this car kept the same wheelbase, track, suspension and basic running gear as the Minx, but had a new frame with side members which passed under the line of the back axle. The engine had a high-compression cylinder head and there was a remote-control gear-change.

The radiator grille was swept forward at its base to give an impression of streamlining (soon, the same treatment would also be applied to other more bread-

By 1938 the Minx Magnificent had been facelifted, with a different front grille, though the other front-end 'sheet metal' and cabin was untouched.

Hillman Aero Minx: the original coupe body (later adapted for the Talbot Ten) was joined by several alternative styles including this 1935 two-seater Cresta sports. (Photo: National Motor Museum, Beaulieu.)

and-butter Minx models). The standard body style was a 2+1 (the rear seat was set crosswise) fastback coupe, lower and quite rakish, so the performance was better than that of the Minx saloon. Prices started at £245 in September 1932.

Within a year, Rootes had added a four-seat open tourer and a close-coupled foursome saloon to the Aero Minx range; from late 1934, when the all-synchromesh gearbox was standardized, it was also given a Streamline open two-seater style.

The Aero Minx was built until 1935, at which point the well-honed Rootes badge-engineering system swung into action and it was converted into the new Talbot 10hp model for 1936!

Hillman 16hp, Hawk and 80 (1935 to 1937)

The technically old-fashioned Wizard/16/20-70 models were dropped in 1935, to be replaced by a new range of Hillmans, complete with new chassis-frames having independent front suspension and box-section side members and with improved six-cylinder engines.

Both William Heynes and Alec Issigonis had been involved in the new chassis design. The new IFS featured a transverse leaf spring and upper wishbones, with radius arms helping to keep the wheels in the right place; this layout was graced with the trade name Evenkeel.

The rest of the chassis layout was conventional, for there was a choice of side-valve six-cylinder engines (these were longer-stroke, enlarged and updated versions of the iron-head Hillman Wizard types). The gearboxes, with synchromesh on top and third gears, were like those of the superseded Wizard-family cars.

Because the wheelbase was 9ft 0in (10ft 6in for the Hillman 80) and the tracks approached 5ft 0in, these were spacious cars, though the squared-up style (the standard saloons were by Pressed Steel and were closely related to those used in the Humber 12hp of the day) won no prizes for its looks. The larger, most powerful, versions were often used by government bodies and companies for managerial transport.

In retrospect, these cars should have been sold as Humbers (they overlapped, somewhat, with current models), because as Hillmans they did not sell well, even though prices were lowered in July 1936. In 1937, after a short life, the 16hp/Hawk models gave way to the much more modern-looking 14hp model, though the 80 carried on for another season.

Hillman 16hp, Hawk, 80 specification

Produced: Humber Road, 1935–38, 5,236 cars built.
General layout: Separate steel chassis-frame, 6-cylinder engine and wide choice of saloon, coupe, DHC and limousine (80 model only) bodies. Front-mounted engine driving rear wheels.
Engine and transmission: Hillman-Humber engine, 6-cylinder, sv, in-line. (16hp) 2,576cc, 67.5 x 120mm, approx 56bhp; torque not revealed; (Hawk, 80) 3,181cc, 75 x 120mm, approx 71bhp; 4-speed gearbox, synchromesh on top and 3rd gears; centre-floor gear-change; live (beam) rear axle with spiral-bevel final drive.
Chassis: Independent front suspension, transverse leaf spring, upper wishbones and radius arms. Worm-and-nut steering. Live (beam) rear axle, half-elliptic leaf springs. Front and rear drum brakes. 6.50-16in tyres.
Dimensions: Wheelbase 9ft 0in (10ft 6in on 80 model); front track 4ft 9.9in; rear track 4ft 11.5in; (typical overall dimensions, 16hp) length 14ft 4in; width 5ft 11in; height 5ft 6in; (typical, 80) length 15ft 10in; width 5ft 11in; height 5ft 6in. Unladen weight (typical, 16hp) 3,750lb (typical, 80) 3,935lb.
Distinguishing features from previous models: Completely different style of Hillman compared with previous models, visually related to contemporary Humber 12hp, with similarities to new-generation Minx.
Typical performance: (16hp) Maximum speed 71mph; 0–50mph 22.4sec; typical fuel consumption 20mpg; (80) maximum speed 71 mph; 0–50mph 18.4sec; typical fuel consumption 18mpg.
Derivatives: 1937 14hp model used modified version of chassis and suspension, but different body style.
Fate: Discontinued in 1937 and 1938 in favour of new 14hp and (in case of 80) large Humber models.

Mid-1930s catalogue for the larger Hillmans typifies publicity material of the period, dramatic and impressionistic in its graphic style. Inside, much was made of the new Evenkeel front suspension.

The Hillman Hawk appeared in 1935, with a solid new body style. There were also '16' and '80' derivatives of this basic design.

The Hillman 14 (which, when redesigned, became the postwar Humber Hawk) was launched in 1938.

Hillman 14 (1937 to 1939)

Even in 1937, Rootes was still shuffling and reshuffling its line-up and the inter-connection of its middle-size models and badges. In the mid-1930s, there had been a Humber 12hp, a Hillman 16hp and a Humber 18hp, which in marketing terms was rather messy.

In the autumn of 1937, therefore, Rootes separated the two makes; henceforth the smallest Humber would be the 16hp and the largest Hillman would be a 14hp. If only to make life easier for dealers and the manufacturing specialists, this ought to have been done years earlier.

The Hillman 14, therefore, was the spiritual descendant of the Humber 12hp and the Hillman 16hp (both of which disappeared at this time), for it drew components from both types.

The box-section side-member chassis of the 14hp model was new; although typical of the Evenkeel type introduced two years earlier on the Hillman 16hp, it had a 6in longer wheelbase than before, but narrow wheel tracks, and there were no radius arms at the front. As usual, there were cable brakes.

The 1,944cc side-valve four-cylinder engine was a simple bored-out stretch of the Humber 12hp unit, and the all-synchromesh gearbox was that of the latest Hillman Minx.

Later changes included deletion of first-gear synchromesh in the autumn of 1938 (at the same time as on the Minx) and the adoption of hydraulic brakes and no running-boards for the proposed but in the event stillborn 1940 models.

Only sold as a saloon, with bodywork by Pressed Steel, this was a value-for-money car (the De Luxe model selling for only £268 in 1938), but it only had a two-year life; after the war, however, it was reborn in modified form as the Humber Hawk (see the Humber chapter), this model being built until 1948.

Hillman 14 specification

Produced: Humber Road, 1937–39, 3,984 cars built.
General layout: Separate steel chassis-frame, 4-cylinder engine and 4-door saloon bodyshell. Front-mounted engine driving rear wheels.
Engine and transmission: Hillman engine, 4-cylinder, sv, in-line. 1,944cc, 75 x 110mm, 51bhp at 3,600rpm; torque not revealed; 4-speed gearbox, all-synchromesh at first, then no 1st-gear synchromesh; centre-floor gear-change; live (beam) rear axle with spiral-bevel final drive.
Chassis: Independent front suspension, transverse leaf spring and upper wishbones. Worm-and-nut steering. Live (beam) rear axle, half-elliptic leaf springs. Front and rear drum brakes. 5.75-16in tyres.
Dimensions: Wheelbase 9ft 6in; front track 4ft 7.5in; rear track 4ft 8in; length 14ft 6in; width 5ft 10in; height 5ft 5in. Unladen weight approx 3,055lb.
Distinguishing features from previous models: Completely different style of Hillman compared with previous models, fitted with 4-door saloon body looking superficially similar to current Minx and large Humbers.
Typical performance: Maximum speed 69mph; 0–50mph 22.5sec; typical fuel consumption 24mpg.
Derivatives: 1945–48 Humber Hawk was same basic car, but updated for postwar use.
Fate: Discontinued on outbreak of war.

Hillman Minx Phase I and II (1939 to 1942 and 1945 to 1948)

Rootes was not the first British company to adopt a monocoque (unit-construction) body-chassis design in its family cars, but was certainly well up in the race to modernize.

For the record, the monocoque Hillman Minx Phase I was revealed in September 1939, was sold in limited numbers to civilians in the early years of the war, latterly to essential users such as doctors and other officials, but was then put into hibernation because of the war. The monocoque Vauxhall 10 had arrived in 1937 and the monocoque Morris Ten in 1938, but the Minx was third in the race.

Although the Phase I was only announced in September 1939, just as the Second World War was beginning in Europe, a considerable number were delivered to meet civilian orders. No fewer than 10,015 examples were produced before November 1942, when Rootes production was finally confined to military machinery; true civilian deliveries then began again in the summer of 1945. Most of the cars were four-door saloons, though a few (Commer-badged) estate cars and a number of drop-head coupes (by Carbodies) were also produced.

At first glance, it was difficult to tell the old (separate-chassis) and the new (monocoque) Minxes apart, for they had the same 7ft 8in wheelbase, tracks and overall dimensions, as well as the same easiclean wheels and similar styling 'signatures'. Except that the monocoque car had a boot bustle where the original car had a smooth tail profile, the lines were virtually identical, and there is no doubt that a considerable proportion of the Magnificent body, as facelifted in 1937, survived in the monocoque car.

Like all Minxes of the 1930s, 1940s and 1950s, this was a solidly reliable family car being sold at very attractive prices. Phase I became Phase II in December 1947, when the front end was restyled to incorporate the headlamps into bulbous wings (in rather the same way as that proposed for the forthcoming Humber Pullman and Super Snipe models a few months hence). At the same time, the Phase II was given an awful Synchromatic steering-column gear-shift, while hydraulic brakes had replaced cables during 1947.

Hillman Minx Phase I and II specification

Produced: Humber Road, 1939–42, Ryton-on-Dunsmore, 1945–48 number built unknown.
General layout: Unit-construction body-chassis structure in saloon, DHC and estate car bodies. Front-mounted engine driving rear wheels.
Engine and transmission: Hillman engine, 4-cylinder, sv, in-line. 1,185cc, 63 x 95mm, 35bhp at 4,100rpm; 54lb ft at 2,400rpm; 4-speed gearbox, no synchromesh on 1st gear; centre-floor gear-change on Phase I, steering-column on Phase II; live (beam) rear axle with spiral-bevel final drive.
Chassis: Beam-axle front suspension, half-elliptic leaf springs. Worm-and-nut steering. Live (beam) rear axle, half-elliptic leaf springs and anti-roll bar. Front and rear drum brakes. 5.00-16in tyres.
Dimensions: Wheelbase 7ft 8in; front track 3ft 10.9in; rear track 4ft 0.5in; length 12ft 9.75in (Phase II, 13ft 0in); width 5ft 0.5in; height 5ft 2.5in. Unladen weight (typical) 1,905lb (Phase II, 2,045lb).
Distinguishing features from previous models: The first unit-construction Hillman, with similar styling to previous Minx model; Phase II model had new full-width nose with faired-in headlamps, and steering-column gear-change.
Typical performance: (Phase II) Maximum speed 63mph; 0–50mph 25.7sec; typical fuel consumption 31mpg.
Derivatives: None.
Fate: Phase I replaced by Phase II in December 1947, Phase II discontinued in 1948 in favour of new Loewy-styled Phase III.

By 1948, however, this type of Minx was beginning to look distinctly old-fashioned; it was replaced by the true postwar generation car, the Minx III, in September 1948.

For 1940, the Minx was redesigned, with a monocoque structure, but the exterior style was virtually unchanged, except for the addition of a boot bulge at the rear.

After the Second World War, Rootes relaunched a Hillman Minx Drophead Coupe. This publicity still shows a 1948 model (complete with revised front style) posed near the J. Arthur Rank film studios at Denham, with contemporary stars Jean Kent and Dermot Walsh adding glamour!

Hillman Minx Phase III, IV and V (1948 to 1953)

Rootes, like other British volume-production car makers, was in no position to produce brand new models immediately after the war in 1945. Work began at once, but it was not until 1948 that the new generation of cars went on sale.

The Phase III Minx, whose styling had been guided by the Loewy studio and much influenced by the Studebakers which Loewy had also produced in the same period, was a smart, full-width family car (but one which still hid essentially mundane mechanical equipment) and it sold at strictly family-car prices. Like the Phase I and II cars before it, a majority were exported for a number of years, which means that few now survive in the UK.

Except for the engine/gearbox/axle assemblies, there was virtually no carry-over from the Phase II car, for the body-chassis unit (sold in saloon, estate car or drop-head coupe form) was entirely new, being altogether more squat and squared-up than before. Power, as ever, was by the famous little side-valve unit which had been designed in 1930. This engine, in fact, would continue to be used in Rootes cars and LCVs until the mid-1950s.

The Minx III became the Minx IV in the autumn of 1949, complete with an enlarged and more powerful engine, plus more substantial bumpers, but the Minx V of October 1951 represented only a minor update.

The first all-postwar Hillman Minx design was the Phase III, launched in the autumn of 1948; it was the first Minx to have independent front suspension.

Styling consultant Raymond Loewy drew inspiration from the postwar Studebaker body style when recommending shapes for the new Hillman Minx.

Hillman Minx Phase III, IV and V specification

Produced: Ryton-on-Dunsmore, 1948–53, 28,619/90,832/59,777 cars built.
General layout: Unit-construction body-chassis structure, 4-cylinder engine and choice of saloon, DHC and estate car bodies. Front-mounted engine driving rear wheels.
Engine and transmission: Hillman engine, 4-cylinder, sv, in-line. (Minx Phase III) 1,185cc, 63 x 95mm, 35bhp at 4,100rpm; 54lb ft at 2,400rpm; (Minx IV and V) 1,265cc, 65 x 95mm, 37.5bhp at 4,200rpm; 58lb ft at 2,200rpm; 4-speed gearbox, no synchromesh on 1st gear; steering-column gear-change; live (beam) rear axle with spiral-bevel final drive.
Chassis: Independent front suspension, coil springs, wishbones. Worm-and-nut steering; worm-and-peg steering on Minx V. Live (beam) rear axle, half-elliptic leaf springs and anti-roll bar. Front and rear drum brakes. 5.00-16in tyres (5.00-15in, estate car).
Dimensions: Wheelbase 7ft 9in; front track 4ft 0.6in; rear track 4ft 0.5in; length 13ft 1.25in; width 5ft 0in; height 5ft 2in. Unladen weight (typical) 2,115lb.
Distinguishing features from previous models: Completely new style of Hillman compared with previous models with modern full-width shape; strong family resemblance to 1949-model Humber Hawk.
Typical performance: (Minx Phase III) Maximum speed 63mph; 0–50mph 24.0sec. typical fuel consumption 35mpg; (Minx IV and V) maximum speed 67mph; 0–60mph 40.2sec; typical fuel consumption 34mpg.
Derivatives: 1953 Minx VI was same basic car but with styling and equipment changes.
Fate: discontinued in 1953 in favour of Minx VI.

Hillman Minx Mk VI and VII (1953 to 1954)

Here was the first of several annual-change Minxes, for the Mk VI was only 17 months behind the Mk V, while Mk VII followed a mere eight months later. Rootes was setting a frenetic pace which it was going to keep up for at least another decade.

The Mk VI was also dubbed the Anniversary Minx, because it was announced 21 years after the original type went on sale. Mechanically, there were virtually no changes, but there were two styling novelties. The new Californian coupe was effectively a permanent hardtop version of the drop-head coupe (and used all the pressings from that car). It was a direct ancestor of what became the Sunbeam Rapier when the next generation of Minx/Sunbeam cars came on stream in 1955–56. The front of all Minxes was jazzed up, with a wide-mouth grille and modified sheet metal surrounding it.

Eight months later, the Mk VII Minx took over, with further styling improvements which included an enlarged rear window and other tail-end detail changes. The big modernization – a new overhead-valve engine – would have to wait until the Mk VIII, which followed in 1954.

Another view of the Phase III Hillman Minx, showing the full-width style combined with a compact overall length.

Even though it had a monocoque structure, the early 1950s Minx was built in several different styles. This was the Convertible, complete with its 1953 facelift front end.

The Thrupp & Maberly stand at the Earls Court Motor Show in 1952 had examples of the latest Minx Drophead Coupe, and the Minx Californian, on display. With them are the latest Sunbeam-Talbot and Humber models of the day.

In 1953 Rootes revealed the Minx Californian, above, really a hardtop version of the existing Convertible. Clearly this was the direct ancestor of the Sunbeam Rapier which followed in 1955. By 1954 the Minx had become Mk VII, below, visually almost exactly the same as when facelifted in 1953.

Hillman Minx Mk VI and VII specification

As for Minx Mk V except for:
Produced: Ryton-on-Dunsmore, 1953–54, 44,643/60,711 cars built.
Engine: 1,265cc engine fitted to all types.
Dimensions: Length 13ft 3.5in.
Distinguishing features from previous models: New nose style with wide-mouth chrome grille. Californian (hardtop) coupe introduced for first time. Mk VII had longer tail and larger boot.
Typical performance: (Californian) Maximum speed 69mph; 0–60mph 34.7sec; standing ¼-mile 24.8sec; typical fuel consumption 29mpg.
Derivatives: 1954 Minx Mk VIII was same basic car as Minx Mk VII, but with overhead-valve engine. Husky of October 1954 was also a short-wheelbase version of established Minx estate car design.
Fate: Discontinued in 1954 in favour of Minx Mk VIII.

Hillman Minx Mk VIII and VIIIA (1954 to 1957)

The most important change made to this generation of postwar Minxes was the adoption of the brand-new overhead-valve engine for the Mk VIII launched in October 1954. This unit, at first with 43bhp from 1,390cc, was to be improved, enlarged and redesigned several times over the next 30 years, eventually to become a 100+bhp 1,725cc unit in the Sunbeam Rapier H120!

In its original Minx form it was a simple three-bearing iron-head unit with a downdraught Zenith carburettor, and it was only fitted to the de Luxe saloon, drop-head coupe and Californian models; for the time being the estate and budget-price Special saloon kept the old side-valve engine, even though these were still known as Mk VIII models.

The Mk VIII became an VIIIA in September 1955 when Gay Look duo-tone paintwork styling was adopted and the side-valve engine was finally abandoned. This model, however, had a very short life, for the new-generation Minx saloon took over in mid-1956; Mk VIIIA estates were made until mid-1957.

Hillman Minx Mk VIII and VIIIA specification

As for Minx Mk VII except for:
Produced: Ryton-on-Dunsmore, 1954–56, 94,123 cars built.
Engine and transmission: Mk VIII except for Special and all Mk VIIIA models, ohv, 1,390cc, 76.2 x 76.2mm, 43bhp at 4,400rpm; 66lb ft at 2,200rpm.
Chassis: Front anti-roll bar, no rear anti-roll bar. 5.60-15in tyres.
Distinguishing features from previous models: Except for Special, all had new ohv engine, plus 15in road wheels. Mk VIIIA saloons had 2-tone paintwork.
Typical performance: Maximum speed 73mph; 0–60mph 29.7sec; standing ¼-mile 23.9sec; typical fuel consumption 35mpg.
Derivatives: None.
Fate: Discontinued in 1956 in favour of new-generation Minx.

Hillman Husky (1954 to 1957)

Almost at the end of the life of the 1954–56 generation of Hillman Minxes, Rootes introduced a short-wheelbase version of the estate car, calling it Husky in passenger-carrying and Commer Cob in plain van form.

The original Husky had a 9in shorter wheelbase than the existing Minx estate car and it retained the old-style side-valve engine until the end of its three-year career. It was a compact car, which could carry very little indeed if the fold-down rear seat was in use, but it was a useful load-carrier if the seat was folded forward. Usefully, too, it had a single-panel rear loading door, hinged at the right side. There was little charisma and the handling was awful, but it seemed to fulfil a need and around 42,000 were sold.

For 1958, however, this type of Husky gave way to a larger model, which was based on the new-generation Minx.

The original Hillman Husky used a shortened version of the Minx estate car's underframe, but there were only two passenger doors, and behind them it used unique body panels.

The long-running Rootes overhead-valve 'four' as used in many Hillmans, Sunbeams and Humbers of the 1950s–1970s period, was revealed in 1954. Weren't engine bays simple in those days!

Hillman Husky specification

Produced: Ryton-on-Dunsmore, 1954–57, 41,898 cars built.
General layout: Unit-construction body-chassis structure, 4-cylinder engine and estate car or van bodies. Front-mounted engine driving rear wheels.
Engine and transmission: Hillman engine, 4-cylinder, sv, in-line. 1,265cc, 65 x 95mm, 35bhp at 4,100rpm; 55lb ft at 2,200rpm; 4-speed gearbox, no synchromesh on 1st gear; centre-floor gear-change; live (beam) rear axle with spiral-bevel final drive.
Chassis: Independent front suspension, coil springs, wishbones. Worm-and-peg steering. Live (beam) rear axle, half-elliptic leaf springs. Front and rear drum brakes. 5.00-15in tyres.
Dimensions: Wheelbase 7ft 0in; front track 4ft 0.6in; rear track 4ft 0.5in; length 12ft 1.5in; width 5ft 2in; height 5ft 1in. Unladen weight approx 1,925lb.
Distinguishing features from previous models: Shorter wheelbase than other models in Minx family, but with strong resemblance to 1954–56 models.
Typical performance: Maximum speed 63mph; 0-50mph 27.5sec; standing ¼-mile 26.3sec; typical fuel consumption 35mpg.
Derivatives: None.
Fate: Discontinued in 1957 in favour of new-generation Husky.

After eight years, Rootes produced a new-generation Minx family, from which several Singers and Sunbeams were also 'cloned'. This was the original Minx style, as announced in 1956.

Hillman Minx Series I and II (1956 to 1957)

Rootes certainly got its money's worth out of the first postwar Minx design, which ran from 1948 to 1956, and it was to do even better with the replacement for that car. The Series Minx design came along in mid-1956 and was last built at the end of 1966 – a very profitable life indeed.

Not only that, but the Minx was the basis from which the two-door Sunbeam Rapier (really a latter-day Californian which got better and better as the years passed), the so-called Singer Gazelle and the second-generation Husky were all developed. Even the smart two-seater Alpine/Tiger models of 1959–68 had definite links and shared quite a lot of running gear with this versatile design. There was no second-generation Californian, of course.

Although the Sunbeam Rapier was revealed first (launched in October 1955, it was seven months ahead of the Minx), it was the Minx which was the central model. The Rapier, of course, was closely related to the forthcoming Minx convertible because it was built with the same underpan, running gear, front end and body panels, but it had a unique two-door saloon/coupe style at first.

With a style inspired by Loewy which was definitely related to early-1950s Studebakers which were also designed in his studio, the new Minx was altogether smarter, sleeker, roomier (with a longer wheelbase), better handling and faster than the cars it replaced. No wonder that Ryton was soon full to overflowing and that Rootes could develop its 'new version every season' philosophy for the next few years. The basic engine/gearbox/axle was carried over from the Mk VIII/VIIIA Minxes of the mid-1950s, but everything else was new.

Saloon and convertible models were launched at once, but the five-door estate car was not ready until June 1957; this type had upper-and-lower tailgate panels. The Series II Minx was launched in August 1957, featuring a slightly revised engine, a floor-mounted gear-change (Husky-type) on the austere Minx Special, the adoption of Lockheeed Manumatic two-pedal transmission and a new front grille.

Nothing, however, lasted for long at Rootes in this period, for the Series III models took over a year later, in the autumn of 1958.

Hillman Minx Series I and II specification

Produced: Ryton-on-Dunsmore, 1956–58, 202,264 cars built.
General layout: Unit-construction body-chassis structure, 4-cylinder engine and choice of saloon, DHC and estate car bodies. Front-mounted engine driving rear wheels.
Engine and transmission: Hillman engine, 4-cylinder, ohv, in-line. 1,390cc, 76.2 x 76.2mm, (SI) 47.5bhp (net) at 4,600rpm; 70lb ft at 2,400rpm; (SII) 47.5bhp (net) at 4,400rpm; 72lb ft at 2,200rpm; 4-speed gearbox, no synchromesh on 1st gear; steering-column gear-change (floor change on SII Special); optional Manumatic semi-automatic transmission on SII models; live (beam) rear axle with spiral-bevel final drive.
Chassis: Independent front suspension, coil springs, wishbones and anti-roll bar. Worm-and-nut steering. Live (beam) rear axle, half-elliptic leaf springs. Front and rear drum brakes. 5.60-15in tyres.
Dimensions: Wheelbase 8ft 0in; front track 4ft 1in; rear track 4ft 0.5in; length 13ft 4.5in; width 5ft 0.75 in; height 4ft 11.5in, estate car 5ft 1in. Unladen weight (saloon) approx 2,185lb.
Distinguishing features from previous models: Completely new style of Hillman compared with previous models with strong family resemblance to 1956-model Sunbeam Rapier.
Typical performance: Maximum speed 77mph; 0–60mph 27.7sec; standing ¼-mile 23.5sec; typical fuel consumption 34mpg.
Derivatives: 1958 Minx SIII was same basic car with styling and equipment changes. Singer Gazelle was same car, originally with own engine, latterly with only decoration differences. 1958 Husky was short-wheelbase version of estate. Sunbeam Rapier was two-door and more highly tuned derivative.
Fate: Discontinued in 1958 in favour of Minx Series III.

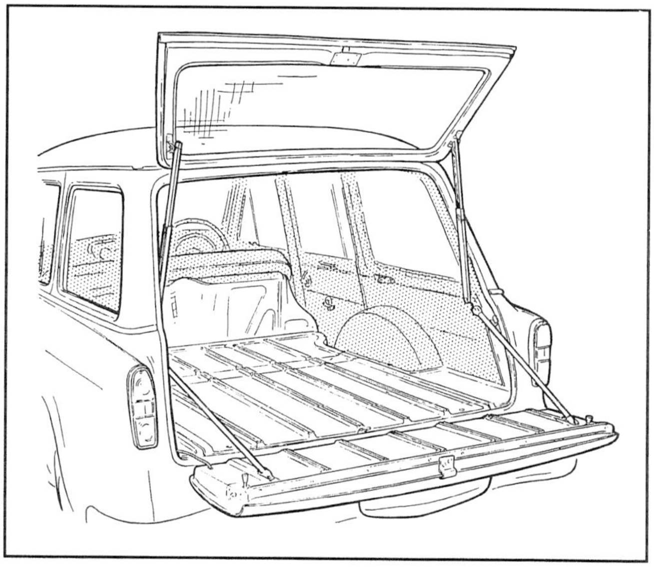

Opposite: Hillman's Minx estate was a smart and versatile derivative of the saloon, with a split tailgate, which had been revealed in mid-1956. In Hillman, and Singer Gazelle, form, this sold strongly for several years. Rootes also produced a convertible version of the Minx, though sales of this type of body were falling away all the time. The Sunbeam Rapier convertible used the same basic structure too. Right: by the end of 1959 the Hillman Minx had been facelifted *and* tail-lifted – the tailfins, in fact, being introduced for the Series IIIA.

Hillman Minx Series III, IIIA and IIIB (1958 to 1961)

Take a deep breath and absorb what Rootes did to the Minx in three years and three model derivatives without basically altering the design....

The Series III of September 1958 received an enlarged (1,494cc versus 1,390cc) version of the modern overhead-valve engine, bringing it into line with the latest Gazelles and Rapiers. At the same time, there was a different grille and a revised facia.

Only a year later, the Series IIIA took over with the option of Smiths Easidrive automatic transmission in place of the Manumatic semi-automatic, together with more engine power, a floor gear-change on all home-market models, new roll-over rear fins and yet another front grille.

The Series IIIB followed less than a year after the IIIA, the most important change being the adoption of a new generation of hypoid-bevel rear axle, instead of the long-established spiral type. Even after all this, a Series IIIC was to follow just one year later!

Hillman Minx Series III, IIIA and IIIB specification

As for Minx Series II except for:
Produced: Ryton-on-Dunsmore, 1958–61, 83,105/78,052/58,260 cars built.
Engine and transmission: 1,494cc, 79 x 76.2mm, (SIII) 49bhp (net) at 4,400rpm; 78lb ft at 2,100rpm; (SIIIA and SIIIB) 53bhp (net) at 4,600rpm; 83lb ft at 2,000rpm; centre-floor gear-change, all models, from start of SIIIA; optional Smiths Easidrive automatic transmission instead of Manumatic from start of SIIIA.
Dimensions: Length 13ft 6in. Unladen weight (saloon) approx 2,200lb.
Typical performance: (SIII) Maximum speed 78mph; 0–60mph 26.6sec; standing ¼-mile 23.2sec; typical fuel consumption 29mpg.
Derivatives: 1961 Minx Series IIIC was revised version of SIIIB. Other Singer Gazelle/Sunbeam Rapier types were also closely related.
Fate: Discontinued in 1961 in favour of Minx Series IIIC.

Hillman Minx Series IIIC (1961 to 1963)

From August 1961, immediately after the factory's summer shut-down, the Minx progressed to Series IIIC. The most significant changes were that the engine was enlarged to 1,592cc and there was a general price reduction. At this stage, a duo-tone paint finish cost an extra £10 (basic) or £14.58 with Purchase Tax.

Rootes started to advertise the car as the Minx 1600 at a time when the range began to be trimmed. There was no stripped-out Special version of the Series IIIC, while to leave the field clear for the newly announced Super Minx, both the estate and convertible types were dropped from the summer of 1962. On this latest model, the Minx name was added to the tail of the cars in a chromed script.

Hillman Minx Series IIIC specification

As for Minx Series IIIB except for:
Produced: Ryton-on-Dunsmore, 1961–63, number of cars built unknown.
Engine and transmission: 1,592cc, 81.5 x 76.2mm, 53bhp (net) at 4,100rpm; 87lb ft at 2,100rpm; Smiths Easidrive automatic transmission optional.
Distinguishing features from previous models: Minx script on tail, single waistline strip instead of twin strips.
Typical performance: Maximum speed 79mph; 0–60mph 23.6sec; standing ¼-mile 22.8sec; typical fuel consumption 25mpg.
Derivatives: Minx Series V was restyled version of Series IIIC. Singer Gazelle followed suit and Rapier was continued.
Fate: Discontinued in favour of Minx Series V in 1963.

From late 1961 the Minx became Series IIIC, with badging changes to denote the use of a 1.6-litre engine (note the '1600' badging on the doors).

The Minx Convertible of the late 1950s (this was a Series IIIA) was a smart style, made more interesting by the use of the roll-over fins. Below: no matter how often the Minx was facelifted, there was always an estate version which was well-packaged and popularly priced. This particular example dates from about 1960.

Hillman Minx Series V (1963 to 1965)

There was no Minx Series IV, for this title had originally been reserved for the car officially launched as the Super Minx in 1961. Instead, the long-running Minx jumped from Series IIIC to Series V in 1963.

Even after seven years, Rootes had not lost interest in the Minx family, for in moving from Series IIIC to V the company indulged in a complete restyle and re-engineering of the cabin and tail end. Out went the rounded roof and the wraparound window, to be replaced by a more angular cabin top having enlarged doors, a simple curved rear window and a more angular roof line.

The roll-over fins, too, had disappeared, to be replaced by simple, rather angular, corners.

There was also a great deal of further rationalization with the Super Minx, for at long last the Minx was given 13in wheels, front-wheel disc brakes, a larger (10-gallon) fuel tank and Borg-Warner instead of Smiths Easidrive automatic transmission as an option. There was also a new all-synchromesh gearbox from autumn 1964.

All chassis grease points had been eliminated, and there was a new low-line bonnet profile, along with a new facia layout.

This well-liked, no-nonsense, version of the Minx ran for just two years before being superseded by the last of the line in the autumn of 1965.

Hillman Minx Series V specification

As for Minx Series IIIC except for:
Produced: Ryton-on-Dunsmore, 1963–65, number of cars built unknown.
Engine and transmission: (Series V) Automatic transmission cars 58bhp (net) at 4,000rpm; 86lb ft at 2,500rpm; all-synchromesh gearbox from late 1964; optional Borg-Warner automatic transmission.
Chassis: Front-wheel disc brakes. 6.00-13in tyres.
Dimensions: Front track 4ft 3.75in; height 4ft 10in.
Distinguishing features from previous models: Restyled upper cabin including enlarged rear doors, non-wraparound rear window plus new facia style, squatter cabin profile and 13in wheels. Closely related to Gazelle V of the period.
Derivatives: 1965 Minx Series VI used same structure, but larger and more powerful engine.
Fate: Discontinued in autumn 1965 in favour of Minx Series VI.

Hillman Minx Series VI (1965 to 1967)

This really *was* the final fling for this successful and long-running Rootes family car. In the autumn of 1965 it was given the latest, enlarged (1,725cc) five-bearing version of the famous overhead-valve engine, and this carried it forward until the beginning of 1967, when it was finally supplanted by the new-generation Arrow style of Minx. There were no styling changes except for the inclusion of '1725' badges to denote the use of the latest engine.

Hillman Minx Series VI specification

As for Minx Series V except for:
Produced: 1965–67, number of cars built unknown.
Engine and transmission: 1,725cc, 81.5 x 82.55mm, originally 65bhp (net) at 4,800rpm; 98lb ft at 2,400rpm, but most cars 59bhp (net) at 4,200rpm; 92lb ft at 2,200rpm.
Distinguishing features from previous models: Series VI had '1725' badges.
Typical performance: Maximum speed 82mph; 0–60mph 20.5sec; standing ¼-mile 21.8sec; typical fuel consumption 25mpg.
Derivatives: None.
Fate: Discontinued early in 1967 in favour of new Arrow type of Minx.

Hillman Husky Series I and II (1958 to 1963)

The original Husky only had a three-year career, and even then it outlived the Minx family on which it had been based by more than a year. A new-generation Husky duly followed in January 1958, about a year and a half after the first of the new-generation Series Minxes appeared in 1956.

From the autumn of 1963 the Minx became Series V, complete with a roof and tail-end restyle. All in all, this shape was simpler, and more successful, than the original.

For the front of the Minx Series V there was another new grille, simple enough to harmonize with the rest of the fresh style.

There was even an attempt to up-date the 1963 facelift, but it was abandoned at the mock-up stage. Roy Axe supplied this Stoke styling studio shot.

The second-generation Husky, like the first, was effectively a short-wheelbase Minx estate car, but with two doors not four, and a side-hinged tailgate.

The Commer Cob was really a van version of the Hillman Husky estate. This was a late-1950s model, based on the second-generation Husky.

The Husky received body modifications, with a lowered roof panel and other changes, from March 1960.

Like the original type, the new-generation Husky was a short-wheelbase, three-door version of the five-door Minx estate car. The new type of Husky therefore had an overhead-valve engine, but it also ran on a 2in longer wheelbase than the original type and was a little more roomy and capacious. Like the original type, it had a one-piece tailgate, hinged at the right side. As before, there was a centre-floor gear-change, and trim standards approximated to those of the Special saloon, with a very simple facia/dashboard layout.

The Series I type was upgraded to Series II in March 1960, at which point it received a slightly lowered roof line, a deeper front screen and better seating. Along with other cars in this wide-ranging family, it gained a new design of hypoid rear axle in August 1960. This car ran through until the summer of 1963, when the final Series III took over.

Hillman Husky Series I and II specification

Produced: Ryton-on-Dunsmore, 1958–63, approx 56,000 cars built.
General layout: Unit-construction body-chassis structure, 4-cylinder engine and short-wheelbase estate car body style. Front-mounted engine driving rear wheels.
Engine and transmission: Hillman engine, 4-cylinder, ohv, in-line. 1,390cc, 76.2 x 76.2mm, (early cars) 40bhp (net) at 4,000rpm; 66lb ft at 1,600rpm; (from mid-1959, including all SIIs) 47bhp at 4,400rpm; 72lb ft at 2,200rpm; 4-speed gearbox, no synchromesh on 1st gear; centre-floor gear-change; live (beam) rear axle with spiral-bevel final drive at first, hypoid-bevel from August 1960.
Chassis: Independent front suspension, coil springs, wishbones. Worm-and-nut steering. Live (beam) rear axle, half-elliptic leaf springs. Front and rear drum brakes. 5.00-15in tyres.
Dimensions: Wheelbase 7ft 2in; front track 4ft 1in; rear track 4ft 0.5in; length 12ft 5.5in; width 5ft 0.5in; height (SI) 5ft 0.9in, (SII) 4ft 11.5in. Unladen weight (typical) 2,080lb.
Distinguishing features from previous models: Completely new style of Husky compared with previous model, now a short-wheelbase version of new (1956-generation) Minx estate car.
Typical performance: (Husky SI) Maximum speed 69mph; 0–60mph 41.4sec; standing ¼-mile 24.3sec; typical fuel consumption 34mpg; (Husky SII) maximum speed 73mph; 0–60mph 30.0sec; standing ¼-mile 23.2sec; typical fuel consumption 27mpg.
Derivatives: 1963 Husky SIII was same basic car with styling and equipment changes.
Fate: Discontinued in 1963 in favour of Husky SIII.

The facelifted second-generation Husky, complete with new grille, was built from 1963 to 1965.

Hillman Husky Series III (1963 to 1965)

In August 1963, Rootes facelifted the Husky in line with the changes made to other cars in the Minx/Gazelle/Rapier family. For the Husky, which became Series III, this meant a lowered bonnet line, a modernized facia/instrument panel layout and the deletion of all chassis greasing points. With ground clearance in mind, however, the Husky retained its 15in wheels (whereas the Minx went to 13in at this juncture).

A year later, from September 1964, the Husky also inherited the new all-synchromesh gearbox, a diaphragm-spring clutch and a front suspension anti-roll bar.

Production of Husky models finally ran out at the end of 1965, well before the Minx itself was dropped. The next-generation Husky was an entirely different type of car, being based on the rear-engined Hillman Imp.

Hillman Husky Series III specification

As for Husky Series III except for:
Produced: 1963–65, number of cars built unknown.
Engine and transmission: 40.5bhp (net) at 4,200rpm; 72lb ft at 1,800rpm; all-synchromesh gearbox from late 1964; hypoid-bevel final drive.
Chassis: Front anti-roll bar from late 1964. Recirculating-ball steering. 5.60-15in tyres.
Distinguishing features from previous models: Lowered bonnet line and revised facia/instrument panel layout.
Typical performance: Maximum speed 73mph; 0–60mph 35.9sec; standing ¼-mile 24.5sec; typical fuel consumption 27mpg.
Derivatives: None.
Fate: Discontinued at end of 1965 and not immediately replaced. Next Husky, introduced in 1967, was based on rear-engined Hillman Imp.

Hillman Super Minx Mk I and II (1961 to 1964)

This model family (which also included the Singer Vogue and the Humber Sceptre) was originally planned as a straight replacement for the existing 'Audax' range of Hillman Minxes, but as development progressed it became clear that the new car would be bigger, heavier and more expensive than originally hoped. Lord Rootes was unwilling to see his profitable Minxes killed off in favour of a more expensive car, so the decision was taken to build both types in parallel. Thus the new Minx, which should have been badged as the Minx Series IV, became the Super Minx.

Technically, it was a conventional series of cars in the familiar Rootes tradition, with saloon, estate car and convertible derivatives, and the well-proven Minx engine and transmission, but there was a new front suspension and many thoughtful detail changes. The style, by Ted White's Humber Road studio without any Loewy influence (those links had become more tenuous in the late 1950s), retained a full wraparound rear window, and the bodies were more spacious than those of the Audax variety of Minx. A bench front seat was standard, though individual seats were available for less than £15.

The Super Minx started life with a 62bhp, 1,592cc version of the familiar four-cylinder engine, and a floor gear-change was standard. It was the first medium-sized Rootes car to use 13in road wheels, and it picked up the more satisfactory Borg-Warner automatic transmission option from 1962. The new car, therefore, was unexciting, not that it was ever intended to be otherwise.

Only a year after its birth, the Super Minx progressed to Mk II, with front discs instead of drums, individual front seats as standard, a relocated petrol tank, and Borg-Warner automatic transmission as an option. The convertible disappeared in June 1964.

Perhaps this should originally have been a 'new Hillman Minx', but in the end the *old* Minx continued, and the new car became the Super Minx, launched in 1961.

The Super Minx was well-packaged, with good rear leg room (though for this publicity shot you may be sure that the front seats had been slid forward to make it look more spacious . . .)

Hillman Super Minx Mk I and II specification

Produced: Ryton-on-Dunsmore, 1961–64, number of cars built unknown.
General layout: Unit-construction body-chassis structure, 4-cylinder engine and choice of saloon, DHC (from June 1962) and estate car (from May 1962) bodies. Front-mounted engine driving rear wheels.
Engine and transmission: Hillman engine, 4-cylinder, ohv, in-line. 1,592cc, 81.5 x 76.2mm, 62bhp (net) at 4,800rpm; 84lb ft at 2,800rpm; 4-speed gearbox, no synchromesh on 1st gear; centre-floor gear-change; optional Easidrive automatic transmission at first, optional Borg-Warner automatic transmission for Super Minx II; live (beam) rear axle with hypoid-bevel final drive.
Chassis: Independent front suspension, coil springs, wishbones, anti-roll bar, half-elliptic leaf springs. Front and rear drum brakes at first, front discs on Super Minx II. 5.90-13in tyres.
Dimensions: Wheelbase 8ft 5in; front track 4ft 3.5in; rear track 4ft 0.5in; length 13ft 9in; width 5ft 2.25in; height 4ft 10.25in. Unladen weight (typical) 2,355lb.
Distinguishing features from previous models: Completely new style of Hillman compared with previous models, with new unit-construction hull. Recognition points included sidelamps tucked under crown of front wings.
Typical performance: Maximum speed 83mph; 0–60mph 22.5sec; standing ¼-mile 22.7sec; typical fuel consumption 24mpg.
Derivatives: 1964 Super Minx Mk III was same basic car with styling and equipment changes. Singer Vogue and Humber Sceptre models were both developed from this basic design.
Fate: Discontinued in 1964 in favour of Super Minx Mk III.

Super Minx Mk III and IV (1964 to 1967)

After only three years, the Super Minx was given a thorough mid-life facelift and became the Mk III. The body cabin was restyled so that the original wraparound rear window was dropped in favour of a near-flat rear screen, while there was an extra quarter-window behind the rear doors and a new roof panel to suit. Only saloon and estate car options were available, Rootes having dropped its convertible type in mid-1964. At the same time, the car was given the new corporate all-

This was the original Super Minx estate car, a style which was built from 1962.

The last of the Super Minx estate cars was produced in 1966/1967, fitted with the five-bearing 1,725cc, engine, and subtle restyling included a deeper windscreen.

The Super Minx convertible was a short-lived model, built only from mid-1962 to mid-1964, as sales were very low.

Hillman Super Minx Mk III and IV specification

As for Super Minx Mk II except for:
Produced: 1964–67, number of cars built unknown.
General layout: Saloon and estate car bodies available.
Engine and transmission: Mk IV version had 1,725cc, 81.5 x 82.55mm, 65bhp (net) at 4,800rpm; 91lb ft at 2,400rpm; 4-speed all-synchromesh gearbox.
Distinguishing features from previous models: In addition to new engine and gearbox, Mk IV also had fully reclining front seats.
Typical performance: (Mk III) Maximum speed 82mph; 0–60mph 19.5sec; standing ¼-mile 21.5sec; typical fuel consumption 25mpg; (Mk IV) Maximum speed 83mph; 0–60mph 17.9sec; standing ¼-mile 20.7sec; typical fuel consumption 22mpg.
Derivatives: Singer Vogue and Humber Sceptre of same period were close relatives.
Fate: Discontinued in 1966/67 in favour of new-generation Hillman Hunter.

synchromesh gearbox and fully reclining front seats became standard.

Only a year later, the Mk IV took over. This used exactly the same hull and general style as before, but was given the newly developed five-main-bearing 1,725cc version of the familiar four-cylinder engine and Laycock overdrive became optional. The last saloon was built in 1966, ahead of the launch of the Hunter, though the estate car carried on into the spring of 1967.

Hillman Imp Mk I and II (1963 to 1976)

The creation, life and subsequent decline of the Linwood project has already been covered in earlier chapters. The all-new rear-engined Imp was the first of many cars in this family for which the Linwood factory was set up.

Rootes had built several economy car prototypes in the 1950s before settling on this design to rival BMC's Mini, Ford's Anglia and Vauxhall's Viva in British and

Would you believe that this astonishingly bulbous prototype was a forerunner of the Hillman Imp, conceived during the bubble-car boom?

world markets. The new car, coded 'Apex', was eventually made in Hillman Imp, Singer Chamois and Sunbeam Imp/Stiletto guises as a saloon, a coupe, a Husky estate car and a van. Sports car versions were also designed, but not put on sale.

The layout was unfashionable (and, as it transpired, unsuccessful) for there was a light-alloy four-cylinder engine behind the line of the rear wheels, driving them through a four-speed all-synchromesh gearbox. The car was tail-heavy, but because it had carefully developed all-independent suspension, allied to rack-and-pinion steering, it handled well and even the least powerful types were true drivers' cars.

The Imp was neither a sales nor a financial success. The main problem was not one of styling or packaging (both of which were thoroughly satisfactory), but of fashion (the small-car world was rapidly turning to front-

Hillman Imp Mk I and II specification

Produced: Linwood, 1963–76, 440,032 of all types of Imp built.
General layout: Unit-construction body-chassis structure, 4-cylinder engine and saloon body style. Rear-mounted engine driving rear wheels.
Engine and transmission: Hillman/Coventry Climax engine, 4-cylinder, ohc, in-line. 875cc, 68 x 60.4mm, 39bhp (net) at 5,000rpm; 52lb ft at 2,800rpm; later recalibrated to 37bhp (DIN) at 4,800rpm; 49lb ft at 2,600rpm; 4-speed gearbox, synchromesh on all forward gears; centre-floor gear-change; transaxle in unit with engine, hypoid-bevel final drive.
Chassis: Independent front suspension, coil springs, swing axles. Rack-and-pinion steering. Independent rear suspension, coil springs and semi-trailing arms. Front and rear drum brakes. 5.50-12in tyres.
Dimensions: Wheelbase 6ft 10in; front track 4ft 1in; rear track 4ft 0in; length 11ft 7in; width 5ft 0.25in; height 4ft 6.5in. Unladen weight approx 1,530lb.
Distinguishing features from previous models: Completely new style of Hillman compared with previous models with squared-up styling and rear engine.
Typical performance: (From late 1965, with more powerful engine) Maximum speed 78mph; 0–60mph 25.4sec; standing ¼-mile 22.8sec; typical fuel consumption 36mpg.
Derivatives: Singer Chamois was same basic car with styling and equipment changes, Sunbeam Imp Sport was more powerful version, Californian was coupe derivative, Husky was estate car type.
Fate: Discontinued in 1976 and not replaced.

This was the Imp as it eventually appeared, distinctively styled with large glass area, the waistline groove reputedly showing the influence of the Chevrolet Corvair design.

A sectioned view of the original Hillman Imp, showing the rear-mounted engine/transmission assembly, and the swing axle independent front suspension.

wheel drive) and poor product reliability. At best, only 29,000 Imps were sold in the UK in a year – about a third of what Rootes had expected.

Within two or three years the cars were much more durable and sensibly detailed than before, but on the 'give a dog a bad name' principle the damage had already been done. To the very end, engines were always liable to blow cylinder-head gaskets and overheat, and there were many detail problems in build quality which were never resolved. Mk II Imps had more lusty engines (though quoted peak figures were not changed) and better finish, while an internal facelift (introduced in October 1968) produced a rather messy instrument layout, but better seats and details.

There were no important changes over the next eight years, with the Imp family gradually dying out as the 1970s progressed.

Apart from the Singer and Sunbeam badged types, the Imp also spawned the smart little Californian coupe which, like the Husky estate car, is described separately.

One feature of the Imp saloons (but not the fastback coupes) was the opening rear window. This allowed luggage to be stowed behind the rear seat backrest which could also be tipped forwards.

The front boot of the rear-engined Imp was rather small because the spare wheel took up a lot of space. This was an early-1970s example of the car, by which time the nose had been facelifted, and radial-ply tyres had been standardized.

The Super Imp was a better-trimmed version of the Imp De Luxe, mechanically unchanged. This was a 1971 model, in what is sometimes called 'Mk 3' form.

One of several restyling studies carried out on the Imp in the late 1960s. It never progressed beyond the mock-up stage.

The Imp Californian featured a lowered roof line in a fastback style, the shell being shared with the Singer Chamois Coupe and the Sunbeam Stiletto.

Inside the Imp Californian was a split-fold rear seat backrest arrangement, useful for light luggage, though the rear window did not open.

Hillman Imp Californian (1967 to 1970)

In January 1967, Rootes/Chrysler revealed the smart little Imp Californian, a far more elegant car than the first Rootes model to carry that name in 1953. Basically this was an upmarket version of the rear-engined Imp, but distinguished by a smart fastback coupe roof line, allied to a more steeply raked windscreen and a lowered steering column. It was a little lower than the saloon, and there was rather less space and headroom in the rear seat.

The seats were fully reclining, and this was the first of the Imps to have de-cambered front suspension. Like the Imp, it was facelifted in October 1968, with a new facia and other details.

In little more than three years, only 6,122 Californians were sold in the UK, which explains why it was dropped in April 1970. The Sunbeam Stiletto version, which was faster, smarter and more exclusive, was a much more appealing proposition.

Hillman Imp Californian specification

As for Hillman Imp saloons except for:
Produced: 1967–70.
General layout: Fastback coupe body style.
Dimensions: Height 4ft 3in. Unladen weight approx 1,560lb.
Distinguishing features from previous models: No relation to 1953–56 Hillman Californian. Compared with Hillman Imp saloon, had lowered roof line in fastback coupe style.
Typical performance: Maximum speed 78mph; 0–60mph 22.1sec; standing ¼-mile 21.9sec; typical fuel consumption 35mpg.
Derivatives: Sunbeam Stiletto used same basic body as Imp Californian, but with more power. Singer Chamois Coupe was close relation.
Fate: Discontinued in 1970 and not replaced.

Hillman Husky (1967 to 1970)

Two years after the last conventional (front-engine/rear-drive) Husky had been dropped, Rootes/Chrysler introduced a third-generation Husky, this being a derivative of the rear-engined Imp. Because it had a loading floor above the engine and transmission, it was by no means an easy design to evolve.

From the nose to the front doors the new-type Husky was based on the existing Imp, but from that point on it was given a square, high-roof, estate car body, which offered 25cu ft of load capacity. There was a one-piece, lift-up tailgate and engine bay cooling slots were provided under the aperture. A van version, the Commer Cob, was also available.

Mechanically, the Husky was like the Imp, though it was the first Hillman derivative to be fitted with radial-ply tyres. Unfortunately, the Husky was launched when the Imp's reputation was already in decline and the Group's new owner, Chrysler, was determined to rationalize at all costs. Accordingly, the Husky was dropped in 1970, only three years after it had appeared.

The Imp-based Hillman Husky of the late 1960s had a high roof and (considering the rear engine location) excellent stowage capacity. A van version was also produced.

Hillman Husky specification

As for Hillman Imp saloons except for:
Produced: 1967–70.
General layout: Estate car body style.
Chassis: 155-12in tyres.
Dimensions: Length 11ft 9in; height 4ft 10in. Unladen weight approx 1,645lb.
Distinguishing features from previous models: Completely new style of Husky compared with previous models, based on Imp layout wtih high-back estate car style.
Typical performance: Maximum speed 76mph; 0–60mph 24.2sec; standing ¼-mile 22.8sec; typical fuel consumption 35mpg.
Derivatives: Van version was called Commer Cob.
Fate: Discontinued in 1970 and not replaced.

Hillman Rallye Imp (1965 to 1967)

For marketing reasons, the Rootes Competitions Department was asked to start rallying Imps in 1964, but it soon became clear that the 875cc-engined car was not quick enough. Accordingly, an enlarged version of the engine, bored out to 998cc, was developed for 1965, and this was used wherever the regulations allowed. Rosemary Smith achieved a startling, but prestigious, outright victory in the Tulip Rally that year.

From the autumn of 1965, in order to gain sporting homologation, a car called the Rallye Imp was officially launched.

Rallye Imps were produced in a small workshop at the Humber Road works, close to the Competitions Department, as conversions of standard cars which had been delivered from Linwood to Coventry. In addition to the enlarged and more powerful engine, these cars

In 998cc form, the Imp became the Rallye Imp and was developed into a very successful class-winning car. This is Rosemary Smith and Val Domleo on their way to yet another Ladies' Award in a dark-blue painted 'works' car.

On the racing circuit too, the 998cc Imp was, for a time, almost unbeatable in its class.

were given suspension revisions, a special facia panel and a servo for the drum brakes. Peak power was boosted from 37bhp to 60bhp, but the conversion cost £250 – a 46% impost on top of the retail price of an Imp de Luxe. Homologation regulations required 500 such cars to be built in a year for sporting approval to be given, and in theory this was duly achieved. However, no actual build figures have ever been released, and it is likely that rather fewer were, in fact, produced. Once the Sunbeam Imp Sport became readily available in the winter of 1966–67, demand for the Rallye Imp conversions died away.

Rallye Imps were very successful in motor racing, where supertuned 998cc engines were eventually persuaded to produce more than 100bhp, but few cars were ever used on the road.

Just to confuse the issue of identity, a number of other Imp derivatives – Singer and Sunbeam-badged saloons or coupes – were given the same treatment, and a number of older cars were retrospectively modified in later life....

Hillman Rallye Imp specification

As for Hillman Imp except for:
Produced: Linwood and Humber Road, 1965–67, number of cars built unknown.
Engine and transmission: 998cc, 72.5 x 60.4mm, 60bhp (DIN) at 6,200rpm; 59lb ft at 3,200rpm.
Distinguishing features from previous models: Lowered and stiffened suspension, extra cooling slats in engine lid, twin-carburettor engine, special instrument and facia panel.
Typical performance: (Works rally car with perhaps 70bhp) Maximum speed 92mph; 0–60mph 14.9sec; standing ¼-mile 19.8sec; typical fuel consumption 30mpg.

Later models

Two important new families of Hillman cars came on to the market after Chrysler's influence over Rootes had become complete. One was the medium-sized Arrow-family Hunters and Minxes and the other was the B-Car, better known as the Avenger series.

These cars, their specifications, and the events which led to their development, are discussed in **Chapter 9**, which covers the period following the takeover by Chrysler.

Chapter 5

HUMBER

In encouraging Humber to merge with Hillman in 1928, then injecting capital and finally taking control of the companies, Rootes was looking ahead to an enlarged, rationalized and altogether more efficient operation at Humber Road, Coventry.

Even so, most of the early effort went into the revival of Hillman, through the launch of the Wizard and then the Minx. There was little sign of the same process at Humber until the arrival of the new four-cylinder 12hp model for 1933.

Real rationalization came three years later with the launch of a new range of side-valve six-cylinder engines and the appearance of a smoothly-profiled six-window bodyshell from Pressed Steel (which was shared, until 1940, with the more expensive Hillman models). By the end of the 1930s, Rootes' product strategy had become clear – Hillman would look after the volume cars, Humber would cater for the middle-classes and middle-incomes, while Sunbeam-Talbot would produce a series of sporty models.

After the Second World War, most Humber activity prior to 1963 was based on one chassis design and body style, built with a choice of four-cylinder or six-cylinder engines. A new Humber Hawk arrived in 1948, soon to

In the 1920s the independent Humber company built a series of sturdy touring cars. This is a nicely maintained 8/18, seen at a Vintage meeting in the 1970s.

be joined by the same style of Super Snipe, and an entirely new generation of large cars arrived in 1957 and 1958, which would be built until 1967.

Rootes also invented a new and smaller range of Humbers, the Sceptres, which were closely linked to the Hillman Super Minx and Hillman Hunter ranges during the period 1963-76. Mercifully, there was no attempt to produce a Humber version of the rear-engined Imp model, though this was proposed at one time!

After the merger

By the time the Humber shareholders had agreed to a merger with Hillman, the 1929 models were already on sale, all with characteristic overhead inlet/side exhaust-valve engines. For 1930, the same cars – 9/28, 16/50 and 20/65 – were carried on, along with a new 25/70 Snipe model, based on the 20/65, but with a 3,498cc version of the six-cylinder engine. The little 9/28 was dropped in 1930, but the other models continued for a further two years.

By this time, the merger process was complete, much investment had been poured into the Coventry factories, the Hillman Wizard and Minx cars had been put on sale, and it was time for the first Rootes Humbers to make their appearance. These epoch-making cars were the all-new 12hp model and the side-valve-engined 16/60hp model (itself developed from the 16/50 Snipe).

The 'Vogue' derivative of the Humber Twelve, early 1930s. The Twelve was the first true 'Rootes-Humber' of all.

Humber 12hp (1932 to 1937)

This was the third all-Rootes new car of the early 1930s – the 1931 Hillman Wizard and the 1931–32 Hillman Minx being the first two of the trio – and it was a neat gap-filler in a carefully thought-out range.

The chassis design of the new car was utterly conventional, with half-elliptic springs and beam axles at front and rear and cable-operated brakes. The standard six-window bodyshell, by Pressed Steel, was like that offered on medium-sized Hillmans of the period, though a selection of special and limited-production shells was also offered, notably the Vogue style and some smart open-top cars.

The engine was an all-new four-cylinder side-valve unit of 1,669cc, which was destined to have a very long life indeed. Enlarged later in the 1930s for the Hillman 14, turned into an overhead-valve engine for the postwar Sunbeam-Talbot 90 and used in light commercial vehicles, it was produced in one form or another until the end of the 1970s!

The Humber 12's gearbox was that of the Hillman Minx (which meant that it was all-synchromesh from late 1934) and was none too strong for its job. There was a freewheel for 1934, a new frame with cruciform centre bracing for 1935 and a new-style six-window body style by Pressed Steel.

There were big price reductions in 1936 to counter falling sales, for the 12 (unlike the large six-cylinder-engined Humbers) never received independent front suspension.

Humber 12hp specification

Produced: Coventry, 1933–37, 8,486 cars built.
General layout: Separate chassis-frame with choice of bodyshells and styles. Front-mounted engine driving rear wheels.
Engine and transmission: Humber engine, 4-cylinder, sv, in-line. 1,669cc, 69.5mm x 110mm, 42bhp at 3,800rpm; maximum torque not revealed; 4-speed gearbox, no synchromesh at first, freewheel from late 1933, all-synchromesh from late 1934; centre-floor gear-change; live (beam) axle with spiral-bevel final drive.
Chassis: Beam-axle front suspension, half-elliptic leaf springs. Cam-and-roller steering. Live (beam) rear axle, half-elliptic leaf springs. Front and rear drum brakes. 5.00-18in tyres.
Dimensions: Wheelbase 8ft 2.5in; front track 4ft 3in; rear track 4ft 3in; length 12ft 2in; width 5ft 1in; height 5ft 9in. Unladen weight approx 2,240lb.
Distinguishing features from previous models: No links with previous Humbers. Standard 6-window style very similar to Hillman Wizard of early 1930s.
Typical performance: Maximum speed 65mph; 0–50mph 26sec; typical fuel consumption 28mpg.
Derivatives: None.
Fate: Discontinued in 1937 and not replaced.

The Snipe 80 (this being a 1934 model) was on sale in the early 1930s.

Humber 16/60 and Snipe 80/Pullman (1933 to 1935)

Although one might think this car to be a direct descendant of the 1928–32 16/50, it was really a new car. Not only did it have a new chassis-frame, but there were different six-cylinder engines and rationalized bodies as well.

The new ladder-type frame had a 10ft 4in wheelbase, boxed-in side members alongside the engine and cruciform members under the passenger cabin. The 16/60 used an enlarged side-valve Hillman Wizard-type engine of 2.3 litres with cast-iron combined block and crankcase. The Snipe 80 used a much-modified (side-valve) development of the previous 3,498cc Humber 25/70 engine which, in that form, had had overhead inlet valves. The Snipe 80 unit had an electron crankcase and a separate cast-iron cylinder block.

The gearbox had no synchromesh at first, but constant-mesh top and third gears; synchromesh on top and third was fitted from late 1933. Then, from the spring of 1935, an optional De Normanville gearbox was revealed, this having epicyclic gears and a column change. Hydraulic lever-arm dampers and cable-operated brakes added up to a strictly conventional layout of running gear.

There was a wide choice of bodies, ranging from a standard Pressed Steel type to coachbuilt shells built in small numbers, one being a smart foursome coupe by Thrupp & Maberly. These cars sold well until 1935, when they were replaced by the new range with the Evenkeel independent-suspension chassis-frame.

For 1936, Rootes advertised in snooty periodicals like *The Sphere*, merely by showing a rendering, with the Humber name – nothing more, they thought, was needed. Detroit styling influence is obvious here.

Humber 16/60 and Snipe 80/Pullman specification

Produced: Coventry, 1932–35, 7,891 cars built.
General layout: Separate chassis-frame with choice of bodyshells and styles. Front-mounted engine driving rear wheels.
Engine and transmission: Humber engine, 6-cylinder, sv, in-line. (16/60) 2,276cc, 67.5mm x 106mm, maximum power and torque not revealed; (Snipe 80 and Pullman) 3,498cc, 80 x 116mm, 77bhp peak power, no other details revealed; 4-speed gearbox, no synchromesh at first, on top and 3rd from late 1933; centre-floor gear-change; optional De Normanville semi-automatic transmission in 1935 (with column change); live (beam) rear axle with spiral-bevel final drive.
Chassis: Beam-axle front suspension, half-elliptic leaf springs; radius-arm location from late 1933. Cam-and-roller steering. Live (beam) rear axle, half-elliptic leaf springs. Front and rear drum brakes. (16/60) 6.00-18in tyres; (Snipe 80) 6.50-17in; (Pullman) 7.00-18in.
Dimensions: Wheelbase 10ft 4in/11ft 0in; front track 4ft 9in; rear track 4ft 9in; length (typical) 15ft 9in; width 5ft 8in; height 5ft 9in. Unladen weight (typical) 3,750lb. (Note: Pullman models used 11ft 0in-wheelbase frames, massive bodies and weighed up to 4,200lb.)
Distinguishing features from previous models: Developed visual links with previous coachbuilt Humbers. Standard 6-window style larger, but similar, to large Hillmans of the period.
Typical performance: (Snipe 80) Maximum speed 77mph; 0–60mph 25.4sec; typical fuel consumption 18mpg; (Pullman) maximum speed 73mph; 0–60mph 26.0sec; typical fuel consumption 16mpg.
Derivatives: 1933 Hillman 16 and 20/70 used many Humber 16/60 components, but shorter wheelbase and different bodies.
Fate: Discontinued in 1935, replaced by new-generation large Humbers with independent front suspension chassis-frame.

Humber 18hp and Snipe (1935 to 1937)

By the mid-1930s, Rootes had transformed the Group, and with production rising steadily was able to promote an entirely new range of large Humbers; technically, however, there was quite a lot of overlap with the latest range of Hillmans, for the Hillman 16/Hawk/80 used the same basic running gear as the new Humber 18/Snipe/Pullman models.

The new box-section chassis-frames (longer wheelbases for the Pullman models) featured Evenkeel independent front suspension, with a transverse leaf spring, upper wishbones and radius arms for location purposes. The six-cylinder engines were distantly related to the earlier type of Wizard and 16/60 units, but were almost entirely new in detail and had longer strokes and a simple side-valve layout. The 18 and Snipe engines were matched to the same choice of transmission as before – synchromesh manual, or De Normanville semi-automatic; another feature was servo-assisted brakes.

This is a 1937 model 27hp Humber Snipe, photographed in the 1980s – the car having been stored from 1967 to 1987! This model was one of the first to use the famous Humber 'Blue Riband' six-cylinder engine.

The Humber Pullman of 1936 looked similar to the Snipe of the period, but was longer, more spacious and, of course, more costly. The location? The famous Brooklands motor racing track premises.

The other major innovation was the smoothly-detailed six-window standard-saloon body style by Pressed Steel, which was shared with the larger Humbers and the large Hillmans.

The 2,731cc Humber 18 was only built for two years before Rootes carried out a further reshuffle, when it gave way to the new 16; the Snipe was also smaller-engined for 1938.

Humber 18hp and Snipe specification

Produced: Coventry, 1935–37, 866/2,652 cars built.
General layout: Separate chassis-frame with choice of bodyshells and styles. Front-mounted engine driving rear wheels.
Engine and transmission: Humber engine, 6-cylinder, sv, in-line. (18hp) 2,731cc, 69.5mm x 120mm, 61bhp at 3,600rpm; maximum torque not revealed; (Snipe) 4,086cc, 85 x 120mm, 100bhp at 3,400rpm; maximum torque not revealed; 4-speed gearbox, synchromesh on top and 3rd; centre-floor gear-change; optional De Normanville semi-automatic transmission with column change; live (beam) rear axle with spiral-bevel final drive.
Chassis: Independent front suspension, transverse leaf spring, upper wishbones, radius arm location. Worm-and-nut steering. Live (beam) rear axle, half-elliptic leaf springs. Front and rear drum brakes. 7.00/7.50-16in tyres.
Dimensions: Wheelbase 10ft 4in; front track 4ft 10.6in; rear track 5ft 0.25in; length 16ft 3in; width 6ft 1in; height 5ft 8in. Unladen weight (typical) 4,465lb.
Distinguishing features from previous models: Completely new rounded 6-window body style, similar to large Hillmans of the period. Note the use of a vee-profile 2-piece windscreen.
Typical performance: (18hp) Maximum speed 67mph; 0–60mph 42.8sec; typical fuel consumption 17mpg; (Snipe) maximum speed 83mph; 0–60mph 24.8sec; typical fuel consumption 15mpg.
Derivatives: Hillman 16, Hawk 20 and 80 models from 1935 onwards used many Humber 18 components, including similar bodies but different wheelbases.
Fate: Discontinued in 1937, replaced by 16hp and smaller-engined Snipe models in same basic structure.

Humber Pullman (1935 to 1939)

By this time, Rootes had established its Pullman line for its largest and most expensive Humbers, and this tradition carried on with the new-style Evenkeel chassis-frames. Using an 11ft 0in wheelbase and various Thrupp & Maberly limousine body styles, this was a very successful business and mayoral car of the late 1930s.

The chassis-frame was stiffened-up for 1939, and the car was finally made obsolete at the end of that year when a new body style was introduced. But this was not sold to private customers until after the war.

Humber Pullman specification

Produced: Coventry, 1935–39, 3,700 cars built, including Snipe/Snipe Imperial models.
General layout: Separate chassis-frame with limousine body style. Front-mounted engine driving rear wheels.
Engine and transmission: Humber engine, 6-cylinder, sv, in-line. 4,086cc, 85 x 120mm, 100bhp at 3,400rpm; maximum torque not revealed; 4-speed gearbox, synchromesh on top and 3rd, centre-floor gear-change; optional De Normanville semi-automatic transmission with column change; live (beam) rear axle with spiral-bevel final drive.
Chassis: Independent front suspension, transverse leaf spring, upper wishbones, radius arm location. Worm-and-nut steering. Live (beam) rear axle, half-elliptic leaf springs. Front and rear drum brakes. 7.50-16in tyres.
Dimensions: Wheelbase 11ft 0in; front track 4ft 10.6in; rear track 5ft 0.25in; length 17ft 0in; width 6ft 1in; height 5ft 9in. Unladen weight (typical) 4,585lb.
Distinguishing features from previous models: New 6-window limousine body style. Vee-shape 2-piece windscreen.
Typical performance: Maximum speed 76mph; 0–60mph 27.2sec; typical fuel consumption 15mpg.
Derivatives: None, this being a derivative of the Snipe.
Fate: Discontinued in late 1939, replaced by new body style which went into civilian production in 1945.

Humber 16/Snipe models featured Evenkeel independent front suspension, and the Rootes 'family' body style of the period.

Humber 16hp and Snipe (1937 to 1940)

From September 1937, Rootes reshuffled its range of larger-bodied cars (Humbers and Hillmans) so that it could provide even more carefully spaced models and prices in this profitable market sector.

The new Hillman 14hp (already described) was really a replacement for the Humber 12, the new Humber 16hp had a chassis and body based on the Hillman and it replaced the 18hp model, and the closely-related Snipe became a 21hp model, with a 3.2-litre version of the engine. (The new Snipe Imperial, described below, was really based on the old Snipe of 1935–37.)

Compared with the old 18hp model, of course, the

Humber 16hp and Snipe specification

Produced: Coventry, 1937–39, 1,925/2,706 cars built.
General layout: Separate chassis-frame with Pressed Steel or Mulliners saloon body styles. Front-mounted engine driving rear wheels.
Engine and transmission: Humber engine, 6-cylinder, sv, in-line. (16hp) 2,576cc, 67.5mm x 120mm, 60bhp at 3,700rpm; (Snipe) 3,181cc, 75 x 120mm, 78bhp at 3,300rpm; maximum torque not revealed; 4-speed gearbox, synchromesh on top and 3rd; centre-floor gear-change; live (beam) rear axle with spiral-bevel final drive.
Chassis: Independent front suspension, transverse leaf spring, upper wishbones. Worm-and-nut steering. Live (beam) rear axle, half-elliptic leaf springs. Front and rear drum brakes. 6.00-16in tyres.
Dimensions: Wheelbase 9ft 6in; front track 4ft 7.5in; rear track 4ft 8in; length 14ft 7in; width 5ft 10in; height 5ft 5in. Unladen weight (typical) 3,390lb.
Distinguishing features from previous models: New Pressed Steel 6-window saloon body style, narrower and more compact than before, closely related to new Hillman 14hp.
Typical performance: (Snipe) Maximum speed 76mph; 0–60mph 22.9sec; typical fuel consumption 19mpg.
Derivatives: These cars were derivatives of the new Hillman 14hp. Postwar Humbers (revealed 1945) were closely based on these cars.
Fate: Discontinued in late 1939 immediately after facelift announced, then revived, modified and renamed as the Hawk/Snipe/Super Snipe range in 1945.

new 16hp was a lighter and more compact car, with a different cabin, shorter wheelbase and narrower tracks, but technically and mechanically there were great similarities to the old types; Bendix cable brakes were retained, there were some front suspension improvements, and an automatic choke was now standardized. From September 1938, the chassis was given extra cruciform stiffening, and hydraulic brakes were specified.

From April 1938, a new Mulliners of Birmingham sports saloon style was put on offer at £380/£395. A general styling facelift, unveiled in December 1939, just after the outbreak of war, which included the addition of a boot bustle and narrow foot/running-boards, plus the addition of a rear anti-roll bar, never worked its way through to civilian customers.

Humber Snipe Imperial (1937 to 1939)

As part of the comprehensive reshuffle of larger Hillmans and Humbers announced in the autumn of 1937, the 1935–37 type of Snipe was reincarnated, suitably modified, as the Snipe Imperial.

This retained the 10ft 4in-wheelbase chassis and the 4.1-litre engine of the original design, plus a modified variety of the original Pressed Steel saloon style, and was also sold with a range of special styles including a Thrupp & Maberly limousine, plus sports saloons and drop-head coupes. Naturally, this meant that the Snipe Imperial was more costly than the Snipe – the 1938-model Snipe cost £345 whereas the Imperial prices spanned £495 to £555.

The same technical and mechanical improvements were made as for the 16hp/Snipe models.

Humber Super Snipe (1938 to 1940)

Still permutating all its possibilities, Rootes combined the 4.1-litre 100bhp engine of the Snipe Imperial with the compact chassis and choice of bodies of the 16hp/Snipe models to produce the Super Snipe. By late-1930s standards, this was a real road-burner and gave Ford's all-conquering V8 models a great deal of competition.

Like the 1939 16hp/Snipe models, the Super Snipe had the cruciform-stiffened frame and hydraulic brakes. In common with the other large Humbers, this car was facelifted for 1940, but almost every car then went straight into military service. Happily, it was put on private sale in 1945 when the postwar range was announced.

The 1939 Humber Super Snipe was a very fast car for its day, for it had a 4.1-litre engine. This was one of several body styles which were available – the Sports Saloon.

Super Snipe in battledress – Field Marshal Montgomery's famous 'Old Faithful' model, with Thrupp & Maberly coachwork, as used throughout the North African and Sicilian campaigns of the Second World War.

The official title of this Second World War machine is 'Car, Scout, Humber Mark I', the Rootes family-car connection being that the side-valve Humber Super Snipe engine was used.

Humber Super Snipe specification

As for Humber 16hp/Snipe except for:
Produced: Coventry 1938–40, approx 1,500 cars built. Many more built in 1939–45 for military use.
Engine and transmission: 4,086cc, 85 x 120mm, 100bhp at 3,400rpm. Dimensions: Unladen weight approx 3,500lb.
Typical performance: Maximum speed 82mph; 0–60mph 16.7sec; typical fuel consumption 17mpg.
Derivatives: None prewar, but this car was reborn as the postwar Super Snipe.

Postwar Humbers

By 1945, Rootes had further rationalized its product plan. In the late 1930s it was still possible to sell a wide range of different models without running out of investment capital. Even so, there had been something of an overlap with Hillman (the Humber 12 and 16 had been uncomfortably similar in size, price, styling and engineering to the Hillman 14 and 80), but the pricing/specification ladder was settling down by 1939.

In postwar years, the business and financial climate had changed considerably and from 1945, therefore, the master plan was revised yet again. Hillman was slated to

After the Second World War, the Humber range was rationalized. This was the 1946–1948 variety of Hawk, which was really a rebadged and slightly developed version of the late-1930s Hillman 14hp.

The postwar (1945–1948) variety of Humber Super Snipe often found use as a police car.

produce only the new range of unit-construction Minx models, while Humber was set to build a slightly redesigned Hillman 14, now to be badged as the Hawk, along with familiar Snipes, Super Snipes and Pullmans. All these cars had been facelifted for 1940, but not sold to civilian motorists. The long-chassis Snipe Imperial, however, was not revived.

New postwar designs (with Loewy-inspired full-width body styles) would come along as soon as the body tooling could be readied, but this would take a great deal of time and the new-generation Hawk was delayed until the 1948 Earls Court Motor Show, while its Super Snipe sister car had to wait until 1952 to fall into line.

As with the Hillman marque, Rootes' marketing strategy was falling into line with the North American ideal of providing an annual change, introducing modifications at the start of every model-year and giving the cars different Phase or Model names to suit. Although one basic type of car would run for much longer than in the 1930s, it would come in for more facelifting and modification.

Humber Hawk Mk I and II (1945 to 1948)

Rootes was ready to announce its postwar Humbers in August 1945. Assembly, at first, began at Humber Road (the Stoke factory), but by 1947 it was transferred to the new Ryton-on-Dunsmore plant.

Humber Hawk Mk I and II specification

Produced: Coventry (Humber Road, then Ryton-on-Dunsmore), 1945–48, Mk I production unknown, 4,000 Mk II cars built.
General layout: Separate chassis-frame with Pressed Steel saloon body style. Front-mounted engine driving rear wheels.
Engine and transmission: Humber/Hillman engine, 4-cylinder, sv, in-line. 1,944cc, 75 x 110mm, 56bhp at 3,800rpm; 97lb ft at 2,000rpm; 4-speed gearbox, synchromesh on top, 3rd and 2nd gears; centre-floor gear-change at first, column change from late 1947; live (beam) rear axle with spiral-bevel final drive.
Chassis: Independent front suspension, transverse leaf spring, upper wishbones. Worm-and-nut steering. Live (beam,) rear axle, half-elliptic leaf springs and anti-roll bar. Front and rear drum brakes. 5.75-16in tyres.
Dimensions: Wheelbase 9ft 6in; front track 4ft 7.8in; rear track 4ft 8in; length 15ft 0in; width 5ft 9in; height 5ft 5in. Unladen weight (typical) 2,970lb.
Distinguishing features from previous models: Almost identical style to late-1930s Hillman 14hp or Humber 16hp/Snipe/Super Snipe of same period, facelifted with extended boot and no running-boards.
Typical performance: Similar to Hillman 14hp of 1937–39. Maximum speed 68mph; 0–50mph 21.8sec; typical fuel consumption 24mpg.
Derivatives: Snipe and Super Snipe of this period were same cars with different engines.
Fate: Discontinued in 1948 in favour of new Hawk Mk III.

The new Hawk of 1945, in fact, was little more than a 1940-model Hillman 14hp, complete with the December 1939 facelift (including the enlarged boot compartment with a bustle and no running-boards), some further slight improvements and appropriately rebadged.

Like the last of the prewar Humber 16/Snipe/Super Snipe models, the Hawk was built on the ubiquitous 9ft 6in chassis-frame, complete with Evenkeel independent front suspension. The engine was the side-valve 1,944cc four-cylinder unit, with an aluminimum cylinder head and a peak power output of 56bhp; the gearbox was as fitted to Hillman Minx models, as was the spiral-bevel final drive and differential.

The big change for all such Humbers was that no alternative body styles were on offer – Hawks were only built with the Pressed Steel Company's style, which had first been seen in the 1930s.

In September 1947, there was an important change which upgraded the Hawk from Mk I to Mk II to cater for fashion and (reputedly) for export markets; the same gearbox cluster was fitted into a new casing and selector mechanism so that instead of a centre gear-change, the gear lever was now placed on the steering column.

Humber Snipe (1945 to 1948)

The second rationalized postwar Humber announced in August 1945 was the Snipe, which was effectively the facelifted-for-1940 Snipe, but fitted with the 2,731cc six-cylinder engine last seen in the Humber 18hp of 1935–37.

From September 1947 the Hawk received 'Synchromatic' transmission, which included a steering column gearchange. Evident in this view is the boot bustle added to the basically prewar body design.

The 1947–1948 variety of Humber Hawk chassis, show prepared for inspection. Note the four-cylinder side-valve engine, the transverse leaf spring front suspension, and the steering column gearchange.

Humber Snipe specification

Produced: Coventry (Humber Road, then Ryton-on-Dunsmore), 1945–48, 1,240 cars built.
General layout: Separate chassis-frame with Pressed Steel saloon body style. Front-mounted engine driving rear wheels.
Engine and transmission: Humber engine, 6-cylinder, sv, in-line. 2,731cc, 69.5 x 120mm, 65bhp at 3,500rpm; 120lb ft at 1,300rpm; 4-speed gearbox, synchromesh on top, 3rd and 2nd gears; centre-floor gear-change; live (beam) rear axle with spiral-bevel final drive.
Chassis: Independent front suspension, transverse leaf spring, upper wishbones, radius arm location. Worm-and-nut steering. Live (beam) rear axle, half-elliptic leaf springs and anti-roll bar. Front and rear drum brakes. 6.00-16in tyres.
Dimensions: Wheelbase 9ft 6in; front track 4ft 7.8in; rear track 4ft 8in; length 15ft 0in; width 5ft 9in; height 5ft 5in. Unladen weight approx 3,330lb.
Distinguishing features from previous models: Slightly modified version of 1937–39 Pressed Steel 6-window saloon body style of Hillman 14/Humber 16/Super Snipe, facelifted for 1940 with extended boot and no running-boards.
Typical performance: Not tested by magazines in this form, but similar to 1935–37 Humber 18hp.
Derivatives: Super Snipe and 4-cylinder Hawk of 1945–48 were to same basic design.
Fate: Discontinued in 1948 and not replaced.

Technically and structurally, therefore, it was like the Humber Hawk Mk I, though it had extra cruciform bracing in the frame, and it kept its centre gear-change to the end, which came in the summer of 1948. In marketing terms, it fell between two stools – the Hawk and the Super Snipe – so it sold slowly.

Humber Super Snipe Mk I (1945 to 1948)

The Super Snipe was the third of the rationalized postwar Humbers and was almost the same car as the facelifted Super Snipe seen briefly at the end of 1939.

Unlike the Snipe, however, the Super Snipe was due for a longer postwar life, for in modified form it eventually rose to Mk III specification and was built until the summer of 1952.

Humber Super Snipe Mk II and III (1948 to 1952)

Three years after postwar production resumed, the Humber Super Snipe was considerably changed for 1949 and became Mk II. Mechanically, the only important changes were that the wheelbase was lengthened by 3.5in, wider front and rear tracks were specified, a new type of gearbox casing and linkage was fitted, and a steering-column change was standardized. The 4.1-litre engine, as ever, was rated at 100bhp.

Humber Super Snipe Mk I specification

Produced: Coventry (Humber Road, then Ryton-on-Dunsmore), 1945–48, 3,909 cars built.
General layout: Separate chassis-frame with Pressed Steel saloon body style. Front-mounted engine driving rear wheels.
Engine and transmission: Humber engine, 6-cylinder, sv, in-line. 4,086cc, 85 x 120mm, 100bhp at 3,400rpm; 197lb ft at 1,200rpm; 4-speed gearbox, synchromesh on top, 3rd and 2nd gears; centre-floor gear-change; live (beam) rear axle with spiral-bevel final drive.
Chassis: Independent front suspension, tranverse leaf spring, upper wishbones. Worm-and-nut steering. Live (beam) rear axle, half-elliptic leaf springs and anti-roll bar. Front and rear drum brakes. 6.00-16in tyres.
Dimensions: Wheelbase 9ft 6in; front track 4ft 7.8in; rear track 4ft 8in; length 15ft 0in; width 5ft 9in; height 5ft 5in. Unladen weight approx 3,360lb.
Distinguishing features from previous models: Slightly modified version of 1937–39 Pressed Steel 6-window saloon body style of Hillman 14/Humber 16/Snipe/Super Snipe, facelifted for 1940 with extended boot and no running-boards.
Typical performance: Maximum speed 80mph; 0–60mph 24.5sec; typical fuel consumption 15mpg.
Derivatives: 1945–48 Snipe and 4-cylinder Hawk were to same basic design.
Fate: Discontinued in 1948 in favour of Super Snipe Mk II.

Rootes, aided and abetted by the Loewy studio, applied a major front-end facelift to the Pressed Steel Company's bodyshell, visually bringing it into line with the recently announced (Thrupp & Maberly) Pullman limousine style. The main passenger cabin was unchanged, but at the front there was an alligator-style bonnet and a new nose incorporating revised wings with the headlamps faired in, rather than standing proud as on the early postwar types. Running-boards, which had been ousted in 1940, reappeared. For the first time since the war, too, alternative bodies (touring limousine and drop-head coupe) became available.

The revised Super Snipe Mk II, therefore, was a bigger, heavier and altogether more impressive car than its predecessor. It progressed yet again, this time to Mk III, in August 1950. The style and chassis were basically unchanged, the important differences being the addition of a Panhard locating rod to the rear suspension and detachable wheel covers at the rear.

Humber Super Snipe Mk II and III specification

As for Humber Super Snipe Mk I except for:
Produced: Ryton-on-Dunsmore, 1948–52, 8,361/8,703 cars built.
Chassis: Panhard-rod rear suspension location on Mk III. 6.50-16in tyres.
Dimensions: Wheelbase 9ft 9.5in; front track 4ft 9.9in; rear track 5ft 1in; length 15ft 7.5in; width 6ft 2.5in; height 5ft 5.7in. Unladen weight (typical) 3,745lb.
Distinguishing features from previous models: Completely new nose style with headlamps faired in to wider and more bulbous wings, plus alligator-style bonnet opening. Running-boards now fitted under doors.
Typical performance: Maximum speed 80mph; 0–60mph 22.7sec; typical fuel consumption 16mpg.
Derivatives: Touring limousine and drop-head coupe.
Fate: Mk II gave way to Mk III in August 1950, the Mk III being discontinued in favour of all-new Mk IV in October 1952.

Humber Pullman Mk I (1945 to 1948)

Rootes' plans for the dignified, middle-class weddings/funerals/managing director/mayoral Pullman were foiled by the outbreak of war, just as the company was ready to reveal the completely new style. The new car was built and used for military purposes between 1939 and 1945.

Accordingly, the 'new' Pullman went on sale in 1945 and sold steadily until 1949, when it was replaced by a completely new style. The chassis was a longer-wheelbase version of that fitted to postwar Super Snipes and the running gear was identical. The bodyshell,

The background, Buckingham Palace, tells us what sort of image Rootes wanted to create for the Humber Super Snipe in facelifted Mk II form. The new bonnet and front wings gave the car a totally different look from the Mk I, though the cabin was substantially unchanged and the mechanical components only revised in detail.

Tickford built a limited number of Super Snipe drophead coupes in the late 1940s and early 1950s, lushly trimmed and equipped.

however, was a lofty and semi-razor edge seven-seater limousine, with a pair of fold-away jump seats.

Like the current Super Snipe, its headlamps still stood proudly at each side of the vertical grille, its front and rear doors both being hinged from the B/C pillar immediately behind the front seats.

It was destined to have a short life, for Thrupp & Maberly was encouraged to come up with a more up-to-date design and the Mk II took over in the spring of 1948.

Immediately after the Second World War, Rootes put the Mk I Pullman on sale, a large and impressive beast, this example having the Thrupp & Maberly landaulette body style.

From 1948 to 1953, the Humber Pullman was sold with a revised front end, all the sheet metal ahead of the windscreen being new.

Humber Pullman Mk I specification

Produced: Coventry (Humber Road, then Ryton-on-Dunsmore) 1945–48, number of cars built unknown.
General layout: Separate chassis-frame with Thrupp and Maberly limousine body style. Front-mounted engine driving rear wheels.
Engine and transmission: Humber engine, 6-cylinder, sv, in-line. 4,086cc, 85 x 120mm, 100bhp at 3,400rpm; 197lb ft at 1,200rpm; 4-speed gearbox, synchromesh on top, 3rd and 2nd gears; centre-floor gear-change; live (beam) rear axle with spiral-bevel final drive.
Chassis: Independent front suspension, transverse leaf spring, upper wishbones. Worm-and-nut steering. Live (beam) rear axle, half-elliptic leaf springs and anti-roll bar. Front and rear drum brakes. 6.50-16in tyres.
Dimensions: Wheelbase 10ft 7.5in; front track 4ft 7.8in; rear track 5ft 1in; length 16ft 6in; width 6ft 1in; height 5ft 10in. Unladen weight approx 4,005lb.
Distinguishing features from previous models: Completely different style from 1935–39 Pullman, launched in December 1939, but only used as military staff car until 1945.
Typical performance: Maximum speed 80mph; 0–60mph 24.5sec; typical fuel consumption 16mpg.
Derivatives: 1948 Pullman Mk II, which used a new body style and an even longer wheelbase.
Fate: Discontinued in 1948 in favour of Pullman Mk II.

Humber Pullman Mk II and III (1948 to 1953)

The Mk II Pullman, unveiled in May 1948, used the same basic running gear as the 1945–48 variety, except that the wheelbase was lengthened by 3.5in and the tracks were both slightly wider than before.

As with the Super Snipe which followed a few months later, the Pullman picked up a new gearbox casing, selector linkage and steering-column control.

The new Thrupp & Maberly limousine shell was massive and impressive and looked superficially like that of the revised Pressed Steel shell soon to be fitted to the Humber Super Snipe Mk II. There was, however, no commonality between the two shells, or between this Pullman and the Pullman Mk I shell which it replaced.

This particular type of Pullman eventually gave way to the short-lived overhead-valve Pullman Mk IV of 1953–54, and it was closely related to the Imperial models (see below) which were built from 1949 to 1954.

Humber Pullman Mk II and III specification

As for Pullman Mk I except for:
Produced: Ryton-on-Dunsmore, 1948–53, 2,200/1,526 cars built.
Engine and transmission: Steering-column gear-change.
Chassis: Panhard rod location of rear suspension from late 1950. 7.00-16in tyres.
Dimensions: Wheelbase 10ft 11in; front track 4ft 10in; rear track 5ft 2in; length 17ft 6.5in; width 6ft 2.5in; height 5ft 9in. Unladen weight (typical) 4,465lb.
Distinguishing features from previous models: Completely different and more rounded style from Pullman Mk I.
Typical performance: Maximum speed 78mph; 0–60mph 26.2sec; standing ¼-mile 23.2sec; typical fuel consumption 16mpg.
Derivatives: Imperial model, introduced in 1949, was really the same car, but without a limousine division. 1953 Pullman Mk IV was same basic car, but fitted with different overhead-valve 6-cylinder engine.
Fate: Discontinued in 1953 in favour of Pullman Mk IV.

Humber Pullman Mk IV (1953 to 1954)

In May 1953, the Pullman was rejuvenated for the last time by the fitment of the modern Rootes overhead-valve engine and all-synchromesh gearbox (described more fully in the Super Snipe Mk IV section), though there were no other major changes.

At the end of its career, in 1953 and 1954, the Humber Pullman became Mk IV, complete with the new overhead-valve six-cylinder engine, but with no change in appearance since the styling was identical to that of the 1948–1953 variety.

Humber Pullman Mk IV specification

As for Humber Pullman Mk III except for:
Produced: Ryton-on-Dunsmore, 1953–54, 414 cars built.
Engine and transmission: Humber Blue Riband engine, ohv, 4,139cc, 89 x 111.1mm, 113bhp at 3,400rpm; 206lb ft at 1,400rpm; synchromesh on all forward gears.
Chassis: 7.50-16in tyres.
Dimensions: Unladen weight approx 4,870lb.
Derivatives: Imperial Mk III was the non-limousine equivalent of this model.
Fate: Discontinued in mid-1954 and never replaced.

Humber Imperial Mk II, III and IV (1949 to 1954)

This model was mechanically identical to the Pullman models of the day and shared the same Thrupp & Maberly body style. However, the Imperial was a seven-seater saloon (with the middle, occasional, row of seats facing forwards, capable of being folded down to provide an enormously spacious rear compartment with nearly 3ft of leg room). Imperials usually had leather upholstery compared with the Pullman's West of England cloth seats.

The Imperial Mk II and III had the side-valve engine and were mechanically the same as the Pullman Mk II and III, while the Imperial Mk IV had the new overhead-valve engine and was mechanically the same as the Pullman Mk IV.

Production of the Pullman/Imperial series finished in 1954.

Humber Hawk Mk III and IV (1948 to 1952)

The 1948 Hawk Mk III was the first truly postwar Humber, for its chassis had no links with previous models, or with any older Hillmans. Like the new Minx announced at the same Earls Court Motor Show, it had simple but well-proportioned full-width styling.

The Loewy studio had been closely involved in the design of the four-door saloon shell, which was made for Rootes by Pressed Steel, and to the *cognoscenti* the new Hawk had a shape which had been influenced by the current Studebakers.

The new car still had a separate chassis-frame, one which had completely boxed side members allied to a cruciform centre section. This, however, was the first Humber to have independent front suspension by coil springs and wishbones. The engine and gearbox were exactly as used in the ousted Hawk Mk II, but there was a new rear axle with a hypoid-bevel final drive; a steering-column gear-change, allied to a bench front seat, was standard.

This Hawk got off to a fine start at home and abroad, but was soon seen to need more power. Accordingly, from September 1950, the Mark IV Hawk was phased in, this having an enlarged side-valve engine.

Humber Hawk Mk V (1952 to 1954)

Four years after it had been put on sale, the Hawk was freshened up yet again, this time becoming Mk V. Mechanically, there were no basic changes, but the front end was given an altogether more flamboyant style, with more brightwork to the grille and separate

The first all-postwar design from Humber was the Hawk Mk III, launched in the autumn of 1948. In styling terms, it was close to the Hillman Minx of the same period. This car is the Mk IV, lightly modified with separately positioned sidelamps.

The Hawk Mk V and Mk VI of 1952 to 1957 had styling changes, including a lengthened tail, and glossier front-end trim.

Humber Hawk Mk III and IV specification

Produced: Ryton-on-Dunsmore, 1948–52, 10,040/6,492 cars built.
General layout: Separate chassis-frame with Pressed Steel saloon body style. Front-mounted engine driving rear wheels.
Engine and transmission: Humber/Hillman engine, 4-cylinder, sv, in-line. (Mk III) 1,944cc, 75 x 110mm, 56bhp at 3,800rpm; 97lb ft at 2,000rpm; (Mk IV) 2,267cc, 81 x 110mm, 58bhp at 3,400rpm; 110lb ft at 1,800rpm; 4-speed gearbox, synchromesh on top, 3rd and 2nd gears; steering-column gear-change; live (beam) axle with hypoid-bevel final drive.
Chassis: Independent front suspension, coil springs, wishbones. Worm-and-nut steering. Live (beam) rear axle, half-elliptic leaf springs and anti-roll bar. Front and rear drum brakes. (Mk III) 5.50-15in, (Mk IV) 6.40-15in tyres.
Dimensions: Wheelbase 8ft 9.5in; front track 4ft 8in; rear track 4ft 9in; length 14ft 6in; width 5ft 10in; height 5ft 4in. Unladen weight (typical) 2,750lb.
Distinguishing features from previous models: Completely different style from 1945–48 Hawk, with full-width body style including faired-in headlamps.
Typical performance: (Mk III) Maximum speed 72mph; 0–60mph 34.4sec; typical fuel consumption 26mpg; (Mk IV) maximum speed 70mph; 0–60mph 30.4sec; typical fuel consumption 22mpg.
Derivatives: Mk III became Mk IV in autumn 1950; Mk V and Mk VI Hawks were further developments of this design. 1952–57 Super Snipe Mk IV models used same basic bodyshell.
Fate: Discontinued in 1952 in favour of Hawk Mk V.

Humber Hawk Mk V specification

As for Humber Hawk Mk IV except for:
Produced: Ryton-on-Dunsmore, 1952–54, 14,300 cars built.
Dimensions: Unladen weight approx 2,920lb.
Distinguishing features from previous models: Facelifted front-end style with more brightwork and full-width supplementary grilles.
Derivatives: Hawk Mk VI was a lineal descendant of this car.
Fate: Discontinued in mid-1954 in favour of Hawk Mk VI.

sidelamps now surrounded by supplementary grilles. This frontal treatment was shared with the Super Snipe Mk IV, which was revealed a few weeks later. A Touring Limousine conversion was also made available, but was very rare.

This car was produced for a further two years until replaced by the overhead-valve Hawk Mk VI.

Humber Hawk Mk VI and VIA (1954 to 1957)

In 1954, at last, it was time for the Humber Hawk to inherit the overhead-valve version of the familiar four-cylinder engine; this, in fact, had been in use in the Sunbeam-Talbot 90 since 1948. There were several other important changes to the design, which had now been on the market for six years.

The engine, a 70bhp version of the 2,267cc unit, approximately 10bhp less powerful than that used in the current Sunbeam-Talbot 90 and Alpine models, was linked to the existing gearbox, but Laycock overdrive was now optionally available. The front suspension was firmer because an anti-roll bar had been added.

Based on the Mk VIA version of the Hawk, the estate car combined the roles of comfortable saloon and roomy luggage carrier. The lower part of the tailgate could be let down to extend the load platform.

Humber Hawk Mk VI and VIA specification

Produced: Ryton-on-Dunsmore, 1954–57, 18,836/9,614 cars built.
General layout: Separate chassis-frame with Pressed Steel saloon or estate car body style. Front-mounted engine driving rear wheels.
Engine and transmission: Humber/Hillman engine, 4-cylinder, ohv, in-line. 2,267cc, 81 x 110mm, 70bhp (later 75bhp for Mk VIA) at 4,000rpm; 119lb ft at 2,200rpm; 4-speed gearbox, synchromesh on top, 3rd and 2nd gears; steering-column gear-change, optional Laycock overdrive; live (beam) rear axle with hypoid-bevel final drive.
Chassis: Independent front suspension, coil springs, wishbones and anti-roll bar. Worm-and-nut steering. Live (beam) rear axle, half-elliptic leaf springs and anti-roll bar. Front and rear drum brakes. 6.40-15in tyres.
Dimensions: Wheelbase 8ft 9.5in; front track 4ft 8in; rear track 4ft 9in; length 15ft 1.5in; width 6ft 0in; height 5ft 4in. Unladen weight (saloon) approx 3,110lb; (estate) approx 3,360lb.
Distinguishing features from previous models: Restyled rear end with more extended wings and enlarged boot. Chrome strip along flanks.
Typical performance: Maximum speed 80mph; 0–60mph 23.8sec; standing ¼-mile 22.5sec; typical fuel consumption 26mpg.
Derivatives: Estate car version announced in September 1955. Super Snipe Mk V used similar main bodyshell.
Fate: Discontinued in 1957 in favour of new Hawk Series I.

The front-end styling of the Mk VI was exactly the same as before, but a longer tail, with a more capacious boot and different tail lamps (similar, but not the same as the tail recently adopted for the Super Snipe Mk IV) was specified. The Mk VIA arrived in April 1956, with de luxe paint and trim options.

A year after the new car was launched, the first-ever Hawk estate car was announced, this being a conventional five-door style on the same wheelbase as the saloon, though with different rear passenger doors.

This was the last of the separate-chassis Hawks, for in the spring of 1957 it gave way to the new unit-construction model.

Humber Super Snipe Mk IV, IVA and IVB (1952 to 1957)

Once the 'full-width' Humber Hawk had been launched in the autumn of 1948, the pundits smugly sat back and waited for the Super Snipe to follow. They had a long wait. Rootes persevered with the revamped Mk II and Mk III models for another four years.

In October 1952, the long-awaited Mk IV appeared, this car not only having a new chassis-frame, a long-wheelbase/long-nose version of the current Hawk design, but also the latest overhead-valve straight-six cylinder engine which had already appeared in some Commer commercial vehicles.

Except that the engine was even more powerful than had been expected, the latest Super Snipe was a thoroughly predictable update and amalgam of Rootes' large-car thinking. The main passenger body of the Pressed Steel Company's Hawk bodyshell was retained, but there was a longer tail and, naturally, there was a longer nose to accommodate the bulky new engine.

Rootes, of course, had no intention of leaving this design alone, so from the autumn of 1953 it was given a little more power (Mk IVA), then from April 1954 it moved on to become Mk IVB, complete with a walnut dashboard and, again, a little more power than before.

Borg-Warner automatic transmission became optional in 1956, but sales of the car were lagging badly by that point, and Rootes was relieved to bring in a brand-new Super Snipe in 1958.

The Super Snipe was completely redesigned in the early 1950s, this shape of car being on sale from 1952 until 1957. This particular car is a Mk IVB model of 1955/1956. The cabin and the tail were similar to the existing Hawk, but the wheelbase, and the nose, were considerably longer.

Humber Super Snipe Mk IV, IVA and IVB specification

Produced: Ryton-on-Dunsmore, 1952–57, 9,785/676/7,532 cars built.
General layout: Separate chassis-frame with Pressed Steel saloon or estate car body style; various coachbuilt and utility derivatives also produced by specialists. Front-mounted engine driving rear wheels.
Engine and transmission: Humber Blue Riband engine, 6-cylinder, ohv, in-line. 4,139cc, 88.9 x 111.1mm, (Mk IV and early Mk IVA) 113bhp, (Mk IVB) 116bhp at 3,400rpm; 206lb ft, (later 211lb ft) at 1,400rpm; (Mk IVB from September 1955) 122bhp at 3,600rpm; 4-speed gearbox; all synchromesh gearbox, steering-column gear-change and optional Laycock overdrive from September 1955, optional Borg-Warner automatic transmission from April 1956; live (beam) rear axle with hypoid-bevel final drive.
Chassis: Independent front suspension, coil springs, wishbones and anti-roll bar. Worm-and-nut steering. Live (beam) rear axle, half-elliptic leaf springs. Front and rear drum brakes. 7.00-15in tyres.
Dimensions: Wheelbase 9ft 7.7in; front track 4ft 9.9in; rear track 4ft 8.25in; length 16ft 5in; width 6ft 1.5in; height 5ft 6in. Unladen weight (typical) 4,025lb.
Distinguishing features from previous models: Completely different shell from Super Snipe Mk III, based on that of contemporary Hawk.
Typical performance: (Mk IV) Maximum speed 90mph; 0–60mph 16.0sec; standing ¼-mile 20.5sec; typical fuel consumption 16mpg.
Fate: Super Snipe Mk IV became Mk IVA in April 1954 and Mk IVB in September 1955. Mk IVB discontinued in 1957, to be replaced by new Super Snipe Series I.

Humber Hawk Series I, IA, II and III (1957 to 1964)

In 1957, the separate-chassis postwar Humber Hawk was pensioned off after a near nine-year career in several different guises. In its place, Rootes introduced a new unit-construction model which was to have an even longer career; in the next 10 years the same basic car, freshened up by a restyle in 1964, would be built in Series I, IA, II, III and IV forms.

For the new generation of Humbers, Rootes designed a new unit-construction shell which was to accept two new engines, the four-cylinder being for the Hawk and a new six-cylinder for the Super Snipe.

The new shell, built at British Light Steel Pressings in workshops previously given over to Sunbeam-Talbot 90 shell assembly, was once placarded as the largest being built in the UK. Although there were still clear signs of Transatlantic influence in its lines (1955 Chevrolet?), these were not completely derivative of any particular Detroit machine. The new Hawk, like the Super Snipe which followed, was a handsome and spacious car, available in saloon and (from October 1957) estate car guise. One neat little detail was that the fuel filler cap was mounted at the bottom of the right-hand tail-lamp

Hawk for 1957 had an all-new unitary shell in saloon or estate form but retained the familiar 2,267cc engine.

Humber Hawk Series I, IA, II and III specification

Produced: Ryton-on-Dunsmore, 1957–64, 15,539/6,813/7,230/6,109 cars built.
General layout: Unit-construction body-chassis structure in choice of saloon, limousine or estate car styles. Front-mounted engine driving rear wheels.
Engine and transmission: Humber engine, 4-cylinder, ohv, in-line. 2,267cc, 81 x 110mm, 73bhp (net) at 4,400rpm; 120lb ft at 2,300rpm; 4-speed gearbox, synchromesh on top, 3rd and 2nd gears; steering-column gear-change, optional Laycock overdrive, optional Borg-Warner automatic transmission until 1962; live (beam) rear axle with hypoid-bevel final drive.
Chassis: Independent front suspension, coil springs, wishbones and anti-roll bar. Recirculating-ball steering. Live (beam) rear axle, half-elliptic leaf springs. Front and rear drum brakes; front discs from October 1962. 6.00-15in or 6.40-15in tyres.
Dimensions: Wheelbase 9ft 2in; front track 4ft 8in; rear track 7.5in; length 15ft 4.7in; width 5ft 9.5in; height 5ft 1in. Unladen weight (typical) 3,080lb.
Distinguishing features from previous models: Completely different shell from Hawk Mk VI, based on that of new Super Snipe.
Typical performance: Maximum speed 83mph; 0–60mph 20.6sec; standing ¼-mile 21.8sec; typical fuel consumption 25mpg.
Derivatives: Super Snipes from 1958 to 1967 used same basic structure and suspension, but different engines. Saloon, limousine and estate car types available.
Fate: Series I became Series IA in October 1959, Series II followed in October 1960 and Series III in September 1962. Discontinued in favour of restyled Series IV model in October 1964.

cluster and had a reflector over it as disguise.

The new car's chassis included coil-spring independent front suspension and recirculating-ball steering; an all-drum brake installation was fitted at first, though front-wheel discs followed for the Series II.

The engine was the familiar old 2,267cc unit, now boasting 73bhp (net), with a choice of four-speed manual, Laycock overdrive, or Borg-Warner automatic transmissions.

Series I became Series IA in October 1959, with slightly different internal gearbox ratios, and Series II followed a year later when the disc brakes were added, but the automatic transmission option was dropped. Series III, from September 1962, meant a minor restyle of the rear window outline.

Series IV (described below), was a much more serious facelift, but the last of its type on this body.

Humber Hawk Series IV and IVA (1964 to 1967)

In the autumn of 1964, Rootes announced a comprehensive facelift on its family of big Humbers, the Hawk and the Super Snipe receiving the same treatment. At the same time (see below), a top-of-the-range six-cylinder Imperial was introduced.

Below the waistline of the Hawk, the only significant change was redesigned bumpers and sidelamps, but like the other big Humbers, there was a much changed upper cabin, with enlarged glass, a flatter rear window and the addition of a rear quarter-window.

Under the skin, the Hawk now had an all-synchromesh gearbox, and an anti-roll bar was added to the rear suspension. It was in this form that the Hawk ended its career in mid-1967.

From late 1964, the Hawk body was restyled to have a flatter roof line, with different rear quarters and window profiles.

Humber Hawk Series IV and IVA specification

As for Hawk Series III except for:
Produced: Ryton-on-Dunsmore, 1964–67, 1,746/3,754 cars built.
Engine and transmission: All-synchromesh manual gearbox; Borg-Warner automatic transmission re-introduced in 1965 on Series IVA.
Chassis: Rear suspension had anti-roll bar (saloon only).
Distinguishing features from previous models: New upper cabin with more glass area, flatter rear window and third quarter-window behind rear passenger doors.
Fate: Discontinued in 1967 and not replaced.

Humber Super Snipe Series I (1958 to 1959)

As part of its long-term strategy, Rootes developed a new pair of large Humbers for the late 1950s and early 1960s. The new Hawk (described above) used the familiar 2.3-litre four-cylinder engine, while the new-generation Super Snipe was equipped with a new in-line six-cylinder engine, which bore a startling resemblance to the existing Armstrong Siddeley Sapphire unit. This design is analyzed in **Appendix D**.

The original Super Snipe of this type had a 2.6-litre version of the new engine coupled to a new all-synchromesh three-speed gearbox. There was also an optional overdrive, or Borg-Warner automatic transmission could be specified.

The Super Snipe's shell, structure and chassis components were all shared with the new type of Hawk, though the new car was not launched until October 1958, more than a year after the old type had been withdrawn from production, and well over a year after the very similar Hawk had been put on sale.

In its original form, the exterior style of the new

Humber Super Snipe Series I specification

Produced: Ryton-on-Dunsmore, 1958–59, 6,072 cars built.
General layout: Unit-construction body-chassis structure in choice of saloon, limousine or estate car styles. Front-mounted engine driving rear wheels.
Engine and transmission: New Humber engine, 6-cylinder, ohv, in-line. 2,651cc, 82.55 x 82.55mm, 105bhp (net) at 5,000rpm; 138lb ft at 2,000rpm; 3-speed all-synchromesh gearbox; steering-column gear-change, optional Laycock overdrive, optional Borg-Warner automatic transmission; live (beam) rear axle with hypoid-bevel final drive.
Chassis: Independent front suspension, coil springs, wishbones and anti-roll bar. Recirculating-ball steering with optional power assistance. Live (beam) rear axle, half-elliptic leaf springs. Front and rear drum brakes. 6.70-15in tyres.
Dimensions: Wheelbase 9ft 2in; front track 4ft 8.5in; rear track 4ft 7.5in; length 15ft 4.7in; width 5ft 9.5in; height 5ft 1in. Unladen weight approx 3,350lb.
Distinguishing features from previous models: Completely different shell from Super Snipe Mk IV, now based on that of new Hawk range.
Typical performance: Maximum speed 92mph; 0–60mph 19.0sec; standing ¼-mile 21.0sec; typical fuel consumption 20mpg.
Derivatives: 1957–67 Hawks used same basic structure and suspension, but different engines. Saloon, limousine and estate car types available.
Fate: Discontinued in favour of modified Series II model in October 1959.

The Humber Super Snipe 'Series' car appeared for the first time in the autumn of 1958, using the same monocoque as that of the current Hawk, but with an all-new six-cylinder engine under the bonnet.

From the autumn of 1960, the nose of the Super Snipe shell (but *not* that of the Hawk) was restyled to incorporate four headlamps. This particular car was registered in 1962.

Super Snipe looked much like the Hawk, except for a more glossy front end, more decoration and larger-section tyres. There was a walnut facia/dashboard, of course, and as with the new-style Hawk, there was a limousine and an estate car option. It was a big, comfortable and spacious car, but Rootes did not leave it unmodified for long!

Humber Super Snipe Series II (1959 to 1960)

After only one year, the new unit-construction Super Snipe became Series II, by the use not only of an enlarged engine (2.96 litres instead of 2.65 litres), but also front-wheel disc brakes and a power steering option. Even so, this was yet another short-lived Super Snipe.

Humber Super Snipe Series II specification

As for Super Snipe Series I except for:
Produced: Ryton-on-Dunsmore, 1959–60, 7,175 cars built.
Engine and transmission: 2,965cc, 87.3 x 82.55mm, 121bhp (net) at 4,800rpm; 162lb ft at 1800rpm.
Typical performance: See Series III.
Derivatives: Series II became Series III in October 1960 with restyled nose.
Fate: Discontinued in favour of Series III Super Snipe in 1960.

Humber Super Snipe Series III and IV (1960 to 1964)

The third unit-construction Super Snipe was revealed in 1960, only two years after the type was launched, and even that was further changed two years later. Life was never dull at Acton, Cricklewood and Ryton in the early 1960s!

For the Series III, Rootes provided the Super Snipe with an impressive new nose in which the car was provided with new sheet metal and four headlamps; this nose was never shared with the Hawk.

Two years later, in September 1962, Series III gave way to Series IV, with a slightly restyled and reshaped rear window and a slightly more powerful engine.

Humber Super Snipe Series III and IV specification

As for Super Snipe Series II except for:
Produced: Ryton-on-Dunsmore, 1960–64, 7,257/6,495 cars built.
Engine and transmission: (Series IV) 124bhp (net) at 5,000rpm; 160lb ft at 2,600rpm.
Dimensions: Length 15ft 8in.
Distinguishing features from previous models: Series III had new four-headlamp nose, Series IV had reprofiled rear window.
Typical performance: (121bhp Series III) Maximum speed 100mph; 0–60mph 14.3sec; standing ¼-mile 19.5sec; typical fuel consumption 20mpg.
Derivatives: Series III became Series IV in September 1962. Series IV gave way to restyled Series V in October 1964.
Fate: Series IV discontinued in October 1964 in favour of new Series V car.

Humber Super Snipe Series V, VA and Imperial (1964 to 1967)

Like the Humber Hawk of the period, the Super Snipe was restyled for the 1965 season with a new cabin and window layout, at the same time the engine being provided with a little more power. Power-assisted steering became standard.

At the same time as the Super Snipe was updated,

A typical Rootes 'mix and match' operation of the early 1960s – the four-headlamp Super Snipe, as sold in estate car form.

At restyle time, in late 1964, the Super Snipe retained its four-headlamp nose, but received the same roof line and rear quarters as the Hawk (and the new Imperial).

Rootes re-introduced an Imperial. This was really a super-specified Super Snipe, with a pvc leathercloth roof, Borg-Warner automatic transmission as standard and a higher level of trim and equipment.

These cars ran out in 1967 and no more large Humbers were ever produced.

Humber Super Snipe Series V, VA and Imperial specification

As for Super Snipe Series IV except for:
Produced: Ryton-on-Dunsmore, 1964–67, 1,907/1,125 cars built.
Engine and transmission: 128.5bhp (net) at 5,000rpm; 167lb ft at 2,600rpm; Borg-Warner automatic transmission standard on Imperial models.
Chassis: Power-assisted steering standard. Rear anti-roll bar standardized (saloons only).
Dimensions: Height 4ft 11.25in. Unladen weight (saloon) approx 3,415lb.
Distinguishing features from previous models: New upper cabin style including flatter roof panel and rear window and extra rear quarter-window behind rear passenger doors.
Typical performance: Maximum speed 100mph; 0–60mph 16.2sec; standing ¼-mile 20.7sec; typical fuel consumption 18mpg.
Fate: Discontinued in 1967 and not replaced.

Humber Sceptre Mk I (1963 to 1965)

At the end of the 1950s, Rootes started the design of a new family of medium-sized cars, which was intended to take over from the existing Minx, Gazelle and Rapier models. However, as has already been made clear in the Hillman chapter, it was subsequently decided to keep the older cars in production and to produce the new series alongside them.

When the new range of cars was designed, the car which became the Sceptre was meant to be a direct replacement for the Sunbeam Rapier; indeed, there are pictures in existence of production-standard Sceptres still being badged as Sunbeams and wearing Rapier IV number-plates. The change from Sunbeam to Humber, therefore, came at a very late stage; there were no mechanical changes, and the only new styling work was to produce new badges and emblems. On the other hand, the carve-up in advertising, marketing and dealer relations terms can be imagined!

The Sceptre of January 1963, therefore, was effectively an up-market version of the existing Hillman

Humber Sceptre Mk I specification

Produced: Ryton-on-Dunsmore, 1963–65, 17,011 built-up, unknown CKD cars built.
General layout: Unit-construction body-chassis structure in four-door saloon style. Front-mounted engine driving rear wheels.
Engine and transmission: Hillman engine, 4-cylinder, ohv, in-line. 1,592cc, 81.5 x 76.2mm, 80bhp (net) at 5,200rpm; 91lb ft at 3,500rpm; 4-speed synchromesh gearbox, no synchromesh on 1st gear in original cars, all-synchromesh from October 1964; centre-floor gear-change, Laycock overdrive standard on top and 3rd gears; live (beam) rear axle with hypoid-bevel final drive.
Chassis: Independent front suspension, coil springs, wishbones and anti-roll bar. Recirculating-ball steering. Live (beam) rear axle, half-elliptic leaf springs. Front disc, rear drum brakes. 6.00-13in tyres.
Dimensions: Wheelbase 8ft 5in; front track 4ft 3.5in; rear track 4ft 0.5in; length 13ft 9.5in; width 5ft 3.25in; height 4ft 9in. Unladen weight approx 2,455lb.
Distinguishing features from previous models: Completely different type of Humber compared with previous models; closely related to Hillman Super Minx/Singer Vogue, with 4-headlamp nose.
Typical performance: Maximum speed 90mph; 0–60mph 17.1sec; standing ¼-mile 20.3sec; typical fuel consumption 23mpg.
Derivatives: 1965 Sceptre Mk II used same basic structure and suspension, but enlarged engine and revised front style. Hillman Super Minx/Singer Vogue were all in same family.
Fate: Discontinued in favour of modified Mk II model in September 1965.

The Humber Sceptre of 1963, its body shell a much-modified version of the Hillman Super Minx type, was originally meant to be a Sunbeam Rapier, but policies changed at a late stage.

Super Minx and Singer Vogue, with Rapier-standard engine and transmission specification. The first cars had twin Zenith carburettors, but like the Rapier and the Alpine of the period (see the Sunbeam chapter), these gave way to a compound dual-choke Solex unit in the middle of 1963.

Humber Sceptre Mk II specification

As for Humber Sceptre Mk I except for:
Produced: Ryton-on-Dunsmore, 1965–67, 11,985 built-up, unknown CKD cars built.
Engine and transmission: 1,725cc, 81.5 x 82.55mm, 85bhp (net) at 5,500rpm; 106lb ft at 3,500rpm; Borg-Warner automatic transmission now optional.
Distinguishing features from previous models: New nose style, using same body sheet metal as Super Minx – still with 4 headlamps, but in different style.
Derivatives: None.
Fate: Discontinued in summer 1967 in favour of new Arrow-type Sceptre.

The bodyshell was by no means that of the Super Minx/Vogue, for Ted White's stylists had been allowed to make it specialized. The wrapover windscreen and the four 'podded' headlamps (both inspired by late-1950s Chrysler Corporation products) were different, while the trim and decoration were well up to expected Sunbeam standards.

The original Sceptre (the smallest Humber for many years) was a successful, but not fast-selling car. It was, however, too specialized to make money, so the Mk II version was modified to cut costs.

Humber Sceptre Mk II (1965 to 1967)

In the autumn of 1965, bringing it into line with other cars in the Minx/Super Minx/Rapier/Alpine families, the Sceptre was given the latest five-bearing 1,725cc engine, this being in the same state of tune as in the Rapier of the day. At the same time, Borg-Warner automatic transmission, not available on the Mk I, became

In 1965 the Sceptre was facelifted, with a new nose and a new headlamp layout. At the same time it received a 1,725cc engine.

Rootes rationalized severely in the late 1960s, which meant that the new Arrow-based Humber Sceptre used all the same body structure and sheet metal as the then-new Hillman Hunter. At the very end of its life, under Chrysler control, the Sceptre was also produced in smart estate car form, from 1974 to 1976.

optional. A negative-earth electrical system was adopted at this point.

Although the wrapover windscreen was retained, the front-end sheet-metal was rationalized so that the same nose as the Super Minx was used, cunningly disguised with a different grille and spaced-out four-headlamp design.

As with the original Sceptre, this was effectively a larger, heavier, four-door Rapier, and it gently faded away in the summer of 1967. Its replacement was the new Arrow type of Sceptre.

Humber Sceptre Mk III (1967 to 1976)

The writer has the dubious distinction of having been booked for speeding on the M1 motorway even before this car was officially announced. He was confirming that the new model handled better and was significantly faster than the Mk II. The occasion was the assessment of a pre-launch car, and the hated 70mph speed limit had already been imposed....

In the 1966–67 period, Rootes-Chrysler swept away its two old families of medium-sized cars (Minx/Gazelle/Rapier and Super Minx/Vogue/Sceptre), replacing them with the smooth but somewhat anonymous Arrow range. In the process, the old Mk II Sceptre was phased-out and a new Arrow-style Sceptre arrived.

This car used the new MacPherson-strut-suspended Arrow-style four-door shell, the power-train of the fastback Rapier and the highest available level of trim developed for this range. For the Sceptre, of course, this included a wooden facia board and plushy seats, plus a four-headlamp nose.

For a time, that four-headlamp nose was unique, but in the 1970s it came to be applied to the Hillman Hunter GLS sports saloon.

As before, overdrive was standard and automatic transmission was optional.

Surprisingly, towards the end of its life (from October 1974), Chrysler also offered a Sceptre estate car, which used the Hunter/Vogue type of shell, but with every expected Sceptre equipment detail as well as a permanent roof rack.

The last Sceptre was built early in 1976, and with it the Humber marque was laid to rest.

Humber Sceptre Mk III specification

Produced: Ryton-on-Dunsmore, 1967–69, Linwood, 1969–76, 43,951 cars built.
General layout: Unit-construction body-chassis structure in four-door saloon or estate car style. Front-mounted engine driving rear wheels.
Engine and transmission: Hillman engine, 4-cylinder, ohv, in-line. 1,725cc, 81.5 x 82.55mm, 88bhp (net) at 5,200rpm; 100lb ft at 3,500rpm (later re-rated to 79bhp DIN at 5,100rpm; 93lb ft at 3,300rpm); 4-speed all-synchromesh gearbox; centre-floor gear-change, Laycock overdrive standard on top and 3rd gears, optional Borg-Warner automatic transmission; live (beam) rear axle with hypoid-bevel final drive.
Chassis: Independent front suspension, coil springs, MacPherson struts and anti-roll bar. Recirculating-ball steering. Live (beam) rear axle, half-elliptic leaf springs. Front disc, rear drum brakes. 6.00-13in tyres.
Dimensions: Wheelbase 8ft 2.5in; front track 4ft 4in; rear track 4ft 4in; length 14ft 1.5in; width 5ft 4in; height 4ft 8in. Unladen weight approx 2,185lb.
Distinguishing features from previous models: Completely different type of Sceptre compared with previous models; closely related to Hillman Hunter, with 4-headlamp nose.
Typical performance: Maximum speed 98mph; 0–60mph 13.1sec; standing ¼-mile 19.3sec; typical fuel consumption 25mpg.
Derivatives: Sceptre Mk III used same basic structure and suspension as Hillman Hunter/Singer Vogue of Arrow family, but with more powerful engine and revised front style. Estate car version launched in 1974 for final 2 years.
Fate: Discontinued in 1976 and not replaced.

Chapter 6

SINGER

When Singer was taken over by Rootes at the end of 1955, it was only building about 30 cars a week. To Rootes, a concern more used to talking in terms of building 30 cars an hour, this was unacceptable; it was no wonder that Singer was currently losing money hand over fist.

At the same time, the only Singer cars still price-listed in establishment magazines such as *The Autocar* were derivatives of the ancient SM1500 saloon range – the stripped-out Hunter S at £919, the Hunter De Luxe at £1,033 and the newly-launched twin-cam-engined Hunter 75 at £1,218.

For comparison, the existing Hillman Minx De Luxe, soon to be dropped in favour of a new model, was priced at £744, while the newly launched Sunbeam Rapier sold for £1,044.

Clearly, the existing Singers were almost unsaleable at those prices. Within weeks, Rootes had killed off the twin-cam-engined Hunter 75 (contemporary reports stated that existing cylinder blocks and heads were smashed up by labourers wielding sledge-hammers) and slashed the prices of the other models. The 'S' (or Special) was reduced to £796 and the De Luxe to £864.

What the public did not know then – but, had they reflected on previous Rootes form, they would have sensed it inevitable – was that this was merely a typically bold move by Lord Rootes to clear the decks for a new Rootes-Singer model to appear.

Singer Hunter (1954 to 1956)

The original postwar new model from Singer was the SM1500 four-door saloon, previewed in 1947, put on sale in 1948 and eventually facelifted and renamed Hunter in 1954.

The SM1500 had a separate chassis-frame, with box-section side members, cruciform stiffening and

independent front suspension by coil springs and wishbones. The engine was a 1.5-litre overhead-cam unit of traditional Singer layout, though brand new in many details; compared with prewar Singer 1½-litre 'fours', it had a bigger bore, a shorter stroke and 48 instead of 43bhp.

The four-speed transmission had synchromesh on top, 3rd and 2nd gears, and like many other so-called export-conscious British cars of the day, it was inflicted with a steering-column gear-change. The new car's top speed was 72mph and average fuel economy was perhaps 26–28mpg.

The full-width four-door bodyshell, neat and unobtrusive in style by 1947 standards, but one which dated rapidly in the early 1950s, was an all-steel design produced for Singer by the Pressed Steel Company of Cowley.

Sales began in 1948, originally for export only. In 1951, the engine was reduced in size to 1,497cc (the stroke was marginally shortened by slightly modifying the crankshaft), and for 1953 there was the option of a 58bhp twin-carb engine, but these were minor updates. The major facelift, from SM1500 to Hunter, came in the autumn of 1954.

For the Hunter, the basic design – separate frame, overhead-cam engine, Pressed Steel body – was not changed, but the front of the car was restyled and there was a different facia. At the front, the original 'dollar grin' was dropped in favour of a traditional-style vertical radiator grille, this being surrounded by glassfibre bonnet top and side valances. The use of GRP was not a success, and conventional steel pressings took over in the spring of 1955 and continued to the end.

The final flourish of this design was the launch of the Hunter 75 in October 1955, just before the Rootes takeover was announced. Singer had productionized the H.R.G. twin-cam design, using cast iron instead of light alloy for the head casting, vertical (Bristol-style) inlet ports instead of the classical horizontal layout, and twin Solex 32 PBI downdraught carburettors; power was increased by up to 50% – to 75bhp instead of 50 or 58bhp.

Singer Hunter specification

Produced: Birmingham, 1954–56, 4,750 cars built.
General layout: Separate chassis-frame, steel bodyshell, in 4-door saloon car style. Front-mounted engine driving rear wheels.
Engine and transmission: Singer engine, 4-cylinder, ohc, in-line. 1,497cc, 73 x 89.4mm, 48bhp at 4,500rpm, or 58bhp at 4,600rpm; 77lb ft at 2,600rpm; 4-speed gearbox, no synchromesh on 1st gear; steering-column gear-change; live (beam) rear axle with hypoid-bevel final drive.
Chassis: Independent front suspension, coil springs, wishbones and anti-roll bar. Worm-and-nut steering. Live (beam) rear axle, half-elliptic leaf springs. Front and rear drum brakes. 5.50-16in tyres.
Dimensions: Wheelbase 8ft 11.5in; front track 4ft 2.5in; rear track 4ft 3in; length 14ft 9in; width 5ft 3in; height 5ft 4in. Unladen weight approx 2,700lb.
Typical performance: (48bhp engine) Maximum speed 70mph; 0–60mph 32.4sec; standing ¼-mile 24.9sec; typical fuel consumption 24.5mpg.
Derivatives: Hunter itself was derivative of SM1500 from 1948–54. Stillborn 75bhp twin-cam version announced in 1955.
Fate: Discontinued in 1956 in favour of new Rootes-style Singer Gazelle.

Opposite: Singer in the mid-1930s, still independent, and making successful sports cars, exemplified by this prize-winning team on the 1934 RAC Rally, but profits were hard to come by. Right: one indulgence of the 1930s which did not sell as well as Singer hoped – the Airstream, based on the 11hp chassis.

After the Second World War, Singer produced the Roadster, which had a four-cylinder overhead camshaft engine and four-seater accommodation.

A proposal in the early 1950s to update the Roadster with full-width bodywork never reached production.

This was the Singer Hunter, a lightly-modified SM1500, which Singer was making in Birmingham at the time of the Rootes takeover at the end of 1955.

However, Rootes cancelled the Hunter 75 before series production could begin – only about 20 Hunter 75s were ever built and none seem to have survived. Existing single-cam Hunters continued to be built in Birmingham until the summer of 1956. A total of 4,750 Hunters were produced (and, before them, 18,666 SM1500s and 542 rolling chassis for coachbuilders).

The Rootes Singers

The Rootes strategy regarding Singer was simplicity itself. Although Sir William had once been a Singer apprentice, he did not allow sentiment to cloud the master plan. For him, Singer could provide two things – a useful fifth marque, which he could use to flesh out the family of cars, and some useful real estate.

Singer's Coventry Road, Birmingham, factory was quite useless for building cars in the modern manner, and once Hunter production ran down, it was redeveloped. By the end of the 1950s, it had become a massive spare parts warehouse for the entire Rootes Group, thus releasing other buildings in Humber Road, Coventry, to expand the manufacturing capability there. Singer's Coventry premises were eventually turned over to component manufacture.

Rootes decided to use the Singer marque as a more up-market version of the Hillman. In a classic example of badge-engineering, the Singer name was progressively applied to cars mechanically identical to other existing or planned Rootes models, usually with a rather better and more complete standard of trim and decoration. The problem was that the marque never really developed its own Rootes identity – not in the way that Humber meant quality and Sunbeam meant sporting.

Once the new Singer Gazelle, which started life as a re-engined Minx, was given the standard Minx engine in 1958, it was no more than an up-market Minx, the Singer Vogue was an up-market Super Minx and eventually the Singer Chamois was born as an up-market Hillman Imp. The only slight inconsistency in all this was that the Singer Chamois Sport was a cross between Hillman Imp, Hillman Rallye Imp and Sunbeam Imp Sport!

Using the Singer badge in this way was a very useful ploy to raise sales and give the salesmen something else to talk about, even if it did nothing for the blood pressure of traditionalists. By the late 1960s, however, as Rootes/Chrysler saw the need to rationalize, the continued existence of Singer came under scrutiny. In the end, in 1970, the marque was abandoned completely, though some of the cars were rebadged as Sunbeams for a few more months.

The Rootes-inspired Singer Gazelle, based on the Hillman Minx and launched in 1956, had already received a (Rootes) engine transplant and a mild front-end facelift by the time this car was photographed in 1958. Saloon, estate car and convertible versions were available.

The Gazelle convertible, complete with the roll-over tail fins applied to all Minx/Gazelle models in the autumn of 1959, could also be supplied with this detachable Alexander hardtop.

Singer Gazelle Mk I and II (1956 to 1957)

Having completed the takeover of Singer at the beginning of 1956, Rootes moved with astonishing speed to produce a new model – the Gazelle – which was launched in September that year. Nor was it simply a rebadged Hillman, but a Minx which had been re-engined, given a walnut-grained facia panel and a different front-style treatment.

Even by the standards to which Rootes operated in the mid-1950s – with changes every model year and a lot of mix-and-match activity with marques, engines and bodies – this was a real achievement.

The basis of the new Gazelle was the new-generation Loewy-styled Hillman Minx, which was still not even in production when Rootes took over Singer. Like the Minx, it was to be sold in saloon and convertible guises.

Compared with the Minx, the original Gazelle used a slightly modified version of the single-carburettor Singer Hunter engine, though this was mated to the Rootes/Minx four-speed gearbox and featured a steering-column gear-change. There was a distinctive vertical grille which lifted up with the bonnet panel, and the interior was better trimmed and finished.

Car-for-car, prices were close – in September 1956, a Gazelle cost £898, whereas a Minx De Luxe cost £774. The Rapier – effectively a two-door version of the same bodyshell – cost £1,044. The carefully structured Rootes pricing philosophy was obvious.

Gazelle became Gazelle Mk II after a year, when the corporate estate car option became available, minor front-end style changes were made and the useful option of Laycock overdrive was offered. This revised car, however, had a short life, for the Minx-engined Mk IIA followed in a matter of months.

Singer Gazelle Mk I and II specification

Produced: Ryton-on-Dunsmore, 1956–58, 4,344/1,582 cars built.
General layout: Unit-construction body-chassis structure in 4-door saloon or estate car and 2-door convertible style (estate only on Gazelle Mk II). Front-mounted engine driving rear wheels.
Engine and transmission: Singer engine, 4-cylinder, ohc, in-line. 1,497cc, 73 x 89.4mm, 49bhp (net) at 4,500rpm; 77lb ft at 2,000rpm; 4-speed gearbox, no synchromesh on 1st gear; steering-column gear-change, Laycock overdrive optional from October 1957 on Gazelle Mk II; live (beam) rear axle with spiral-bevel final drive.
Chassis: Independent front suspension, coil springs, wishbones and anti-roll bar. Worm-and-nut steering. Live (beam) rear axle, half-elliptic leaf springs. Front and rear drum brakes. 5.60-15in tyres.
Dimensions: Wheelbase 8ft 0in; front track 4ft 1in; rear track 4ft 0.5in; length 13ft 7.5in; width 5ft 0.75in; height 4ft 11.5in. Unladen weight (saloon) approx 2,255lb.
Distinguishing features from previous models: Completely different type of Singer compared with previous models; closely related to Hillman Minx of mid-1956, with own-make engine.
Typical performance: Maximum speed 78mph; 0–60mph 23.6sec; standing ¼-mile 22.9sec; typical fuel consumption 30mpg.
Derivatives: Gazelle Mk II used same basic structure and suspension with slightly revised front style and with additional estate car option.
Fate: Discontinued in 1958 in favour of Minx-engined Gazelle Mk IIA.

Singer Gazelle Mk IIA, III, IIIA and IIIB (1958 to 1961)

As already mentioned in the Hillman chapter, Rootes was well into its annual-change routine by the end of the 1950s. In less than four years, no fewer than four slightly different types of Singer Gazelle were sold, and all can be grouped together in the same description.

Compared with the original type, the big change from Mk II to IIA was that the overhead-valve Minx engine was standardized, the old-style overhead-cam Singer unit being abandoned.

The Mk IIA, revealed in February 1958, looked just like the Mk II, but had a single-carburettor Minx-style engine, and recirculating-ball steering was adopted. The

Singer Gazelle Mk IIA, III, IIIA and IIIB specification

As for Singer Gazelle Mk I and II except for:
Produced: 1958–61, 3,824/10,929/12,491/13,272 cars built.
Engine and transmission: Hillman Minx engine, ohv, 1,494cc, 79 x 76.2mm, 56bhp (60bhp on Mk IIIA) at 4,600rpm; 83lb ft at 2,300rpm; centre-floor gear-change for Mk IIIA and IIIB, optional automatic transmission for Mk IIIA and IIIB; hypoid-bevel rear axle for Mk IIIB.
Chassis: Recirculating-ball steering.
Distinguishing features from previous models: Mk IIA looked identical to Mk II, but had Hillman engine under bonnet; Mk III had new 2-tone paint treatment; Mk IIIA had roll-over rear fins and centre-floor gear-change.
Typical performance: (Mk IIA) Maximum speed 82mph; 0–60mph 21.4sec; standing ¼-mile 22.4sec; typical fuel consumption 31mpg; (Mk IIIB) maximum speed 84mph; 0–60mph 23.9sec; standing ¼-mile 22.2sec; typical fuel consumption 26mpg.
Derivatives: 1961 Gazelle Mk IIIC was like Mk IIIB, but with enlarged and more powerful engine.
Fate: Discontinued in summer 1961 in favour of larger-engined Gazelle Mk IIIC.

Mk III, announced in September 1958, only varied from its predecessor in that it had different two-tone paint treatment, some trim changes and a price reduction for the estate car.

The Mk IIIA was put on sale in September 1959 with the same style changes as the 1960-model Minx, including the roll-over rear fins and deeper front screen. The engine had slightly more power by virtue of using twin downdraught Zenith carburettors, and there were closer-ratio gears and a centre-floor gear-change (though the column change continued on export models and as an option at home). A new option was the Easidrive automatic transmission.

Last of all in this quick-change sequence was the Mk IIIB of August 1960, with a reversion to a single-carburettor engine, and with the new corporate hypoid-bevel rear axle instead of the original spiral-type.

Even this version lived for only a year, being replaced by the Mk IIIC in July 1961.

Singer Gazelle Mk IIIC (1961 to 1963)

Why did the Gazelle family simply not progress through Mks III, IV, V and so on, instead of going into subdivisions like IIIA, IIIB and now – in July 1961 – IIIC? Does it even matter? Only, perhaps, to historians and archivists, for such numbers never appeared as badges on the cars.

The Gazelle Mk IIIC, therefore, was put on sale less than a year after the Mk IIIB had been launched, and was the seventh different type of Gazelle to be launched in five years.

Technically, the changes were confined to the fitment of an enlarged engine (1,592cc instead of 1,494cc, which brought it into line with other cars in this family), which was slightly less powerful than that of the Mk IIIB, to distance it from the recently announced Vogue model, and a slight reshuffling of gearbox and axle ratios. In marketing terms, however, there was a small but significant price reduction (£23 for the saloon, for instance).

The convertible version was dropped in February 1962 and the last estate car was produced a month later. Thereafter, only the four-door saloon was built.

Singer Gazelle Mk IIIC specification

As for Singer Gazelle Mk IIIB except for:
Produced: 1961–63, 15,115 cars built.
Engine and transmission: 1,592cc, 81.5 x 76.2mm, 53bhp (net) at 4,100rpm; 87lb ft at 2,100rpm.
Distinguishing features from previous models: Mk IIIC had a '1600' badge on the doors, otherwise no styling changes.
Typical performance: Maximum speed 79mph; 0–60mph 23.6sec; standing ¼-mile 22.8sec; typical fuel consumption 25mpg.
Derivatives: 1963 Gazelle Mk V was a restyled version of the Mk IIIC.
Fate: Discontinued in autumn 1963 in favour of the restyled Gazelle Mk V.

The Gazelle became IIIC in the autumn of 1961, complete with a 53bhp 1,592cc engine.

This was the rear aspect of the roll-over-fin variety of Singer Gazelle, which was built from 1959 to 1963.

Singer Gazelle Mk V (1963 to 1965)

Why was there no Gazelle Mk IV? Although this was never spelt out in public, it was because the Vogue, launched in 1961, was to have been the Gazelle Mk IV before the policy changes already described saw not one, but two, medium-sized Singers remaining on sale in the 1960s.

One week after the restyled Series V Hillman Minx had been launched, the near-identical Gazelle Mk V was also revealed. Like the Minx, it featured the revised style which included a squared-up cabin top and enlarged rear doors, a Borg-Warner instead of Smiths-type automatic transmission, 13in wheels, front-wheel disc brakes and a 'no-greasing' chassis. Inside the car there was a new and neater facia style and fully reclining front seats were standard.

Autocar summed up the new car perfectly: 'The role of the Singer Gazelle has always been that of a luxury version of the Hillman Minx'....and so it was.

Like the Minx Series V, therefore, the Gazelle Mk V also inherited an all-synchromesh gearbox and a diaphragm-spring clutch from the autumn of 1964, plus a floor-mounted selector for automatic-transmission models.

Singer Gazelle Mk V specification

As for Singer Gazelle Mk IIIC except for:
Produced: 1963–65, 20,022 cars built.
Engine and transmission: (Manual) 53bhp (net) at 4,100rpm; 87lb ft at 2,100rpm; (Automatic) 58bhp (net) at 4,000rpm; 86lb ft at 2,500rpm; all-synchromesh gearbox from late 1964, optional Borg-Warner automatic transmission.
Chassis: Front disc brakes. 6.00-13in tyres.
Dimensions: Front track 4ft 3.75in; height 4ft 10in.
Distinguishing features from previous models: Restyled upper cabin including enlarged rear doors and non-wraparound rear window, plus new facia style and smaller road wheels. Closely related to Minx Series V of same period.
Typical performance: Maximum speed 79mph; 0–60mph 24.9sec; standing ¼-mile 22.5sec; typical fuel consumption 28mpg.
Derivatives: 1965 Gazelle Mk VI used same structure, but enlarged engine.
Fate: Discontinued in 1965 in favour of Gazelle Mk VI.

Singer Gazelle Mk VI (1965 to 1967)

As ever, Gazelle development in the mid-1960s was closely tied to that of the Hillman Minx. When the Minx was given its 1,725cc engine and negative-earth electrics in the autumn of 1965, so did the Gazelle, and it was in this form, complete with slightly restyled nose (and a grille fixed to the front panel rather than swinging up with the opening bonnet) that it was produced in small numbers until the beginning of 1967. Then, after more than 10 successful years, the original Gazelle family gave way to the Arrow type of Gazelle.

Like the Hillman Minx, the Gazelle was considerably restyled in the autumn of 1963, becoming Gazelle V with the help of a new and more angular roof line, larger rear passenger doors, and a flatter rear window.

Singer Gazelle Mk VI specification

As for Singer Gazelle Mk V except for:
Produced: 1965–67, 1,482 cars built.
Engine and transmission: 1,725cc, 81.5 x 82.55mm, (originally) 65bhp (net) at 4,800rpm; 98lb ft at 2,400rpm; (most cars) 59bhp (net) at 4,200rpm; 92lb ft at 2,200rpm.
Distinguishing features from previous models: Mk VI had restyled nose with squat Singer-type grille and '1725' badges.
Typical performance: Maximum speed 82mph; 0–60mph 20.5sec; standing ¼-mile 21.8sec; typical fuel consumption 25mpg.
Derivatives: None – this was the last of the line for this particular family.
Fate: Discontinued early in 1967 in favour of new Arrow type of Gazelle.

Singer Vogue I and II (1961 to 1964)

As already explained in earlier chapters, Rootes were so preoccupied with the evolution of existing Minx/Gazelle/Rapier models that by the time the Super Minx/Vogue models were finally revealed, five years had passed without a new shape being shown.

The Vogue, launched in July 1961, was the first of a new family of medium-sized Rootes cars to make its bow – it actually pre-dated the Hillman Super Minx by three months. When conceived, it had been intended as a straight replacement for the Gazelle (and it was to have been the Gazelle Mk IV). Because it was larger, heavier and – most important – more expensive than the Gazelle, it was given a new name (Vogue was actually a Humber trademark from the 12hp model of the 1930s), and it was eventually decided to run it alongside the existing Gazelle for several years.

The Singer Vogue, larger, more expensive and significantly better equipped than the Gazelle, joined the Singer line-up in the summer of 1961. It was closely based on the Hillman Super Minx design, and there were obvious links, too, with the forthcoming Humber Sceptre.

The original Singer Vogue, of 1961, showing off its wrap-round rear window and the prominent tail fins.

The 'office' of the Singer Vogue of 1961, complete with wood veneer instrument panel and centre gear-change.

In most respects, the Vogue was an up-market Hillman Super Minx and shared that car's bodyshell, chassis structure and choice of basic power trains and transmissions. Ahead of the screen, however, it had a unique style featuring two pairs of cowled headlamps (the visual link with late-1950s Chrysler Corporation products was obvious, as the pictures make clear), while there was a walnut-trimmed facia panel and more luxurious seating and appointments. Like the Super Minx, it was a practical rather than sporting car.

At first there was an all-drum braking installation, and there were Smiths Easidrive and Laycock overdrive transmission options. The roomy estate car was put on sale in May 1962. Unlike the Super Minx, however, there was never a convertible option.

From October 1962, the second-series Vogue (Vogue II) took over, this having all the improvements introduced coincidentally on the Hillman Super Minx II. These included front-wheel disc brakes, a Borg-Warner automatic transmission option instead of Easidrive, the elimination of greasing and a new and larger fuel tank.

Better things, however, were in store, so Vogue III then took over from the autumn of 1964.

Singer Vogue I and II specification

Produced: Ryton-on-Dunsmore, 1961–64, 7,423/20,021 cars built.
General layout: Unit-construction body-chassis structure in 4-door saloon or estate car styles. Front-mounted engine driving rear wheels.
Engine and transmission: Hillman engine, 4-cylinder, ohv, in-line. 1,592cc, 81.5 x 76.2mm, 62bhp (net) at 4,800rpm; 86lb ft at 2,800rpm; 4-speed gearbox, no synchromesh on 1st gear; centre-floor gear-change, optional Laycock overdrive, optional Smiths Easidrive on Vogue I, optional Borg-Warner automatic on Vogue II from late 1962; live (beam) rear axle with hypoid-bevel final drive.
Chassis: Independent front suspension, coil springs, wishbones. Recirculating-ball steering. Live (beam) rear axle with half-elliptic leaf springs. Front and rear drum brakes on Vogue I, front discs on Vogue II. 5.90-13in tyres.
Dimensions: Wheelbase 8ft 5in; front track 4ft 3.5in; rear track 4ft 0.5in; length 13ft 9.3in; width 5ft 2.3in; height 4ft 10.3in. Unladen weight (saloon) approx 2,410lb.
Distinguishing features from previous models: Completely different type of Singer compared with previous models, closely related to Hillman Super Minx of 1961, but with 4-headlamp nose style.
Typical performance: Maximum speed 83mph; 0–60mph 20.9sec; standing ¼-mile 21.5sec; typical fuel consumption 24mpg.
Derivatives: Vogue III used same basic structure and suspension with revised and more powerful engine.
Fate: Discontinued in 1964 in favour of Vogue III.

Singer Vogue III (1964 to 1965)

In the autumn of 1964, Rootes repeated its Minx/Gazelle restyling trick and carried out the same type of facelift on the Super Minx/Vogue models. Like the Super Minx, the latest Vogue, called Series III, had an altogether squatter upper cabin which featured a rear quarter-window behind reshaped rear doors, and a flatter rear window and roof.

Under the skin, however, was the most important change of all – the adoption of the much more powerful

Singer Vogue III specification

As for Vogue I and II except for:
Produced: 1964–65, 10,000 cars built.
Engine and transmission: 78bhp (net) at 5,000rpm; 91lb ft at 3,500rpm; all-synchromesh gearbox.
Chassis: 6.00-13in tyres.
Dimensions: Height 4ft 9in.
Distinguishing features from previous models: Restyled upper cabin, including flatter roof and rear window, restyled sides, including extra quarter-window behind reshaped rear doors.
Typical performance: Maximum speed 90mph; 0–60mph 14.1sec; standing ¼-mile 19.9sec; typical fuel consumption 22mpg.
Derivatives: 1965 Vogue IV had style changes and 1,725cc engine.
Fate: Discontinued in autumn 1965 in favour of Vogue IV.

The Vogue became Vogue IV in the autumn of 1965, when it received the 85bhp 1,725cc engine. The roof/window restyle had first appeared on the Vogue III of 1964.

Humber Sceptre/Sunbeam Rapier type of engine, complete with aluminium cylinder head, and the latest Rootes all-synchromesh gearbox. The automatic transmission now had a centre-floor operating lever and reclining front seats had become standard.

Singer Vogue IV (1965 to 1966)

The last derivative of the original Vogue family, built for a mere 12 months, was the Series IV. Like the other cars in this family, it picked up the long-stroke, five-bearing, 1,725cc engine, which was the same as that fitted to Rapiers and Humber Sceptres of this period.

Apart from the fitment of '1725' badges to the bodywork, there were no visual changes.

Singer Vogue IV specification

As for Singer Vogue III except for:
Produced: 1965–66, 10,325 cars built.
Engine and transmission: 1,725cc, 81.5 x 82.55mm, 85bhp (net) at 5,500rpm; 106lb ft at 3,500rpm.
Distinguishing features from previous models: '1725' badges on the front wings and tail.
Derivatives: None – replaced by new-generation Arrow-type Vogue in late 1966.
Fate: Discontinued in 1966 in favour of new Arrow-type Vogue.

Singer Vogue (Arrow-type – 1966 to 1970)

As explained in earlier chapters, Rootes, egged on by Chrysler, severely rationalized its medium-sized family of cars in the late 1960s. In place of two types, both of which dated in styling from the late 1950s, one new family, the Arrow-type, was introduced. The New Vogue was first and the New Gazelle soon followed.

The new-generation Vogue was even more closely related to a Hillman than before. In all but grille design, headlamps (rectangular instead of circular), badging, trim and the facia details, the Vogue saloon was the same as the Hillman Hunter.

The Vogue estate car was launched in April 1967, at first with an iron-headed engine producing 68bhp (instead of the 74bhp of the saloon), but from October 1967 the 74bhp aluminium-headed engine was standardized.

The New Vogue sold well enough, but when Chrysler rationalized further in the spring of 1970, the Singer badge was abandoned completely.

Singer Gazelle (Arrow-type – 1967 to 1970)

Unless you looked carefully, it was difficult to work out the difference between the New Vogue and the New Gazelle, as both were effectively badge-engineered from the same Hillman (Arrow) Minx/Hunter style and structure.

From late 1966 there was a new Singer Vogue, this being very closely based on the Arrow type of Hillman Hunter. This style would be unchanged until the Singer marque disappeared in 1970.

Rootes produced a very smart estate car version of the Arrow structure from the end of 1966. This was the Singer Vogue estate; the author owned one of these cars in 1969/1970.

The new-generation Singer Gazelle of 1967–1970 was really a rebadged version of the latest Hillman Minx, less powerful and slightly less well equipped than the contemporary Vogue. This particular car was a 1969 model.

The New Gazelle, however, was powered by iron-head rather than aluminium-head engines. Manual-transmission cars had the short-stroke five-bearing 1,496cc engine, whereas automatic-transmission cars had five-bearing 1,725cc engines.

Like the New Vogue, the New Gazelle sold steadily, but was not further developed after it was launched and it was dropped in the spring of 1970.

Singer Vogue (Arrow-type) specification

Produced: Ryton-on-Dunsmore and Linwood, 1966–70, 47,655 cars built.
Fate: Discontinued in April 1970 but rebadged for a short time as Sunbeam Vogue. Not replaced.
For all technical details, see Hillman Hunter Series I and II specifications.

Singer Gazelle (Arrow-type) specification

Produced: Ryton-on-Dunsmore and Linwood. 1967–70, 31,482 cars built.
Fate: Discontinued in April 1970. Not replaced.
For all technical details, see Hillman New Minx (1967–70 model) specification.

The 1967 Gazelle's facia style differed considerably from that of the Hillman Hunter, but the Vogue style was similar. This, of course, is an artist's impression.

Singer Chamois (1964 to 1970)

The only real novelty in this rear-engined saloon was its name. Unlike other Rootes names of the period, it had not been picked out of the 'old trademarks' file, and was a neat way of pointing out that here was a lightweight Singer which had a genuine sure-footed character.

Except that it had a slightly higher level of trim and equipment and – strange this – wider-rim wheels, the Chamois was a clone of the Hillman Imp/Super Imp models which have already been described.

Mk I became Mk II in autumn 1965, the front suspension was decambered in the spring of 1967, while a different facia style and twin headlamps were added from October 1968.

Like all other Singers, the Chamois was dropped in April 1970.

Singer Chamois specification

Produced: Linwood, 1964–70, 40,678 cars built.
Fate: Discontinued in 1970 when Singer marque dropped. Not replaced.
For all technical details, see Hillman Imp/Super Imp specification.

Singer Chamois Sport (1966 to 1970)

The Chamois Sport was a slightly better trimmed and furnished version of the Sunbeam Imp Sport, but was mechanically identical.

Like all other Singers, it was dropped in April 1970.

The Singer Chamois appeared in 1964, being a slightly up-market derivative of the rear-engined Hillman Imp. This is the 'Mark 2' type, which appeared in 1965.

The Chamois Sport combined the trim and equipment of the Chamois with the 50bhp 875cc twin-carburettor engine of the Sunbeam Imp Sport. The four headlamps, initially, were unique to this particular version in the Imp family.

Smartest of all the Singer Chamois types, but only on sale from 1967 to 1970, was the Coupe. This shared its body style with the Hillman Imp Californian and the Sunbeam Stiletto.

Singer Chamois Sport specification
Produced: Linwood, 1966–70, 4,149 cars built. **Fate:** Discontinued in 1970 when Singer marque was dropped. Not replaced. For all technical details, see Sunbeam Imp Sport/ Sunbeam Sport specification.

Singer Chamois Coupe (1967 to 1970)

The Chamois Coupe was mechanically identical to the Hillman Imp Californian of the 1967–70 period, with the same fastback coupe style but slightly more up-market trim and fittings.

Like all other Singers, the Californian Coupe was dropped in April 1970.

Singer Chamois Coupe specification
Produced: Linwood, 1967–70, 4,971 cars built. **Fate:** Discontinued in 1970 when Singer marque was dropped. Not replaced.

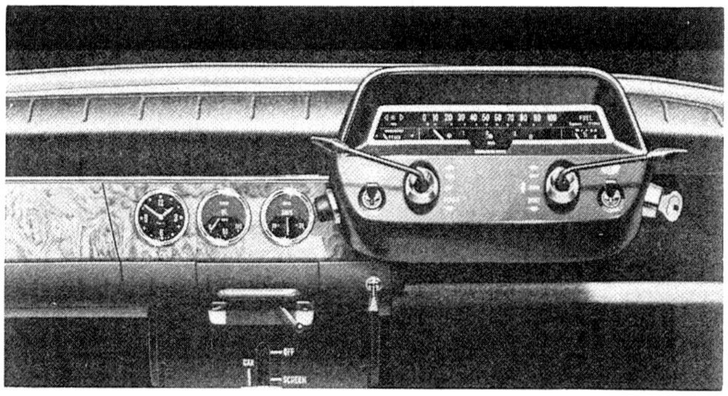

The two Chamois saloons, but not, of course, the Coupe, shared the Imp's useful opening rear window, adorned with more bright trim than the basic Hillman version. Two renderings of the interior, in this case a Chamois Sport, show the neat instrument display, and the unobstructed floor provided by the rear-engined design.

Chapter 7

SUNBEAM

Although Sunbeam was a going concern when bought by Rootes in the summer of 1935, the car-manufacturing business was rapidly closed down and the marque title was allowed to go into cold storage.

One prototype 30hp car was shown in 1936, but nothing came of it, and the next appearance of the name was in the newly invented Sunbeam-Talbot marque in 1938. Sunbeam-Talbot, under Rootes sponsorship, was in existence from 1938 to 1954, and its short life is covered in the next chapter. Just to confuse matters, for some export markets the British-badged Sunbeam-Talbots carried Sunbeam badges.

The Sunbeam name reappeared on its own in the UK in 1953 on the Alpine sports car, and the Talbot part of Sunbeam-Talbot was dropped entirely at the end of the 1954 model-year, which meant that the 1954 Sunbeam-Talbot 90 Mk IIA, when slightly modified and improved, but visually almost unchanged, became the 1955 Sunbeam Mark III.

After the takeover

For its 1935 model-year, at takeover time, the Sunbeam Motor Car Company Ltd, of Wolverhampton, was offering the 1.6-litre four-cylinder Dawn at £425 and a closely-related family of six-cylinder Twenty, Twenty-One Sports and Twenty-Five models at prices ranging from £725 to £875. The company was losing money steadily and no major new models were in preparation.

One reason for Rootes taking over Sunbeam, it seems, was that the family wanted to capitalize on a great name by developing a flagship to add to the prestige of its other marque names – Hillman, Humber and (most recently) Talbot. The fact that Rootes already controlled Thrupp & Maberly, the coachbuilding concern which was ideally suited to building the bodies for such cars, must have been a factor; it all made a great deal of sense.

That, however, was for the future. In the meantime, Rootes could see little merit in the existing models (the Dawn was too expensive, too complex and too slow, and the six-cylinder cars were old-fashioned designs dating back to the late 1920s). Accordingly, the car production lines in Wolverhampton were swiftly emptied and stocks cleared and as a result there were no Sunbeams at the Olympia Motor Show in October 1935.

The stillborn Sunbeam Thirty (1936)

Billy Rootes does not seem to have considered giving any new design work to the staff at Wolverhampton. In any case, H.C. Stephens, the prime mover behind the Dawn, had gone; Rootes had other plans for Georges Roesch of Talbot (who had been looking after both marques for a time); and engine designer Hugh Rose had already moved on to work on new engine designs for Riley in Coventry.

Instead, having secured control of Talbot, he presented Roesch, Talbot's technical genius, with a fascinating challenge. At short notice, and with the minimum of facilities, he was asked to produce a new Sunbeam flagship. It was to look magnificent and was to have a 100mph top speed.

The object was to have the first cars on display at Olympia in 1936. Roesch's original brief – one which horrified him – was that he could design a new engine and arrange for bodies to be coachbuilt designs, but he had to use the large Humber chassis and its Evenkeel independent front suspension, which had been revealed in October 1935. This chassis was already being criticized for its roadholding problems so, during the development stages of the new Sunbeam, long radius arms were added to the front suspension.

One hoary old motor industry legend, as quoted by

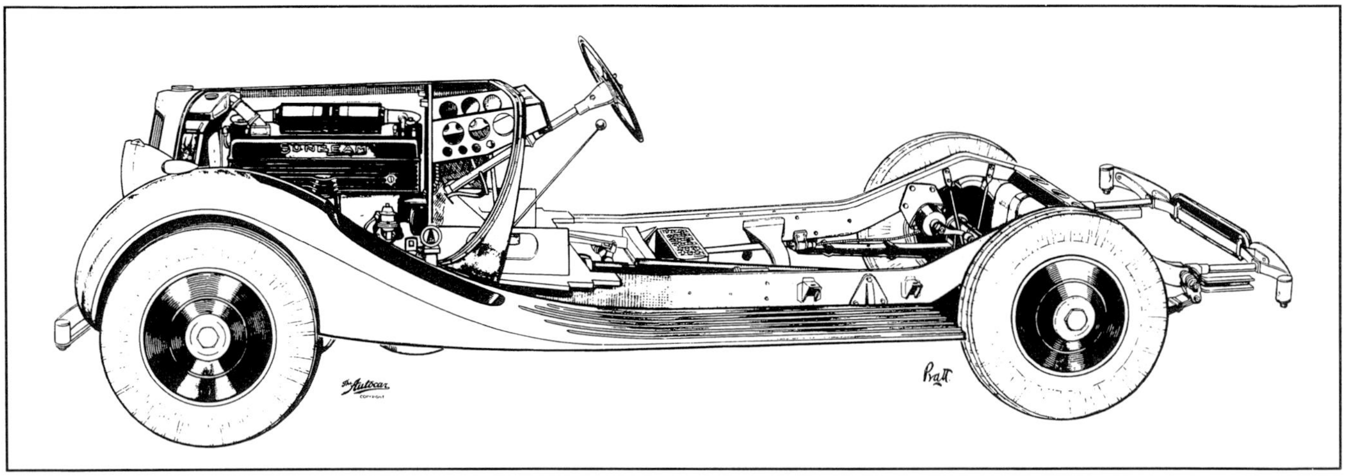

Georges Roesch's Sunbeam Thirty had a brand-new eight-cylinder engine but used a modified Humber chassis frame. At the Olympia Motor Show in 1936, Rootes showed this large and impressive drophead-coupe body style for the new flagship, but in the event the car did not go into production.

Details of the Sunbeam Thirty 'straight-eight' engine, with carefully detailed valve gear, and with twin downdraught carbs, one at each end of the gallery inlet manifold. No trace of this engine in the metal has survived for posterity.

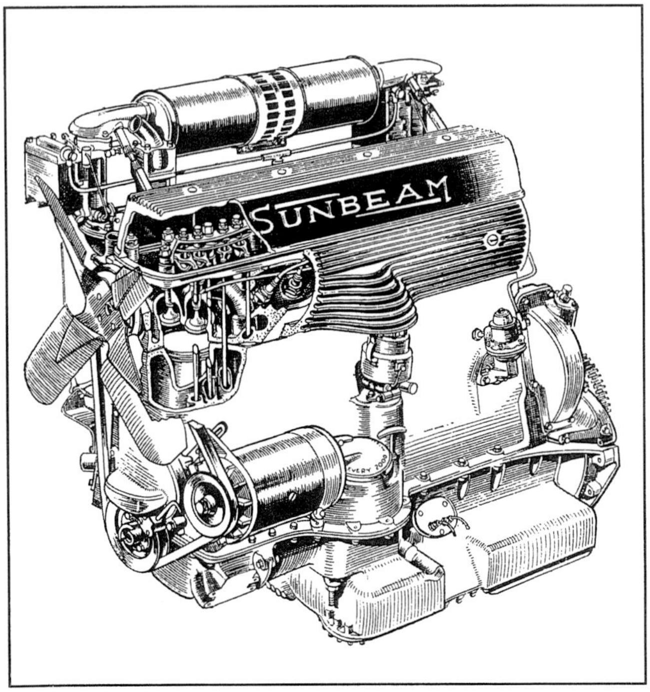

Michael Sedgwick in *Cars of the 1930s*, is worth repeating:

'[Rootes] already held a sizeable percentage of the directorial and mayoral market with their Humber Pullman, and the story goes that William Rootes was determined to produce a ceremonial carriage for King Edward VIII. The consequence was the Sunbeam Thirty....'

It might not have been true, but it makes a good story! This was the car which appeared at Olympia in 1936, and was without doubt the star of that exhibition. Yet to this day it remains a project that has always been an enigma, for it was exhibited, priced, but never seen again. No car, not even an engine, survives.

Prototypes first ran in the summer of 1936, there were completed cars at Olympia (one with a Thrupp & Maberly six-window saloon, one an H.J. Mulliner Sedanca de Ville), and a show chassis. The most outstanding feature of the design was Roesch's new engine and the most disappointing was the barely modified Humber-type chassis.

Right from the start, Roesch reckoned that the car

needed at least 150bhp to produce a 100mph top speed. His existing Talbot 3,377cc six-cylinder engine was near the limit of its development and could not produce that much power so, nothing daunted, he set about converting the 'six' into a straight-eight!

While retaining the same bore and stroke (80 x 112mm) of the Talbot 110 engine, Roesch detailed a new block and cylinder head, reshuffled all the components and speedily designed a compact 4,503cc engine which would comfortably fit into the Humber chassis. The new unit looked sleek and streamlined, with its twin carburettors mounted one at each end of a gallery inlet manifold. At the same time, Roesch also schemed out ways of developing six and four-cylinder variants from the same basic design.

For the new Sunbeam, the engine was matched to the existing Humber four-speed gearbox and back axle. The Humber frame was stretched to its limits, for wheelbases of up to 11ft 4in were to be offered.

In his monumental study of Talbot (*Georges Roesch and the Invincible Talbot*), Anthony Blight tells us that 'the climax came when the Rootes brothers decided to take the car on their Continental holiday. Somewhere near Maidstone, the over-stressed Humber frame broke and the Sunbeam was testily abandoned; from that moment its fate was sealed, though a final decision on its future was postponed for a little longer....'

The Thirty, once it had been shown at Olympia, was never seen again. King Edward VIII, already a Humber owner, abdicated from the British throne in December 1936, to be replaced by King George VI, who rode around in Daimlers or near-identical Lanchesters. Were the two abdications connected?

That is the romantic notion, but it is probably not the real story. What is sometimes forgotten is that at this time Rootes was also becoming embroiled in the vital, but time-consuming, shadow factory scheme. As was stated by Rootes publicists in 1938, when the Sunbeam-Talbot marque was created:

'The original intention of Messrs W.E. and R.C. Rootes was to make the Sunbeam a large and expensive type of car. Production of this, however, was held up by Government activities....'

David Scott-Moncrieff, in his important book *The Thoroughbred Motor Car*, opined that: 'One can only assume that, like many far-sighted men, they saw the gathering war clouds, and decided, wisely, that the tail end of the 1930s would not be a propitious time to launch a new, relatively expensive luxury car....they could hardly risk their shareholders' money on what might easily have been a very doubtful project.'

In other words, the death of the Sunbeam Thirty was all due to priorities and market forces. What a tragedy.

Sunbeam Thirty specification

Produced: London, 1936. Only prototype cars built.
General layout: Separate chassis-frame, coachbuilt bodyshells in a variety of styles. Front-mounted engine driving rear wheels.
Engine and transmission: Talbot engine, 8-cylinder, ohv, in-line. 4,503cc, 80 x 112mm, 150bhp at 4,500rpm; maximum torque not revealed; 4-speed gearbox, no synchromesh on 1st gear; centre-floor gear-change; live (beam) rear axle with spiral-bevel final drive.
Chassis: Independent front suspension, transverse leaf spring and upper wishbones, radius arms. Worm-and-nut steering. Live (beam) rear axle, half-elliptic leaf springs. Front and rear drum brakes. 7.00-17in tyres.
Dimensions: Wheelbase 10ft 4in or 11ft 4in; front track 4ft 10.6in; rear track 5ft 0.25in; length (typical) 16ft 4in; width 6ft 2in; height depending on coachwork fitted. Unladen weight not established.
Fate: Not put into production; all prototypes broken up.

Sunbeam Alpine (1953 to 1955)

The Alpine quite definitely was aimed at the North American market. Billy Rootes, aided and abetted by the Loewy studio, was convinced that an open-top car of the right type would sell in large numbers, and the Alpine was the result.

The new car's styling, it has often been stated, was inspired by a special competition car rigged up by that long-term Rootes family friend (and dealer) George Hartwell. The definitive product, however, was detailed by the Loewy studio.

Basically, the Alpine was a simple two-seater tourer version of the existing Sunbeam-Talbot 90 saloon. It used the same basic chassis and running gear, and the same front-end and side-on styling lines, but it had a two-seater cockpit and a long, graceful, sweeping tail.

To make up for a lack of rigidity in the open-top shell, the chassis was further stiffened with an additional bolt-on tubular cross-member behind and under the engine sump, while the side members were further plated and made deeper. The front suspension had stiffer springs, the anti-roll bar was beefed-up, the steering was made more direct, the 2,267cc engine was further tuned and the gearbox ratios were altered. A new cylinder head, with better breathing, helped produce more power than the saloon, but even though this was supposed to be a sporting car, the steering-column gear-change was retained.

Originally, the Alpine was for export only, though right-hand-drive UK-market deliveries began in autumn 1953. Laycock overdrive was standardized in the autumn of 1954. Even though it was a big and heavy car, the Alpine fared well in motorsport, winning several

The Sunbeam Alpine of 1953–1955 was effectively a two-seater derivative of the contemporary Sunbeam-Talbot 90 Mk IIA. The shells were built for Rootes by Mulliners of Birmingham. Show model's cut-down windscreen, left, emphasized the sporting image.

Hood and sidescreens were neat though more spartan than on the convertible 90. The dash layout reflected the Alpine's intended American market destination.

coupes in the Alpine rallies and setting a 120mph top speed (with Stirling Moss at the wheel) on the Jabbeke road in Belgium.

Unhappily, it was a lot more expensive than new rivals like the Triumph TR2 and the Austin-Healey 100. Not even its use by Grace Kelly in the film *To Catch a Thief* could save it. It was dropped in 1955 – the next-generation Alpine would be a completely different kind of car.

Racing driver Mike Hawthorn, at the wheel, and Rootes competition manager Norman Garrad pose in an Alpine on display at London's Earls Court Motor Show.

Because the two-seater Alpine used the same chassis as the four-seater saloon, there was a long, though shallow, boot compartment.

Sunbeam (-Talbot) Alpine specification

Produced: Ryton-on-Dunsmore, 1953–55, approximately 3,000 cars built.
General layout: Separate chassis-frame, pressed-steel bodyshell. Front-mounted engine driving rear wheels.
Engine and transmission: Hillman/Humber engine, 4-cylinder, ohv, in-line. 2,267cc, 81 x 110mm, 80bhp at 4,200rpm; 124lb ft at 1,800rpm; 4-speed gearbox, no synchromesh on 1st gear (overdrive fitted from late 1954); steering-column gear-change; live (beam) rear axle with hypoid-bevel final drive.
Chassis: Independent front suspension, coil springs, wishbones, anti-roll-bar. Recirculating-ball steering. Live (beam) rear axle, half-elliptic leaf springs, Panhard rod. Front and rear drum brakes. 5.50-16in tyres.
Dimensions: Wheelbase 8ft 1.5in; front track 3ft 11.5in; rear track 4ft 2.5in; length 13ft 11.5in; width 5ft 2.5in; height 4ft 8in. Unladen weight approx 2,900lb.
Distinguishing features from previous models: Same basic chassis-frame and style as contemporary Sunbeam-Talbot touring cars, but with 2-seater open tourer version of familiar body style.
Typical performance: Maximum speed 95mph; 0–60mph 18.9sec; standing ¼-mile 21.1sec; typical fuel consumption 24mpg.
Derivatives: Closely related to Sunbeam-Talbot 90 Mk IIA and Sunbeam Mk III of the period.
Fate: Discontinued in 1955 and not replaced. Sunbeam Alpine, reintroduced in 1959, was an entirely different type of car.

Sunbeam(-Talbot) Mk III (1954 to 1957)

This model was more properly a Sunbeam-Talbot 90 Mk III, developed to succeed the Mk IIA of 1952–54, but it came along just as the Talbot name was being dropped from home-market cars.

Compared with the Mk IIA, the Mk III had a minor front-end facelift, the addition of 'hot air outlet portholes' in the sides of the engine compartment (these, in fact, were Loewy-studio affectations, influenced by similar slots found on contemporary Buicks....) and new wheel trims. There was a revised facia style with an

At the end of 1954, the Sunbeam-Talbot 90 Mk IIA was revamped, and renamed Sunbeam Mk III. It had new front-end decoration and, for the saloon, a two-tone colour scheme. The basic sheet metal, of course, was not altered.

Rootes called the drophead version of the Sunbeam Mk III a Convertible Coupe. It shared the minor styling revisions of the saloon.

Facia of the Sunbeam Mk III: the central circular ornament could be replaced by an optional rev counter. The layout was similar but not identical to that of the Alpine.

Sunbeam Mk III specification

Produced: Ryton-on-Dunsmore, 1954–57, 5,249 cars built, including Mk II Alpines (see above).
General Layout: Separate chassis-frame, pressed-steel bodyshell. Front-mounted engine driving rear wheels.
Engine and transmission: Hillman/Humber engine, 4-cylinder, ohv, in-line. 2,267cc, 81 x 110mm, 80bhp at 4,200rpm; 124lb ft at 1,800rpm;
4-speed gearbox, no synchromesh on 1st gear, with optional overdrive; steering-column gear-change (some car dealer-converted with centre-floor change); live (beam) rear axle with hypoid-bevel final drive.
Chassis: Independent front suspension, coil springs, wishbones, anti-roll-bar. Recirculating-ball steering. Live (beam) rear axle, half-elliptic leaf springs, Panhard rod. Front and rear drum brakes. 5.50-16in tyres.
Dimensions: Wheelbase 8ft 1.5in; front track 3ft 11.5in; rear track 4ft 2.5in; length 13ft 11.5in; width 5ft 2.5in; height 4ft 8in. Unladen weight approx 2,950lb.
Distinguishing features from previous models: Same basic chassis-frame and style as final Sunbeam-Talbot 90 Mk IIA models, but with facelifted front and 3 'portholes' in each valance at bonnet sides.
Typical performance: Maximum speed 91mph; 0–60mph 18.4sec; standing ¼-mile 21.4sec; typical fuel consumption 24mpg.
Derivatives: Very closely related to 1952–54 Sunbeam-Talbot 90 Mk IIA (see Sunbeam-Talbot chapter) and Sunbeam Alpine of the period.
Fate: Discontinued in 1957 and not replaced. Sunbeam Rapier introduced in 1955 was an entirely different type of car.

(optional) rev-counter in the centre of the display. Engine power went up from 77 to 80bhp, in common with the Alpine (see above), while Laycock overdrive became optional. Still with bodywork built at BLSP, this car carried on until 1957, by which time it was thoroughly obsolete. A version produced by Castles of Leicester, a Rootes dealer, featured a different gear-change and a revised boot-opening arrangement, but this, called the Mk IIIS, was a private venture.

Sunbeam Rapier Series I (1955 to 1957)

Rootes commissioned an entirely new family of cars for the mid and late 1950s. The Hillman Minxes and Singer Gazelles of this family have already been described; it is sometimes forgotten, however, that the closely related Sunbeam Rapier was the first of the newcomers to be revealed.

The new Rapier was a two-door, four-seater sports saloon, based on the same basic style (inspired, via Loewy, by the new-generation Studebakers of 1953 which he had also created) as the Hillman Minx. Because it had no B/C pillars, and a two-tone colour scheme, it was in many ways the direct descendant of the Hillman Minx Californian, which had the same sort of character and packaging, but nothing like as much performance and panache.

But how about this for complication? The bare bodyshell was produced by Pressed Steel, shipped to Thrupp & Maberly in North London for painting and trimming, then shipped to Ryton for final assembly!

The Rapier's chassis was almost pure new-generation

The Sunbeam Rapier of 1955 was really a tuned-up two-door version of the new-generation Hillman Minx. The pundits, though, were a little confused when it appeared several months *before* the Minx!

The original Rapier of 1955 had a neat, but definitely mid-Atlantic, style, with a fully wrap-round rear window. In the years to come, it was to be a formidable sports saloon.

Sunbeam Rapier Series I specification

Produced: Ryton-on-Dunsmore, 1955–57, 7,477 cars built.
General layout: Pressed-steel unit-construction body-chassis shell. Front-mounted engine driving rear wheels.
Engine and transmission: Hillman engine, 4-cylinder, ohv, in-line, 1,390cc, 76.2 x 76.2mm, 62.5bhp at 5,000rpm; 73lb ft at 3,000rpm (from autumn 1956, 67bhp at 5,400rpm; 74lb ft at 3,000rpm); 4-speed gearbox, no synchromesh on 1st gear, with overdrive; steering-column gear-change; live (beam) rear axle with spiral-bevel final drive.
Chassis: Independent front suspension, coil springs, wishbones, anti-roll-bar. Worm-and-nut steering. Live (beam) rear axle, half-elliptic leaf springs. Front and rear drum brakes. 5.60-15in tyres.
Dimensions: Wheelbase 8ft 0in; front track 4ft 1in; rear track 4ft 0.5in; length 13ft 4.5in; width 5ft 0.75in; height 4ft 10in. Unladen weight approx 2,280lb.
Distinguishing features from previous models: No relationship to previous or existing Sunbeams and Sunbeam-Talbots. New Rapier effectively a 2-door version of forthcoming mid-1956 Hillman Minx. Superficial styling references to Hillman Minx Californian of early 1950s.
Typical performance: (Original model) Maximum speed 85mph; 0–60mph 21.7sec; standing ¼-mile 22.4sec; typical fuel consumption 34mpg; (R67, 67bhp model) maximum speed 85mph; 0–60mph 19.4sec; standing ¼-mile 21.5sec; typical fuel consumption 30mpg.
Derivatives: Closely related to new range of Hillman Minx cars introduced in 1956 (see Hillman chapter) and to 2-seater Sunbeam Alpine sports car introduced in 1959. Rapier design progressed to Mk V, last built in 1967.
Fate: Discontinued for 1958 and replaced by Sunbeam Rapier Series II.

Minx at first, complete with coil spring and wishbone front suspension and a massive curved cross-member. The engine was a much-modified new-generation overhead-valve Minx unit with a downdraught Stromberg carburettor; a modified Humber Hawk-style gearbox and overdrive were standard equipment.

It soon became clear that the original Rapier was not fast enough so, from October 1956, the R67 type of engine, using twin Zenith carbs and producing 67bhp instead of 62.5bhp, was fitted.

Better things, however, were to come, for the Rapier Series II took over in 1958.

Sunbeam Rapier Series II (1958 to 1959)

The revised Rapier, released immediately after the 1958 Monte Carlo Rally, in which Peter Harper's Series I car had finished a storming fifth overall, was a great improvement over the original. In addition to styling changes there were mechanical improvements and a new convertible option.

The basic style and package was not altered, but at the front there was now a traditional type of vertical Sunbeam grille, and a pair of sharply detailed fins had appeared on the rear quarters. The parent car, the Hillman Minx, had already gained its convertible body option, so the same option for the Rapier was widely expected.

Mechanically, the Rapier became the first Rootes car to receive the 1,494cc version of the modern overhead-valve four-cylinder engine. This was done by enlarging the cylinder bore; the twin Zenith carbs were retained and peak power went up by 6bhp. At the same time, a floor gear-change was standardized, the overdrive became optional rather than standard, a recirculating-ball steering box was specified and the front suspension was stiffened up.

In the mid-1950s, a unique-to-Rootes feature was this type of wind-down rear quarter window, which effectively provided open-air motoring, yet still with a fixed roof panel. Original Rapier facia, right: the steering-column gear-change persists, but at least the rev counter is in front of the driver. This export car has lhd and a kph speedometer.

Sunbeam Rapier Series II specification

As for Sunbeam Rapier Series I except for :
Produced: 1958–59, 15,151 cars built.
Engine and transmission: 1,494cc, 79 x 76.2mm; 73bhp (gross)/68bhp (net) at 5,200rpm; torque 81lb ft at 3,000rpm.
Chassis: Recirculating-ball steering.
Dimensions: Front track 4ft 1in; length 13ft 6.5in.
Distinguishing features from previous models: New front style with traditional vertical Sunbeam grille, and tail fins. Convertible body option for first time.
Typical performance: Maximum speed 90mph; 0–60mph 20.2sec; standing ¼-mile 21.1sec; typical fuel consumption 32mpg.
Derivatives: Coupe and drop-head coupe versions now available. As before, Rapiers closely related to Hillman Minx and Singer Gazelle models of the period. Rapier Series III was natural development of this model.
Fate: Discontinued in 1959 in favour of improved Rapier Series III.

Sunbeam Rapier Series III specification

As for Sunbeam Rapier Series II except for:
Produced: 1959–61, 15,368 cars built.
Engine and transmission: 73bhp (net) at 5,400rpm; 83lb ft at 3,500rpm; hypoid-bevel back axle from September 1960.
Chassis: Front disc brakes, rear drums.
Dimensions: Front track 4ft 1.75in. Unladen weight (saloon) approx 2,340lb.
Distinguishing features from previous models: Minor styling decoration changes, plus new facia style.
Typical performance: Maximum speed 92mph; 0–60mph 16.5sec; standing ¼-mile 20.7sec; typical fuel consumption 29mpg.
Derivatives: Rapier Series IIIA was natural development of this model.
Fate: Discontinued in 1961 in favour of Rapier Series IIIA.

Sunbeam Rapier Series III (1959 to 1961)

The Series III was a well-signalled (and substantial) improvement over the Series II, for most of the features introduced had already been seen on the brand-new Alpine sports car which had been launched a few weeks earlier.

Like the Alpine, the Series III Rapier had a new aluminium cylinder head, more power, closer-ratio gears and front-wheel disc brakes. There were no styling sheet-metal changes, but new for the Series III was a narrower side-colour spear along the flanks, and there was now a wooden veneer finish to the facia and a full horn ring on the steering wheel. A year after launch, a new design of hypoid-bevel back axle replaced the original spiral-bevel type.

Even though many people thought this was the definitive Rapier, it was to last for less than two years, for Rootes had yet more improvements in mind.

Sunbeam Rapier Series IIIA (1961 to 1963)

After the Alpine became the Alpine Series II, in October 1960, it was inevitable that the Rapier would soon follow suit and take on the enlarged engine of the sports car. In April 1961, therefore, the Rapier became Series IIIA, with no styling changes of any type, nor any obvious signal that the engine had been made more powerful. The evidence was in the figures – 75bhp (net) instead of 73bhp and 88lb ft torque instead of 83lb ft.

Sunbeam Rapier Series IIIA specification

As for Sunbeam Rapier Series III except for:
Produced: 1961–63, 17,354 cars built.
Engine and transmission: 1,592cc, 81.5 x 76.2mm; 75bhp (net) at 5,100rpm; torque 88lb ft at 3,900rpm.
Typical performance: Maximum speed 90mph; 0–60mph 19.3sec; standing ¼-mile 21.8sec; typical fuel consumption 24mpg.
Derivatives: Rapier Series IV was directly developed from this model.
Fate: Discontinued in 1963 in favour of Rapier Series IV.

The Rapier SII of 1958 had neat and distinctive tail fins, and for the first time there was a convertible option, its shell very closely based on that of the contemporary Hillman MInx and Singer Gazelle models. Also new was the radiator grille in 'traditional' style, retained for subsequent Rapiers and seen, right, on an SIII convertible, distinguished externally by the straight side stripes.

Below, the Sunbeam Rapier SIII in saloon form. Below right, the interior of the SIII version, with restyled seats and a wood veneer facia.

Sunbeam Rapier Series IV (1963 to 1965)

By this stage, the Rapier should have been dropped, for the original Rapier Series IV became the Humber Sceptre for 1963. Competition from other sports saloons, notably from Ford with the Cortina GT and Vauxhall with the VX4/90, made it imperative that further improvements should be made.

The Series IV, therefore, was launched in October 1963 – at the Earls Court Motor Show, incidentally, which also saw the Rover 2000 and Triumph 2000 models for the first time. It was quite a year for new models....

Compared with the Series IIIA, the latest car received significant engine improvements, including the use of

By the early 1960s, Rootes was using the Rapier for its front-line rally car. This was a pre-race scene on the 1961 RAC Rally, with Peter Procter (holding the door), author Graham Robson (who was co-driving number 12), and Paddy Hopkirk awaiting the 'off'. The team won the manufacturers' team prize on that occasion.

the Solex compound-choke carburettor which had already been 'blooded' on the Humber Sceptre. The latest 78.5bhp engine, therefore, was almost identical to that of the Sceptre.

Like all other Rootes cars in the medium-size category, the new Series IV was given 13in instead of 15in road wheels, with revised gearing to take account of this change, and at the same time a diaphragm-spring clutch was standardized. The new corporate medium-range all-synchromesh gearbox was fitted from October 1964, half-way through the run of the Series IV.

At the same time, styling changes included a lowered bonnet line, new front-end grille treatment, different side flashing and an 'SIV' badge on the tail and front wings. Inside the car, the Alpine's adjustable steering column was fitted, along with a revised facia, adjustable-backrest front seats and many other detail improvements.

There was no convertible option, however, this having been discontinued when the Series IIIA was phased out.

Sunbeam Rapier Series IV specification

As for Rapier Series IIIA except for:
Produced: 1963–65, 9,700 cars built.
Engine and transmission: 78.5bhp (net) at 5,000rpm; 91lb ft at 3,500rpm; all-synchromesh gearbox from October 1964.
Chassis: 6.00-13in tyres.
Dimensions: Front track 4ft 3.75in. Unladen weight (approx) 2,300lb.
Distinguishing features from previous models: 13in wheels instead of 15in, new front grille and details, 'SIV' badges on tail, adjustable steering column and revised facia layout. No convertible option.
Typical performance: Maximum speed 92mph; 0–60mph 17.0sec; standing ¼-mile 20.8sec; typical fuel consumption 24mpg.
Derivatives: Mechanically similar to new Humber Sceptre; Rapier Series V was developed from this model.
Fate: Discontinued in 1965 and replaced by Rapier Series V.

Sunbeam Rapier Series V (1965 to 1967)

Ten years after its launch, the Rapier was effectively obsolete, by now outpaced in motorsport *and* in the showrooms by newer, lighter and faster rivals. Even so, Rootes made one final, important, change to the well-liked old design, turning the Series IV into Series V from September 1965.

The Rapier Series V was the only member of this family to receive the five-bearing 1,725cc version of the famous old engine, a size which was specified for several other Rootes models at this time. Because the block/crankshaft installation was more rigid, it was a smoother engine than the 1,592cc unit, but it was clearly at the end of its development – compared with the Series IV there was 85bhp instead of 78.5bhp.

There were no styling changes except that 'Rootes 1725' badges were standardized. A negative-earth electrical system with alternator was standardized.

This car sold much less well than previous models, and was finally dropped in 1967. Its successor was the completely different fastback model, based on the Hillman Hunter Arrow range.

The Rapier Series IV arrived in 1963, with more power, better equipment, and yet another minor decorative facelift to give distinction to the appearance.

When Rootes stylists were considering the Series V, thought was given to revising the fins, as this mock-up shows. In the end, it was abandoned, and only the larger, 1,725cc engine featured in the revision.

Sunbeam Rapier Series V specification

As for Rapier Series IV except for:
Produced: 1965–67, 3,759 cars built.
Engine and transmission: 1,725cc, 81.5 x 82.55mm, 85bhp (net) at 5,500rpm; 99lb ft at 3,500rpm; all-synchromesh gearbox.
Distinguishing features from previous models: 'Rootes 1725' badging, and minor changes to instrument styling. Alternator fitted instead of dynamo.
Typical performance: Maximum speed 95mph; 0–60mph 14.1sec; standing ¼-mile 19.5sec; typical fuel consumption 22mpg.
Derivatives: None.
Fate: Discontinued in summer 1967 and replaced by fastback Rapier based on new corporate Hillman Hunter Arrow design.

Sunbeam Alpine I (1959 to 1960)

The original Alpine, of 1953 to 1955, had not sold as well as the Rootes family had hoped, but the second attempt was much more successful. This time the car was not to be lumbered with an old-fashioned chassis; it would have an ultra-modern style, and it was clearly aimed at the very lively USA market sector where the MG MGA, Triumph TR3A and six-cylinder Austin-Healeys were selling so well.

As ever, Rootes spent no more money on new design than was absolutely necessary. The running gear was almost pure (updated) Rapier and was meant to be shared with that car, while the underpan and some inner body pressings were those of the Hillman Husky II. For that reason, obviously, the Alpine's wheelbase was 10in less than that of the Rapier – but, then, it was only meant to be a two-seater sports car. There was also a '+2' rear seat, but this was more of a padded shelf for carrying bags, for there was virtually no leg room ahead of it.

To stiffen up the chassis there was extra cruciform bracing under the floorpan, the shells being assembled from major sub-assemblies at Bristol Siddeley. Styling, distinguished by prominent but attractive tail fins, was a contract job by Kenneth Howes (who is not credited with any other Rootes work) and Geoff Crompton, both aided by Roy Axe, who was to go on to much higher things in the years which followed. A rounded, aluminium hardtop was optional. The soft-top, when furled, was hidden away behind hinged flaps.

The car was designed in 1957, when the Rapier Series II was about to be announced. Compared with this car, it was given a new aluminium cylinder head, a new hypoid-bevel rear axle, front disc brakes and 13in road wheels, all of which were eventually fitted to the Rapiers. The optional centre-lock wire wheels, however,

Proof positive that Bristol Siddeley actually assembled Alpine sports car shells in the Burlington works, in Parkside, Coventry. The picture was taken on July 6, 1959.

The original Alpine two-seater of 1959 was well-equipped, with a full display of instruments. It would become glossier, and even neater, in the years to come.

were always exclusive to the Alpine.

It was not only the car, but the way it was assembled, which was notable. As *The Autocar* commented, it was: '....a unique example of co-operation between two motor manufacturers. Assembly takes place entirely at the Coventry works of Bristol Siddeley Engines Ltd, where production capacity is available. This arrangement breaks fresh ground for that company, which for so long has been engaged solely in the production of large quality cars in limited numbers....'

Sunbeam Alpine I specification

Produced: Bristol Siddeley Engines, Coventry, 1959–60, 11,904 cars built.
General layout: Unit-construction pressed-steel body/chassis structure, available as 2-seater open sports car, or with optional hardtop. Front-mounted engine driving rear wheels.
Engine and transmission: Hillman-type engine, 4-cylinder, ohv, in-line. 1,494cc, 79 x 76.2mm, 78bhp (net) at 5,300rpm; 89lb ft at 3,400rpm; 4-speed gearbox, no synchromesh on 1st gear; centre-floor gear-change; optional Laycock overdrive; live (beam) rear axle with hypoid-bevel final drive.
Chassis: Independent front suspension, coil springs, wishbones, anti-roll bar. Recirculating-ball steering. Live (beam) rear axle, half-elliptic leaf springs. Front disc, rear drum brakes. 5.60-13in tyres.
Dimensions: Wheelbase 7ft 2in; front track 4ft 3in; rear track 4ft 0.5in; length 12ft 11.25in; width 5ft 0.5in; height 4ft 3.5in. Unladen weight approx 2,135lb.
Distinguishing features from previous models: No relationship to previous Sunbeams or Sunbeam-Talbots. New Alpine, however, was closely linked to current Sunbeam Rapiers.
Typical performance: Maximum speed 98mph; 0–60mph 14.0sec; standing ¼-mile 19.8sec; typical fuel consumption 26mpg.
Derivatives: Closely related to contemporary Sunbeam Rapier models introduced in 1955. Chassis engineering closely related to other existing Hillman models. Gave way to Alpine II in 1960.
Fate: Discontinued in 1960 in favour of further developed Alpine II.

The Alpine of 1959 was a smart two-seater sports car, using a modified Hillman Husky underpan with the running gear of the latest Sunbeam Rapier.

The Bristol Siddeley assembled Alpine featured this well filled engine bay, complete with two downdraught carburettors, and with bracing bars between the inner wheelarches and the scuttle structure.

Between the distinctive tail fins of the Alpine was this shallow boot, under which was stowed the spare wheel.

Sunbeam Alpine II (1960 to 1963)

The Alpine had only been on sale for 15 months when Rootes began its habitual process of improving the product. Compared with the original, the Alpine II had a larger and more powerful engine – 1,592cc and 80bhp, instead of 1,494cc and 78bhp. Apart from the use of a smaller steering wheel, support channels for the door glass and more robust suspension details, there was very little change to an already successful design.

Final assembly was moved back from Bristol Siddeley to Ryton in the spring of 1962.

Above left: not a wasted line, not a wasted crease – the Alpine looked good from every angle. Centre-lock wire wheels were optional extras. Above: Personalities help sell cars. F1 World Champion Jack Brabham, whose company developed performance conversions for the Alpine, with one of the early hardtop examples.

A very special Alpine indeed: one of the heavily modified Series II cars prepared by Rootes for motor sport in the early 1960s. Events contested included the Le Mans 24-hour race, where this car ran in 1962.

Sunbeam Alpine II specification

As for Sunbeam Alpine I except for:
Produced: Bristol Siddeley Engines, Coventry, to spring 1962, Ryton-on-Dunsomore, 1962–63, 19,956 cars built.
Engine and transmission: 1,592cc, 81.5 x 76.2mm; 80bhp (net) at 5,000rpm; 94lb ft at 3,800rpm.
Distinguishing features from previous models: Support channels ahead of door glasses.
Typical performance: Maximum speed 97mph; 0–60mph 14.8sec; standing ¼-mile 19.7sec; typical fuel consumption 22mpg.
Derivatives: 1963 Alpine III was a direct descendant of this car.
Fate: Discontinued in spring of 1963 and replaced by Alpine III.

Sunbeam Alpine III (1963 to 1964)

The third type of Alpine was really a halfway-house development between the original car and the restyled Series IV which followed less than a year later. Nevertheless, the Alpine III was a real advance over its predecessor in several ways.

The basic style, drive-line and running gear were all unchanged. However, the line was now split into two – the original type of tourer, and an altogether more up-market GT, for which a new and angular style of detachable hardtop was standard, the soft-top and mechanism being removed completely. Better-trimmed and specified '+2' accommodation was provided, and the engine was more softly tuned than before. However, the engine of the tourer was slightly more powerful than previously. The gearbox's internal ratios were also revised.

Chassis changes included a reinforced front cross-member, a stiffer front anti-roll bar, telescopic instead of lever-arm rear dampers and an adjustable-length steering column. Twin fuel tanks (one tucked into each rear wing) were fitted instead of the previous under-floor tank, thereby nearly doubling the luggage accommodation.

There were new, more comfortable, fully reclinable front seats, and a more plush interior. The Alpine was better trimmed and furnished than ever before. The de-tuned GT version, however, was not popular.

When the Alpine progressed to Series III, Rootes also announced a 'Gran Turismo' version, for which the hardtop was standard.

This three-quarter rear view of the Alpine Series III GT shows off the neat lines of the new-style detachable hardtop.

Also new for the Series III was this much improved instrument panel and facia layout.

Sunbeam Alpine III specification

As for Sunbeam Alpine II except for:
Produced: Ryton-on-Dunsmore, 1963–64, 5,863 cars built.
Engine and transmission: (Tourer) 82bhp (net) at 5,200rpm; 94lb ft at 3,800rpm; (GT) 77bhp (net) at 5,000rpm; 91lb ft at 3,500rpm.
Chassis: 5.90-13in tyres.
Dimensions: Unladen weight (Tourer) approx 2,220lb, (GT) approx 2,240lb.
Distinguishing features from previous models: Revised windscreen, new fixed quarter-lights in doors, new angular steel hardtop.
Typical performance: (GT) Maximum speed 98mph; 0–60mph 14.9sec; standing ¼-mile 19.8sec; typical fuel consumption 25mpg.
Derivatives: 1964 Alpine IV was a direct descendant of this car.
Fate: Discontinued in January 1964 and replaced by Alpine IV.

Sunbeam Alpine IV (1964 to 1965)

Less than a year after launching the Alpine III, Rootes replaced it with Alpine IV. The new derivative was prettier, better and a more popular car than the model it replaced.

Why was it not all done at once? As has already been indicated in other chapters, Rootes moved in mysterious ways in the early 1960s....

The big and obvious change for Alpine IV was that the tail had been restyled, the fins cropped back, new tail-lamp designs fitted, and the car made to look even better balanced than before. A new front grille completed the visual change, along with 'SIV' badges on the flanks and tail.

There was also a change in marketing emphasis. On the one hand, the short-lived experiment with two levels

For the Series III Alpine, the boot area was redesigned, with twin fuel tanks tucked into the wings and a relocated spare wheel, to provide more stowage space.

The obvious visual clue to the launch of the Series IV Alpine was that the rear fins had been cropped and new tail lights were used. There were 'Series IV' badges on the boot lid and on the wings.

Series IV (and, later, Series V) Alpines had a revised front grille style.

The Series IV Alpine had a nicely trimmed interior, the modified Microcell-type seats having reclining backrests.

Harrington made several different types of modified Alpine over the years. This was the Harrington Le Mans, in which the tail of the shell was newly styled. It provided a permanently fixed roof with rear hatch, and a lot of stowage space, predating the MGB GT by some years, but very few were sold.

of engine tune had been abandoned, and on the other, an automatic transmission option was made available for the first time. The new corporate Rootes medium-range all-synchromesh gearbox was standardized from the autumn of 1964. It was enough to revive the Alpine's flagging fortunes and keep it going, happily, for another two seasons.

Sunbeam Alpine IV specification

As for Sunbeam Alpine III except for:
Produced: Ryton-on-Dunsmore, 1964–65, 12,406 cars built.
Engine and transmission: Solex compound-choke carburettor instead of twin Zeniths; optional 3-speed Borg-Warner automatic transmission; 4-speed all-synchromesh gearbox from autumn 1964.
Distinguishing features from previous models: Restyled tail with lowered fins and new tail-lamps, plus new front grille.
Typical performance: (Automatic transmission version) Maximum speed 92mph; 0–60mph 18.8sec; standing ¼-mile 22.5sec; typical fuel consumption 22mpg.
Derivatives: Tiger I and Tiger II were both developed from the structure of this and Alpine V models. Alpine V was a direct descendant of Alpine IV.
Fate: Discontinued in 1965 and replaced by Alpine V.

Sunbeam Alpine V (1965 to 1968)

As with similar changes made at the same time to the Rapier (IV to V), Alpine IV became Alpine V in a final attempt to keep an ageing model going for another couple of years.

There were no styling changes (except that the new 'Rootes 1725' badges took over), though the folding panel covers for the soft-top had finally been abandoned, to be replaced by a fixed wall with soft covers. The new corporate five-bearing 1,725cc engine was standardized, in this case with twin semi-downdraught Zenith-Stromberg carburettors and no less than 92.5bhp. The alternator and oil cooler were both unusual standard

fittings for the period. The automatic transmission option, which had only been introduced for the Series IV, had been abandoned.

Stubbornly, still, the Alpine was not quite a 100mph car, this being one of the marketing problems which always held it back, *vis-à-vis* the MGBs and the TR4/TR4A types. The last of these well-liked cars was built in the first weeks of 1968.

Sunbeam Alpine V specification

As for Sunbeam Alpine IV except for:
Produced: Ryton-on-Dunsmore, 1965–68, 19,122 cars built.
Engine and transmission: 1,725cc, 81.5 x 82.55mm, 92.5bhp (net) at 5,500rpm; 103lb ft at 3,700rpm; 2 Zenith-Stromberg carburettors; no automatic transmission option.
Distinguishing features from previous models: 'Rootes 1725' badges for identification.
Typical performance: Maximum speed 98mph; 0–60mph 13.6sec; standing ¼-mile 19.1sec; typical fuel consumption 26mpg.
Derivatives: Tiger I and Tiger II models used the same basic structure and styling, year on year. There was no connection between this Alpine and the fastback Alpine of 1969–76.
Fate: Discontinued in 1968 and not replaced.

Laying claim to the heritage in the early 1960s: an Alpine and a Rapier bracketing two Sunbeam racing cars, the 1912 *Coupe de l'Auto* model (right) and the 1924 supercharged Grand Prix car (left). Nice picture, but quite clearly there were no real links of heritage! In the same vein, a 1926 4-litre V12-engined machine with which Segrave took the World Land Speed Record was the *first* car to be called a Sunbeam Tiger . . .

Sunbeam Tiger I (1964 to 1966)

The life story and short career of the Sunbeam Tiger is well-documented. Its birth was inspired by the instant success of the AC Cobra. The 'quart-into-a-pint-pot' one-off Sunbeam produced in California came back to Coventry, was approved and went into production in 1964. Unhappily for Rootes (and for Tiger enthusiasts), the Tiger used a Ford-USA V8 engine, yet within months Rootes went into partnership with Chrysler, and the clash of interests soon became obvious. That, and the fact that the Tiger was never visually different enough from the Alpine IV/V models, helped to make its career very short. Assembly of all Tigers was carried out by Jensen, at West Bromwich, north-west of Birmingham.

The Tiger used the same basic structure, style and layout as the Alpine IV (which is to say that it featured the cropped-down fins), but was powered by a 4.2-litre Ford engine driving through a different and stronger gearbox and rear axle. At the front there was rack-and-pinion steering, while a Panhard rod helped to keep rear axle movement in check.

Rootes could afford neither the time nor the money to make the styling different, the only way to pick a Tiger I being by the badging and the addition of a chrome strip along the flank of the body.

This car went on UK sale in 1965, but the later Tiger II was never officially sold on the UK market.

Sunbeam Tiger I specification

Produced: Jensen, West Bromwich, 1964–66, 6,495 cars built.
General layout: Unit-construction pressed-steel body/chassis structure, available as 2-seater open sports car, or with optional hardtop. Front-mounted engine driving rear wheels.
Engine and transmission: Ford-USA engine, V8-cylinder, ohv, 4,261cc, 96.5mm x 73mm, 164bhp (gross) at 4,400rpm; 258lb ft at 2,200rpm; 4-speed gearbox, all-synchromesh; centre-floor gear-change; live (beam) rear axle with hypoid-bevel final drive.
Chassis: Independent front suspension, coil springs, wishbones, anit-roll bar. Rack-and-pinion steering. Live (beam) rear axle, half-elliptic leaf springs, Panhard rod. Front disc, rear drum brakes. 5.90-13in tyres.
Dimensions: Wheelbase 7ft 2in; front track 4ft 3.75in; rear track 4ft 0.5in; length 13ft 2in; width 5ft 0.5in; height 4ft 3.5in. Unladen weight (Tourer) approx 2,525lb, (GT) approx 2,575lb.
Distinguishing features from previous models: Visually, very close relationship to contemporary Alpine IV and V models except for use of chrome strip on flanks and different badges.
Typical performance: Maximum speed 117mph; 0–60mph 9.5sec; standing ¼-mile 17.0sec; typical fuel consumption 17mpg.
Derivatives: Replaced by Tiger II in 1967.
Fate: Discontinued at end of 1966 in favour of further developed Tiger II.

Compared with the current Alpine, the Tiger I had a chrome strip along the flanks, different wheel trims, different badges, and of course it also had twin exhaust outlets.

The 90-degree Ford V8 engine was a compact design (except for that overhanging dynamo!), and it turned out that it could *just* be squeezed under the Alpine's bonnet, set well back towards the bulkhead, to form the basis of the Tiger, as launched in 1964.

This was the cockpit of a Tiger I. To distinguish it from that of the Alpine IV, you should note the 'T-bar' under the gear lever knob, and the rev counter red-lined at 4,750rpm.

A tigress reclining on the Tiger – shot at Earls Court Motor Show press day in 1965.

Sunbeam Tiger II (1967)

Once again, a lack of time and development cash got in the way of a comprehensive restyle for the Tiger, especially as it was known that the existing Alpine V (on which it was based) only had a limited life.

The Tiger II, therefore, looked virtually the same as the Tiger I, except that it had a different 'egg-crate' grille and stick-on racing stripes. Under the skin there was a larger and more powerful version of the Ford V8 engine, wider-ratio gears in the box, and radius arms to hold the rear axle firmly in place.

The Tiger II had a very short life, the last car being produced in mid-1967. Tentative efforts to slot a Chrysler V8 engine into the car in place of the Ford came to nothing.

Rootes only had one and a half seasons to turn the Tiger into a very successful rally car. Peter Harper and Ian Hall pushed ADU 312B into a magnificent fourth overall in the Monte Carlo Rally of 1965.

Rootes got together with Lister to prepare two much-modified Tigers for the Le Mans 24-hour race in 1964. Both cars retired with engine failure after the first few hours.

The Tiger II was a short-lived model, sold only in 1967, and then officially only in the USA. It had a 4.7-litre version of the Ford V8 engine, a different grille, and side stripes. Rally driver Rosemary Smith is behind the wheel in this studio shot.

A gathering of Tigers at a 1970s 'classic' meeting. Tiger Is have headlamp hoods, Tiger IIs do not.

The Venezia in small-scale production at the Touring factory in Italy. Hillman Super Minxes are being assembled on the adjoining production line.

Sunbeam Tiger II specification

As for Tiger I except for:
Produced: Jensen, West Bromwich, 1967, 571 cars built.
Engine and transmission: 4,727cc, 101.6 x 73mm, 200bhp (gross) at 4,400rpm; 282lb ft at 2,400rpm.
Chassis: Rear axle located by radius arms.
Distinguishing features from previous models: Egg-crate grille, and 'speed stripes' along flanks make the car visually different from Tiger I.
Typical performance: Maximum speed 122mph; 0–60mph 7.5sec; typical fuel consumption 19mpg.
Fate: Discontinued in 1967 and not replaced.

Sunbeam Venezia (1963 to 1965)

During 1961, Carrozzeria Touring of Milan signed a deal with Rootes to begin assembling Alpines for sale in Europe. Almost immediately this co-operation was extended, with Touring developing a smart new 2+2 coupe on the basis of the Humber Sceptre underframe and running gear. The engine was actually more powerful than the Sceptre's and overdrive was standard, but there were no other significant changes. It was only officially sold on the Italian market, though a handful of cars later came to the UK.

Why the Sceptre, and not a Sunbeam? As mentioned previously, what became the Sceptre was *meant* to be the new Sunbeam Rapier IV....

Like all such Superleggera Touring bodies of the period, the new superstructure had a small-tubular framework, clad in aluminium sheeting. The styling was somewhat anonymous, and included Sceptre windscreen and headlamps, a Rapier grille and the latest Alpine type of tail-lamps.

The Venezia was not a success, and when Touring struck financial problems in 1965 it was dropped.

Sunbeam Venezia specification

Produced: Milan, Italy, 1963–65, 145 cars built.
General layout: Unit-construction pressed-steel body/chassis underframe with Superleggera steel tube/aluminium sheet superstructure, available as 4-seater coupe. Front-mounted engine driving rear wheels.
Engine and transmission: Hillman-type engine, 4-cylinder, ohv, in-line, 1,592cc, 81.5mm x 76.2mm, 88bhp (net) at 5,800rpm; 95lb ft at 3,500rpm; 4-speed gearbox, no synchromesh on 1st gear, Laycock overdrive on top and 3rd; centre-floor gear-change; live (beam) rear axle with hypoid-bevel final drive.
Chassis: Independent front suspension, coil springs, wishbones, anti-roll bar. Recirculating-ball steering. Live (beam) rear axle, half-elliptic leaf springs. Front disc, rear drum brakes. 6.00-13in tyres.
Dimensions: Wheelbase 8ft 5in; front track 4ft 3.5in; rear track 4ft 0.5in; length 14ft 8.8in; width 5ft 1.4in; height 4ft 5.9in. Unladen weight approx 2,475lb.
Distinguishing features from previous models: No links with any past or contemporary Alpine or Rapier models.
Typical performance: (Claimed) Maximum speed 100mph.
Derivatives: None.
Fate: Discontinued in 1965 when Carrozzeria Touring hit financial problems.

The Venezia of 1963–1965 was based on the underpan and running gear of the newly-launched Humber Sceptre (which *should* have been badged as a Sunbeam, before a late policy change), but the body was built by Touring of Italy.

The Venezia was a two-door coupe, styled by Touring, though the tail lamps are ex-Alpine IV, and those also look like Tiger wheeltrims.

The Venezia had four-seater accommodation, and was fitted with fully reclining seats.

The rear aspect of the Sunbeam Rapier of the 1967–1976 period showed the tail lamps which were shared with the Arrow estate cars, and the twin exhaust pipe outlets.

This new-generation Rapier coupe was based on the floorpan and the running gear also used for the Hillman Hunter and Humber Sceptre.

Sunbeam Rapier (Arrow-type – 1967 to 1976)

By the mid-1960s, with Chrysler about to take full control of Rootes, the company was ready to drop the old Minx/Gazelle/Rapier family of cars, and the Hillman Hunter (Arrow) range was destined to take its place. Central to this strategy was the design of a new generation of Rapiers.

The Arrow Rapier, launched in 1967, had a smart four-seater fastback coupe style of superstructure on the underpan and basic chassis of the new Hillman Hunter. Cynics have said that it bore a resemblance to the current Plymouth Barracuda, but stylist Roy Axe insists that this was not so. The tail-lamps, incidentally, were those of the new Minx/Hunter estate, but the superstructure was otherwise quite new.

Like the Hunter, the Rapier had a slightly angled-over 1,725cc engine, with a creditable 88bhp peak rating. Close-ratio gears and overdrive were standard and Borg-Warner automatic transmission was an optional extra.

Except in detail, this smart but less sporting Rapier than the last type continued unchanged until 1976, when it faded gently away. It also formed the inspiration for the more powerful H120, and for the rather more down-market Alpine of this period, and its running gear was also used in the Arrow-type Sceptre and the Hillman GT/Hillman Hunter GT models.

Sunbeam Rapier (Arrow-type) specification

Produced: Ryton-on-Dunsmore, 1967–69, Linwood, 1969–76, 46,204 cars (including H120 and Arrow-type Alpine models) built.
General layout: Unit-construction pressed-steel body/chassis structure, available as 4-seater coupe. Front-mounted engine driving rear wheels.
Engine and transmission: Hillman-type engine, 4-cylinder, ohv, in-line. 1,725cc, 81.5mm x 82.55mm, 88bhp (net) at 5,200rpm (later re-rated to 76bhp DIN at 5,100rpm; 100lb ft at 4,000rpm (later re-rated to 93lb ft at 3,300rpm); 4-speed gearbox, all-synchromesh, Laycock overdrive on top and 3rd; centre-floor gear-change; optional 3-speed Borg-Warner automatic transmission; live (beam) rear axle with hypoid-bevel final drive.
Chassis: Independent front suspension, coil springs, MacPherson struts, anti-roll bar. Recirculating-ball steering. Live (beam) rear axle, half-elliptic leaf springs. Front disc, rear drum brakes. 155-13in tyres.
Dimensions: Wheelbase 8ft 2.5in; front track 4ft 4in; rear track 4ft 4in; length 14ft 6.5in; width 5ft 4.75in; height 4ft 7in. Unladen weight approx 2,275lb.
Distinguishing features from previous models: Completely new fastback style. No links with any past or contemporary Alpine or Rapier models.
Typical performance: Maximum speed 103mph; 0–60mph 12.8sec; standing ¼-mile 18.7sec; typical fuel consumption 28mpg.
Derivatives: More powerful 1968 H120 Rapier and less-powerful 1969 Alpine both used this body structure and basic chassis.
Fate: Discontinued in 1976 and not replaced.

The Rapier H120, announced in October 1968, was based on the Rapier layout, but had a more highly-tuned engine, Rostyle wheels, and distinctive side striping.

The Rapier H120 not only had more power than the ordinary Rapier, but it also had a spoiler on the boot lid.

Sunbeam Rapier H120 (1968 to 1976)

To produce an even faster and more specialized car than the new-generation Rapier, Rootes/Chrysler then developed the H120. Based on the design of the Arrow-style Rapier, the H120 had a more powerful version of the familiar 1,725cc engine, developed by Holbay and fitted with twin dual-choke Weber carburettors.

To add to the sporty image, the H120 was given Rostyle wheels and a neat boot-lid spoiler so that it was instantly distinguishable.

Sunbeam Alpine (Arrow-type – 1969 to 1975)

Although this car was developed under the control of Chrysler, it was a close relative of the fastback Sunbeam Rapier and must therefore be described here. It was essentially a Rapier with a simplified specification, with the single-carburettor type of Hunter/Vogue engine, less lavish equipment and lower performance.

It was also, of course, significantly cheaper than the Rapier, and helped plug the gap between this car and the Sunbeams and Singers in the range.

Sunbeam Rapier H120 specification

As for 1967–76 style of Rapier except for:
Engine and transmission: 105bhp (net) at 5,200rpm; 120lb ft at 4,000rpm (later re-rated to 93bhp DIN at 5,200rpm; 106lb ft at 4,000rpm); automatic transmission option not available.
Chassis: 165-13in tyres.
Dimensions: Unladen weight approx 2,300lb.
Distinguishing features from previous models: Compared with existing Rapier, fitted with Rostyle wheels, side colour flashes and boot-lid spoiler.
Typical performance: Maximum speed 105mph; 0–60mph 11.1sec; standing ¼-mile 17.7sec; typical fuel consumption 24mpg.
Derivatives: Hillman Hunter GLS used same twin-Weber-carburettor engine and related transmission.
Fate: Discontinued in 1976 and not replaced.

Sunbeam Alpine (Arrow-type) specification

As for 1967–76 type of Rapier except for:
Engine and transmission: 74bhp (net) at 5,500rpm; 96lb ft at 3,000rpm (in 1972, retuned and re-rated to 72bhp DIN at 5,500rpm; 90lb ft at 3,000rpm); overdrive optional rather than standard.
Chassis: 6.00-13in tyres at first, 155-13in from 1972.
Dimensions: Unladen weight approx 2,220lb.
Distinguishing features from previous models: No visual or technical connection with previous Alpine range. Closely based on current Arrow type of Rapier, with different trim and badging details.
Typical performance: Maximum speed 91mph; 0–60mph 14.6sec; standing ¼-mile 19.9sec; typical fuel consumption 28mpg.
Derivatives: None.
Fate: Discontinued in 1975 and not replaced.

The 1970-model Sunbeam Alpine was completely different from the 1959–1968 variety, being based on the new-generation Rapier, but with a less powerful engine, and simplified trim and furnishings.

Sunbeam Imp Sport/Sunbeam Sport (1966 to 1976)

Rootes had a positive flurry of new-car announcements in October 1966. Not only did the company launch the new Hunter and Vogue models, it also revealed the first of the sporting rear-engined Imps, which it badged as a Sunbeam. The Imp Sport was built until 1970, and when the Singer Chamois Sport was dropped the range was rationalized into one model; it was rebadged, given slightly different trim and styling details and called, simply, Sunbeam Sport.

Very closely based on the Hillman Imp itself, the Imp Sport had a more powerful twin-carb engine, slightly more sporty handling aided by the wider wheels, and better engine bay cooling due to the use of a slatted engine cover. Before 1970, the Imp Sport had two 7in headlamps, but as a Sport it inherited four smaller headlamps, as used for the Stiletto coupe.

Sunbeam Rallye Imp (1965 to 1969)

In certain markets, and in certain motorsport events, the ubiquitous Rallye Imp of the 1960s was given a Sunbeam nomenclature. For all details of this car, see the entry for the Rallye Imp in the Hillman chapter.

Sunbeam Stiletto (1967 to 1973)

The last of the Imps to be launched, in October 1967, was the smart little Sunbeam Stiletto, one of which was owned by the author for several enjoyable years. The Stiletto combined the fastback style of the Hillman Imp

Sunbeam Imp Sport/Sport specification

Produced: Linwood, 1966–76, estimated 10,000 cars built.
General layout: Unit-construction pressed-steel body/chassis structure, available as 4-seater saloon. Rear-mounted engine driving rear wheels.
Engine and transmission: Hillman Imp-type engine, 4-cylinder, ohv, in-line. 875cc, 68mm x 60.35mm, 51bhp (net) at 6,100rpm; 53lb ft at 4,300rpm; 4-speed gearbox, all-synchromesh, centre-floor gear-change; combined gearbox and hypoid-bevel transaxle ahead of rear-mounted engine.
Chassis: Independent front suspension, coil springs, swing axles. Rack-and-pinion steering. Independent rear suspension coil springs, semi-trailing arms. Front and rear drum brakes. 155-12in tyres.
Dimensions: Wheelbase 6ft 10in; front track 4ft 1.1in; rear track 3ft 11.9in; length 11ft 9in; width 5ft 0.25in; height 4ft 6.5in. Unladen weight approx 1,640lb.
Distinguishing features from previous models: Closely linked in style to current Hillman Imps. No other link with previous Sunbeam models.
Typical performance: Maximum speed 90mph; 0–60mph 16.3sec; standing ¼-mile 20.2sec; typical fuel consumption 34mpg.
Derivatives: Singer Chamois Sport was virtually the same car; Sunbeam Stiletto used same chassis and running gear, but with fastback coupe style. Rallye Imp was also based on this package, but with enlarged engine.
Fate: Discontinued in 1976 and not replaced.

The Sunbeam Imp Sport, really a hotted-up Hillman Imp, was launched in October 1966; it had a twin-carb 50bhp engine in the tail.

By the 1970s, the Sunbeam Imp Sport had four headlamps instead of the original two, adopting the style first seen on the Singer version. Mechanically, though, it remained unchanged.

Sunbeam Imp Sports had a manual choke control lever (just ahead of the gear lever), extra instruments (compared with the normal Hillman Imp) – and not nearly as much interior space as these artist's impressions suggest!

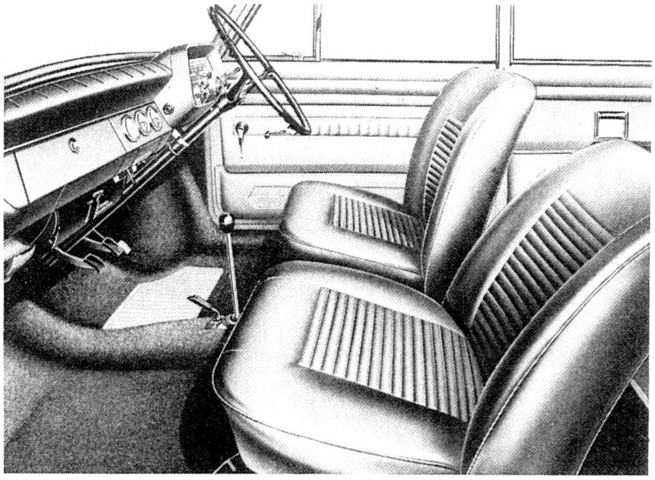

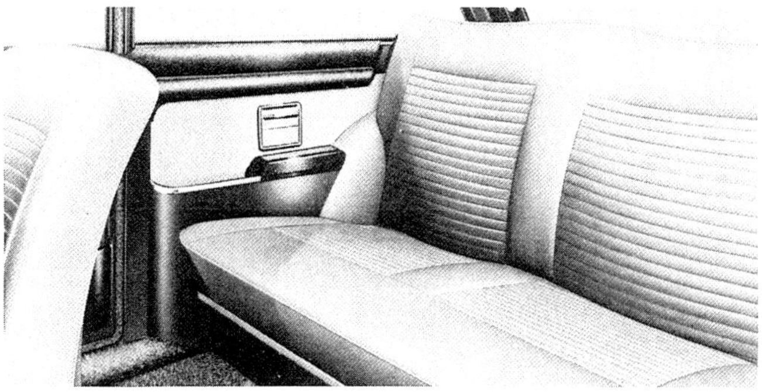

Californian with the chassis and running gear of the Imp Sport, but it was also treated to a four-headlamp nose style, the reduced-camber front suspension and an up-market interior featuring a unique dashboard, reclining front seats and a padded steering wheel rim.

It was an attractive and good handling little car which never sold as well as it should have done. Consequently, when Chrysler began to rationalize its range of cars in the early 1970s, the Stiletto was one of the first to go.

The dashboard was never used on any other Imp derivative.

Sunbeam Stiletto specification

As for Sunbeam Imp Sport except for:
Produced: Linwood, 1967–73, approx 10,000 cars built.
Dimensions: Height 4ft 4.25in. Unladen weight approx 1,625lb.
Distinguishing features from previous models: Closely related in styling to the Hillman Californian, but with a 4-headlamp nose, the slatted Sport engine bay cover and a vinyl roof covering, plus unique dashboard layout.
Typical performance: Maximum speed 87mph; 0–60mph 17.6sec; standing ¼-mile 20.5sec; typical fuel consumption 34 mpg.
Fate: Discontinued in 1973 and not replaced.

The Sunbeam Stiletto was the smartest of all the Imps, with Imp Sport running gear and a better furnished version of the Californian bodyshell. It had four headlamps and a leathercloth-covered roof.

Stiletto rear view shows the vented engine cover which came with the Sport engine in both saloons and coupes. Badge indicates that this enthusiast-owned example also has the 998cc engine conversion developed for the Rallye Imp.

Sunbeam Vogue (1970)

For a very short period, following the death of the Singer Vogue (Arrow-type), the car was renamed Sunbeam Vogue. For all details, see the entry for the Singer Vogue of 1966–70 in the Singer chapter.

Sunbeam Harrington Alpine (1961 to 1963)

Strictly speaking, the Harrington Alpine was not a Sunbeam production car. However, since it was produced by Thomas Harrington Ltd, a Sussex-based coachbuilder which was controlled by the Rootes-owned Robins & Day dealer chain, and was always approved by the Rootes Group, it should be mentioned here.

Several versions of Type A Harrington Alpine were produced, all being based on the two-seater Alpine sports car of the day. The initial model, launched in March 1961 on the basis of the Alpine II, had a smoothly-style glassfibre hardtop bolted to the basic structure; the boot area and the boot-lid were considerably modified to suit. Inside the cabin, the standard equipment was modified by fitting a pair of Microcell seats and a wood-rimmed steering wheel.

Although three stages of engine tune were offered on the 1,592cc engine, of which the most powerful featured twin dual-choke Weber carbs and 100bhp, sales were held back by high costs. At a time when standard Alpine prices started at £986, initial Harrington Alpine prices were £1,225, £1,300 and £1,440, depending on engine tune. Only 150 were built.

From October 1961 the Type B, or Harrington Le Mans type (no Alpine name, please note), was announced. This featured a body which was completely restyled aft of the screen and doors, including new rear quarters, with the roof firmly bonded to the basic structure. No fewer than five stages of engine tune were available, and UK prices started at £1,495. Some 250 of these cars were built.

In 1963, because sales were slow, the Type C Harrington was put on sale, this being something of a cross between the Le Mans and the notchback GT. The intended price was £1,196 (there had been government-imposed purchase tax reductions in the meantime), but very few were made. One or two further Harrington-modified Alpines were produced on the Series III and Series IV models.

Like the Triumph TR4 Dove, the Harrington Alpine was too heavy and too expensive to sell well. It was not until BMC's MGB GT came along in 1965 that a truly successful GT emerged in this size and performance bracket.

Chapter 8

SUNBEAM-TALBOT

Whereas Rootes usually grew by absorbing existing marques, Sunbeam-Talbot was a name established by the Group several years after it had acquired the trademarks and rights to the titles.

As is made clear in other chapters, Rootes bought Sunbeam of Wolverhampton in July 1935 and Talbot of London in January 1935 – both of them from the financial wreckage of the once-proud Sunbeam-Talbot-Darracq combine. Existing Sunbeam models were phased out in a matter of weeks, while existing Talbot products were progressively 'Rootesified' in the next three years.

By 1938, Rootes had wrung the last out of the old Roesch Talbots, which were still being built at the Barlby Road factory in Kensington, London. In the opinion of the Rootes family, it was now time to move ahead to the obvious rationalization. Starting in August 1938, therefore, a new range of cars called Sunbeam-Talbots was progressively introduced.

At one and the same time, the birth of the Sunbeam-Talbot horrified the purists and old-style traditionalists and cheered those who saw how much new investment and security of employment Rootes was bringing into its businesses. The new cars, of course, were based on existing Hillman and Humber chassis engineering, and had no technical links with the old Sunbeams and Talbots, but in some ways their styling was a direct development of late-1930s Talbots.

On balance, and to use 1980s parlance to illustrate their reception, the new Sunbeam-Talbots were awarded two cheers....

In the beginning there were three cars – the Ten, the 3-Litre and the 4-Litre – and a year later, on the eve of war, a 2-Litre was added to the range.

After the Second World War, Rootes took stock, decided it had to cut down the number of models it could build, and only reintroduced the Ten and 2-Litre models, with minor changes and updates. The 3-Litre and 4-Litre models were dropped after a very short life indeed.

This was the magnificent Roesch-Talbot which inspired the invention of the Sunbeam-Talbot marque. 'B. Bira', the famous racing driver from the Siamese royal family, is here seen collecting a new Talbot in 1935.

By the mid-1930s, genuine Roesch-Talbots not only had excellent chassis, but splendid styling. This 1935-model four-seater tourer was clearly the inspiration for early Sunbeam-Talbot tourers which followed a few years later. The backdrop, by the way, is the splendidly detailed 'Clement Talbot Motor Works' in West London (see the plate, between the pillars, immediately above the radiator and headlamps).

The first Rootes-owned Talbot to be announced was the Talbot Ten of late 1935, a car which combined much Hillman Aero MInx chassis engineering with an engine improved by Georges Roesch and with this neat two-door body style. The Sunbeam-Talbot Ten of 1938 was a direct descendant.

The anatomy of the Talbot Ten (later Sunbeam-Talbot Ten) laid bare, showing the 'over-axle' position of the rear seats and the underslung chassis frame.

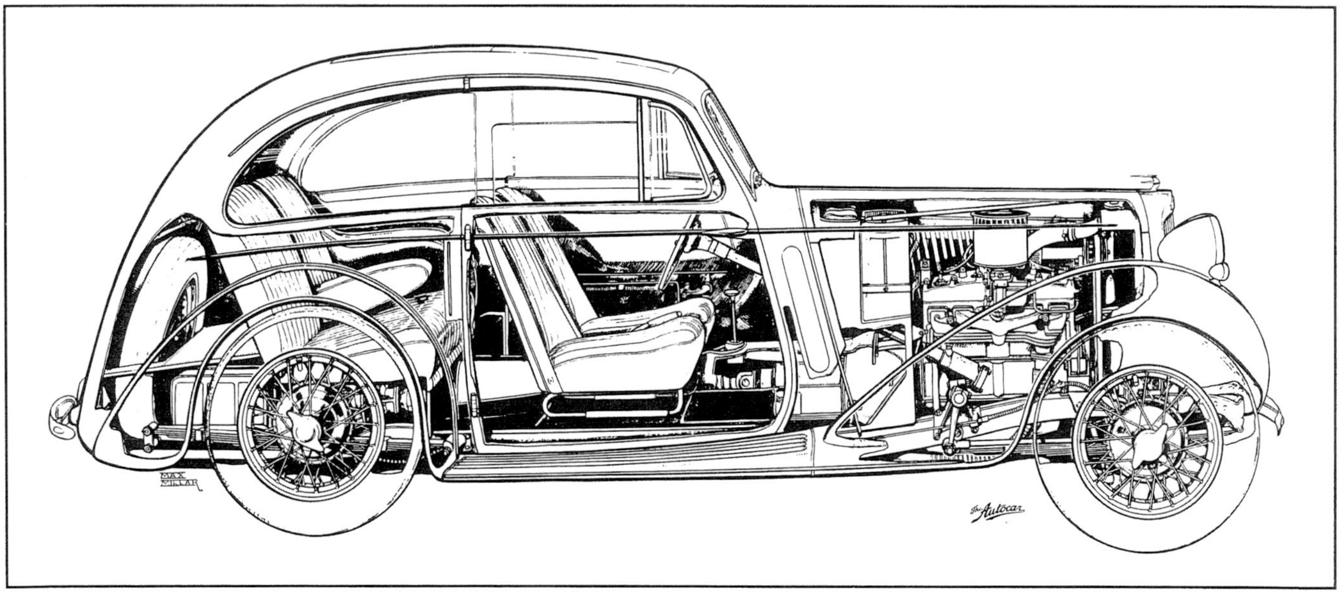

Police forces used the small Talbot/ Sunbeam-Talbot tourers for a time, but they could surely not have been able to catch crooks in Jaguars, Lagondas and other large-engined cars of the period.

As before the war, the drop-head coupes were produced by Carbodies and the tourers by Whittingham & Mitchell. Final assembly was moved from Barlby Road, Kensington, to the new Ryton-on-Dunsmore plant in 1946–47.

In the summer of 1948, the new postwar cars, the 80 and 90 models, were ready for sale, though for the first two years the sleek new styles were fitted to old-type 2-Litre chassis. Saloon shells were produced by British Light Steel Pressings and convertibles by Thrupp & Maberly. Then, after two years, new chassis-frames with independent front suspension were phased in, at which point the slow-selling 80 model was dropped.

The 90, in ever more developed form, was built until the end of the 1954 model-year, at which point it was further improved and named Sunbeam Mk III. A two-seater sports car version, called Sunbeam Alpine, had already appeared in 1953.

In some export markets, a postwar Sunbeam-Talbot had always been badged as a Sunbeam, so it was no surprise that the double-barrelled Sunbeam-Talbot marque name was finally laid to rest in 1954.

The Talbot part of the title, incidentally, would resurface in mid-1979 to replace the Chrysler name on cars then being produced by the companies which came to succeed the Rootes Group. For further clarification of this, please refer to **Chapter 9**.

Sunbeam-Talbot Ten (1938 to 1939 and 1945 to 1948)

When Rootes launched this car in August 1938, it was advertised as 'Britain's Most Exclusive Light Car'. The advertising profession always insists that if you shout something loud enough the public will eventually believe it – in this case it was necessary, for the 'new' Sunbeam-Talbot was only an obvious, lineal descendant of the Talbot Ten.

That chassis had itself evolved from the Hillman Aero Minx, with main members under the line of the back axle, and had a 7ft 9in wheelbase, with simple half-elliptic leaf-spring suspension at front and rear, but it was stiffened up for its latest application. The engine and gearbox, almost pure side-valve Hillman Minx (but with 38bhp and an aluminium cylinder head), had been moved forward in the frame by $3^{1}/_{2}$in.

Thc important innovation was the use of three freshened-up body styles, a four-door saloon, a foursome drop-head coupe (by Carbodies) and a sports tourer (by Whittingham & Mitchell). The most praiseworthy feature of the saloon was the way that rear passenger door glasses overlapped the rear quarter-glasses *without* a pillar to get in the way of vision – this feature was to be carried on to the Sunbeam-Talbot 80s and 90s of postwar years.

After a short prewar run, the Ten was reintroduced in

The Sunbeam-Talbot Ten, launched in 1938, was an updated version of the Talbot Ten, now with the latest body style including that famous Sunbeam-Talbot 'trade mark', the lack of a pillar behind the rear doors.

August 1945 with several improvements and ran through to mid-1948 before being replaced by the new 80 models. It was not a quick car, for in 1947 *The Autocar* only wrung 66mph out of the saloon, but it was neat, smart and very definitely a car with a great deal of character.

Sunbeam-Talbot Ten specification

Produced: London, 1938–39 and 1945–46, Ryton-on-Dunsmore, 1946–48, 4,719 cars (3,304 prewar) built.
General layout: Separate chassis-frame, coachbuilt bodyshells, in a variety of styles. Front-mounted engine driving rear wheels.
Engine and transmission: Hillman engine, 4-cylinder, sv, in-line. 1,185cc, 63 x 93mm, 38bhp, later 41bhp at 4,500rpm; 58lb ft at 2,700rpm; 4-speed gearbox, no synchromesh on 1st gear; centre-floor gear-change; live (beam) rear axle with spiral-bevel final drive.
Chassis: Beam-axle front suspension, half-elliptic leaf springs. Worm-and-nut steering. Live (beam) rear axle, half-elliptic leaf springs. Front and rear drum brakes. 5.25-16in tyres.
Dimensions: Wheelbase 7ft 9in; front track 3ft 11.5in; rear track 4ft 0.5in; length (saloon) 12ft 11.5in; width 5ft 0in; height (saloon) 4ft 10in. Unladen weight (saloon) approx 2,185lb.
Typical performance: (Saloon) Maximum speed 66mph; 0–60mph 35.2sec; standing ¼-mile 25sec; overall fuel consumption 30mpg.
Derivatives: Saloon, foursome DHC, 4-seater tourer. 2-Litre model shared much common engineering and choice of bodies, but with different (Humber Hawk-type) engine and longer wheelbase.
Fate: Discontinued in 1948 in favour of new Sunbeam-Talbot 80.

Sunbeam-Talbot 2-Litre (1939 and 1945 to 1948)

The 2-Litre model, so closely related to the Ten, was launched on the very eve of the Second World War and really did not go on sale until it was reintroduced in August 1945.

Although, both visually and technically, the 2-Litre was based very closely on the Ten and its chassis design was the same, the wheelbase was 3.5in longer, this being necessary to accommodate a 52bhp (56bhp after the war) version of the Hillman 14hp/Humber Hawk side-valve engine.

The 2-Litre shared the same postwar improvements as the Ten, but only 1,124 cars were built before it was made obsolete by the much better Sunbeam-Talbot 90 in 1948; this car, incidentally, used the same basic frame and some of the body panels of the 2-Litre.

Sunbeam-Talbot 2-Litre specification

Produced: London, 1939 and 1945–46, Ryton-on-Dunsmore, 1946–48, 1,124 cars built from 1945.
General layout: Separate chassis-frame, coachbuilt bodyshells in a variety of styles. Front-mounted engine driving rear wheels.
Engine and transmission: Hillman/Humber engine, 4-cylinder, sv, in-line. 1,944cc, 75 x 110mm, 52bhp (postwar 56bhp) at 3,800rpm; 97lb ft at 2,000rpm; 4-speed gearbox, no synchromesh on 1st gear; centre-floor gear-change; live (beam) rear axle with spiral-bevel final drive.
Chassis: Beam-axle front suspension, half-elliptic leaf springs, anti-roll bar. Worm-and-nut steering. Live (beam) rear axle, half-elliptic leaf springs. Front and rear drum brakes. 5.25-16in tyres.
Dimensions: Wheelbase 8ft 0.5in; front track 3ft 11.5in; rear track 4ft 0.5in; length (saloon) 13ft 4.5in; width 5ft 0in; height (saloon) 4ft 10in. Unladen weight (saloon) approx 2,490lb.
Typical performance: Maximum speed 72mph; 0–60mph 22.1sec; standing ¼-mile 24sec; typical fuel consumption 27mpg.
Derivatives: Saloon, foursome DHC, 4-seater tourer. Closely related to Sunbeam-Talbot Ten of the period, which had shorter wheelbase, different (Hillman Minx-type) engine.
Fate: Discontinued in 1948 in favour of new Sunbeam-Talbot 90 model.

Rootes advertising claimed that the new Sunbeam-Talbot 2-Litre was 'In the First Flight for Performance'. The Sports Saloon body was very similar to that of the Ten.

There were several alternative open body designs available for the 2-Litre including this Dropehad Foursome Coupe, a four-seater Sports Tourer . . .

. . . and this Sports 2-Seater, clearly showing the stylistic influence of mid-1930s Talbots.

Sunbeam-Talbot 3-Litre (previously Talbot 3-Litre) (1938 to 1939)

Rootes began the process of rationalization at Barlby Road by adding a variety of Rootes components to existing Talbot models, then, from October 1937, launched the new Talbot 3-Litre. This car, as historian Michael Sedgwick noted, was something of a fraud:

'The bodies were authentic Talbot, and in sports saloon guise the car looked the part – but engine, gearbox, brakes, frame and wheels were equally authentic Humber....'

For 1939, therefore, this car was relaunched, in lightly modified form, as the *Sunbeam*-Talbot 3-Litre model, without styling changes and with few mechanical improvements.

Except that the wheelbase of the separate chassis was 4in longer than that of the contemporary Hillman 14hp/Humber 16/Humber Snipe models, the chassis was like those cars, with the Evenkeel transverse-leaf-spring independent front suspension. The engine was an 80bhp, aluminium-headed version of the 3.2-litre Humber 'six', and the same gearbox had synchromesh on top and third gears.

There was a wide choice of body styles, starting from the six-window saloon, which had a Talbot-style nose, but a standard Pressed Steel Company/'big Rootes' shell from the screen backwards. The sports saloon, complete with pillarless construction as already described for the Tens, was very smart, as were foursome drop-head coupes and tourers.

For 1939, and the relaunch as a Sunbeam-Talbot, the frame was given cruciform stiffening and the brakes became hydraulic instead of Bendix. Prices started at £415 (they had started at £398 for the Talbot 3-Litre cars), which was good value for such good looks, but the car's roadholding and steering did not really match up to its straight-line performance. Top speed was about 80mph.

Sunbeam-Talbot (and Talbot) 3-Litre specification

Produced: London, 1937–39, number of cars built unknown.
General layout: Separate chassis-frame, steel or coachbuilt bodyshells in variety of styles. Front-mounted engine driving rear wheels.
Engine and transmission: Hillman/Humber engine, 6-cylinder, sv, in-line. 3,181cc, 75 x 120mm, 80mph at 3,800rpm; maximum torque not revealed; 4-speed gearbox, no synchromesh on 1st or 2nd gear; centre-floor gear-change; live (beam) rear axle with spiral-bevel final drive.
Chassis: Independent front suspension, transverse leaf springs, upper wishbones. Worm-and-nut steering. Live (beam) rear axle, half-elliptic leaf springs. Front and rear drum brakes. 6.25-16in tyres.
Dimensions: Wheelbase 9ft 10in; front track 4ft 7.5in; rear track 4ft 8in; length (saloon) 15ft 8in; width 5ft 9.5in; height 5ft 4in. Unladen weight approx 3,625lb.
Distinguishing features from previous models: No relationship to previous Talbots and Sunbeam-Talbots, but very similar to new 4-Litre model. New 3-Litre, however, effectively a rebodied version of existing large Hillman/Humber chassis of the period.
Typical performance: Maximum speed 81mph; 0–60mph 20.1sec; typical fuel consumption 17–20mpg.
Derivatives: Closely related to 1939 range of Sunbeam-Talbot 4-Litre models introduced in 1938, which had larger engine. Chassis engineering closely related to existing large Hillman/Humber models.
Fate: Discontinued in 1939 at outbreak of war and never reintroduced.

Sunbeam-Talbot 4-Litre specification

Produced: London 1938–39, number of cars built unknown.
General layout: Separate chassis-frame, steel or coachbuilt bodyshells in variety of styles. Front-mounted engine driving rear wheels.
Engine and transmission: Hillman/Humber engine, 6-cylinder, sv, in-line. 4,086cc, 85 x 120mm, 100bhp at 3,400rpm; maximum torque not revealed; 4-speed gearbox, no synchromesh on 1st or 2nd gear; centre-floor gear-change; live (beam) rear axle with spiral-bevel final drive.
Chassis: Independent front suspension, transverse leaf spring, upper wishbones. Worm-and-nut steering. Live (beam) rear axle, half-elliptic leaf springs. Front and rear drum brakes. 6.25-16in tyres.
Dimensions: Wheelbase 9ft 10in; front track 4ft 7.5in; rear track 4ft 8in; length (saloon) 15ft 8in; width 5ft 9.5in; height 5ft 4in. Unladen weight approx 3,625lb.
Distinguishing features from previous models: Closely related to previous Talbot 3-Litre model and new Sunbeam-Talbot 3-Litre. New 4-Litre effectively a rebodied version of existing large Hillman/Humber chassis of the period.
Typical performance: Maximum speed 82mph; 0–60mph 18.2sec; typical fuel consumption 17–19mpg.
Derivatives: Closely related to 1939 range of Sunbeam-Talbot 3-Litre models, which had smaller engine. Chassis engineering closely related to existing large Hillman/Humber models.
Fate: Discontinued in 1939 at outbreak of war and never reintroduced.

Sunbeam-Talbot 4-Litre (1938 to 1939)

No sooner had Rootes unveiled the 3-Litre than it added the 4-Litre model. This, effectively, was the same car with the same choice of body styles except that it was fitted with the largest version of the Rootes six-cylinder engine, the 4,086cc side-valve unit, which came complete with an aluminium cylinder head. Effectively, therefore, this was a dressed-up version of the newly-launched Humber Super Snipe. Although many people tend to think that what later became known as 'badge engineering' is a postwar phenomenon, it was clearly well established as a central part of Rootes policy by this time.

Compared with the 3-Litre, the 4-Litre had significantly better acceleration, slightly heavier fuel consumption, and was sold at prices starting from £455 – £70 more than the equivalent 4-Litre Humber and £40 more than the Sunbeam-Talbot 3-Litre.

Like the smaller car, its looks and acceleration were let down by its handling capabilities. Production was suspended in the autumn of 1939 and never revived after the war.

Sunbeam-Talbot 80 (1948 to 1950)

Rootes launched the first postwar Sunbeam-Talbots in July 1948. These cars also qualified as the first true postwar-design Rootes cars, for the new-generation Hillman Minx and Humber ranges were still months away from the market.

There were two new sister cars – the 80 and the 90 – the difference being purely that the 80 had an overhead-valve version of the side-valve Minx engine and the 90 a similarly modified version of the larger Hawk engine. The 80's engine was unique in that it was never used in any other Rootes car.

Except that their rear axle was wider, these cars retained the chassis-frame of the obsolete Sunbeam-Talbot 2-Litre model, which is to say that there was a beam front axle with half-elliptic leaf springs all round. Most of the running gear was modified Hawk/modified Minx, for Rootes had its rationalization act well developed by this time.

The saloon shells were produced by BLSP and the drop-head coupes finished off by Thrupp & Maberly, all paint and trim also being carried out at Thrupp &

Norman Garrad drove this Sunbeam-Talbot 90, an ex-sales-demo car, in an early postwar Alpine Rally, thus effectively founding the famous Rootes rally team of the postwar period.

Sunbeam-Talbot 80 specification

Produced: Ryton-on-Dunsmore, 1948–50, 3,500 cars built.
General layout: Separate chassis-frame, pressed-steel bodyshells. Front-mounted engine driving rear wheels.
Engine and transmission: Hillman/Humber engine, 4-cylinder, ohv, in-line. 1,185cc, 63 x 95mm, 47bhp at 4,800rpm; 4-speed gearbox, no synchromesh on 1st gear; steering-column gear-change; live (beam) rear axle with spiral-bevel final drive.
Chassis: Beam axle front suspension, half-elliptic leaf springs. Worm-and-nut steering. Live (beam) rear axle, half-elliptic leaf springs. Front and rear drum brakes. 5.50-16in tyres.
Dimensions: Wheelbase 8ft 1.5in; front track 3ft 11.5in; rear track 4ft 2.5in; length 13ft 11.5in; width 5ft 2.5in; height (saloon) 5ft 0.75in. Unladen weight approx 2,605lb.
Distinguishing features from previous models: Same basic chassis-frame as 1939–48 Sunbeam-Talbots, but with all-new full-width, all-steel body styles.
Typical performance: Maximum speed 73mph; 0–60mph 36.4sec; typical fuel consumption 30mpg.
Derivatives: Saloon, DHC. Closely related to Sunbeam-Talbot 90 of the period, which had different engine and transmission. 80 model not continued beyond 1950.
Fate: Discontinued in 1950 and not replaced.

Maberly; final assembly, as with the last of the Tens and 2-Litres, was at Ryton.

The facia style was very American in feel, and featured the latest type of Rootes steering-column gear-change.

The 80, frankly, was under-powered and not a success – it was asking too much for a 47bhp engine to drag a 2,600lb car along. After only two years, therefore, it was dropped.

Sunbeam-Talbot 90 Mk I (1948 to 1950)

Except that it had the overhead-valve version of the Sunbeam-Talbot 2-Litre/Humber Hawk engine and different back-axle gearing to suit, the first of the 90s was little different from the 80. This engine, of course, would eventually be fitted to the Humber Hawk, but not until 1954.

The 90 was a much better car than the 80, for it had a top speed of at least 80mph instead of 73mph and much better acceleration; in the UK its original basic price was only £102 (about 11%) higher than that of the 80.

This was the first of a series of smart and increasingly faster Sunbeam-Talbots, which would remain in production until 1957. A determined works motorsport programme helped to improve the chassis – the Mk II of 1950 would demonstrate this in no uncertain fashion.

Sunbeam-Talbot 90 Mk I specification

Produced: Ryton-on-Dunsmore, 1948–50, 4,000 cars built.
Engine and transmission: Hillman/Humber engine, 4-cylinder, ohv, in-line, 1,944cc, 75 x 110mm, 64bhp at 4,100rpm; 4-speed gearbox, no synchromesh on 1st gear; steering-column gear-change; live (beam) rear axle with spiral-bevel final drive.
Chassis: Beam-axle front suspension, half-elliptic leaf springs. Worm-and-nut-steering. Live (beam) rear axle, half-elliptic leaf springs. Front and rear drum brakes. 5.50-16in tyres.
Dimensions: Wheelbase 8ft 1.5in; front track 3ft 11.5in; rear track 4ft 2.5in; length 13ft 11.5in; width 5ft 2.5in; height (saloon) 5ft 0.75in. Unladen weight approx 2,830lb.
Distinguishing features from previous models: Same basic chassis-frame as 1939–48 Sunbeam-Talbots, but with all-new full-width, all-steel body styles.
Typical performance: Maximum speed 80mph; 0–60mph 22.5sec; standing ¼-mile 22.5sec; typical fuel consumption 25mpg.
Derivatives: Saloon, DHC. Closely related to Sunbeam-Talbot 80 of the period, which had different (Hillman Minx-type) engine. 80 model not continued beyond 1950.
Fate: Discontinued in 1950, replaced by new Mk II type.

Sunbeam-Talbot 90 Mk II (1950 to 1952)

Here, at least, was the definitive postwar Sunbeam-Talbot, for underneath the already familiar style of the original 90 model was an entirely new chassis-frame, featuring coil spring-and-wishbone independent front suspension.

Not only did the latest car, now officially called Mk II, have a modern frame and better handling, it was also treated to an enlarged and improved version of the familiar engine. This became a 2,267cc unit – a size already applied to the latest Humber Hawk Mk IV announced the previous month – but the Sunbeam-Talbot was still the only Rootes model to have the overhead-valve layout.

A raised final-drive ratio, now by hypoid-bevel instead of spiral-bevel, closer intermediate gears and variable-ratio steering gear all helped to improve an already-attractive car. As to the styling, the only important change was that the headlamps were raised by 3in (with the front wings reprofiled to suit), the fog/driving lamps were abandoned and extra air intakes were let into the front panel in their place.

The postwar Sunbeam-Talbot – in 80 and 90 forms – was launched in 1948. Some panels from the prewar style were retained, along with the rear door window arrangement, but most of the shell was absolutely new, sleek and modern in appearance.

In September 1950, Rootes finally unveiled a modern chassis for the Sunbeam-Talbot 90 (which therefore became Mk II), complete with coil spring independent front suspension, and cruciform bracing under the seats.

A famous occasion. Stirling Moss (standing by the car), Desmond Scannell (driving) and John *The Autocar* Cooper drove this Sunbeam-Talbot 90 Mk II into second place in the 1952 Monte Carlo Rally.

The scene – Monte Carlo Rally 1953. The crew – Sheila Van Damm's team, and their works 90 Mk IIA needing a wheel change on one of the regularity sections. In the event they finished as runners-up for the *Coupe des Dames*.

Not only was the 90 built as a four-door saloon, but also as a two-door drophead coupe. This was a Mk IIA model, pictured in 1952.

Sunbeam-Talbot 90 Mk II specification

As for original Sunbeam-Talbot 90 except for:
Produced: Ryton-on-Dunsmore, 1950–52, 5,493 cars built.
Engine: 2,267cc, 81 x 110mm, 70bhp at 4,000rpm; 113lb ft at 2,400rpm.
Transmission: Hypoid-bevel final drive.
Chassis: Independent front suspension, coil springs, wishbones, anit-roll bar. Rear suspension had Panhard rod location. Recirculating-ball steering.
Dimensions: Unladen weight (saloon) approx 2,905lb.
Typical performance: Maximum speed 86mph; 0–60mph 24.3sec; standing ¼-mile 23sec; typical fuel consumption 23mpg.
Fate: Discontinued in 1952, replaced by further-modified Mk IIA type.

Sunbeam-Talbot 90 Mk IIA (1952 to 1954)

Two years after the independent-front-suspension chassis was introduced for the Sunbeam-Talbot 90, the specification was improved once again, this time to Mk IIA. There was no doubt that the changes had been inspired by experience gained by the works rally team.

The main mechanical improvements were to the engine and the braking, much larger brake drums being specified, with perforated road wheels to assist in the circulation of cooling air, and with the rear spats deleted so that it was easier for fresh air to circulate around the rear wheels. The 2,267cc engine was once again improved, now being rated at 77bhp. This, in fact, was the last Sunbeam-Talbot, for the next improvement of this basic design was badged Sunbeam Mk III.

Sunbeam-Talbot 90 Mk IIA specification

As for Sunbeam-Talbot Mk II except for:
Produced: Ryton-on-Dunsmore, 1952–54, 10,888 cars built, including 1953-54 Sunbeam Alpines.
Engine: 77bhp at 4,100rpm.
Typical performance: Maximum speed 81mph; 0–60mph 20.8sec; standing ¼-mile 22.2sec; typical fuel consumption 28mpg.
Fate: Discontinued in 1954, replaced by the further-modified Mk III type, rebadged as a Sunbeam.

Chapter 9

Chrysler and Peugeot

Rootes' successors and the cars they inherited

Although Rootes was clearly in financial trouble by 1964 – it had lost £2 million in 1961–62 and another £224,000 in 1962–63 – the question of merging with another company was never canvassed in the newspapers and never surfaced until a deal was actually announced – with Chrysler! On reflection, this was really a logical tie-up – at least for Chrysler, since Ford and General Motors (with Vauxhall) were already well established in the UK.

Lord Rootes had been familiar with Chrysler's top managers for a long time, and had cheerfully been pillaging styling ideas from the Corporation for some years. Have a look at the quad-headlamps and the wrap-over screen of the Humber Sceptre, or the fins of the 1958 Sunbeam Rapier, to get the picture....

By this time in failing health, Lord Rootes held a series of talks with Chrysler's president, Lynn Townsend, before flying to New York with Sir Reginald and clinching a deal on June 4, 1964. This was a surprise to everyone, not least to the 10,000 Rootes workers in Coventry, the *Coventry Evening Telegraph* and the *Financial Times*, all of whom might be said to have a vested interest in such goings-on.

Chrysler agreed to pay £12.3 million for a large stake, but not a controlling interest, in Rootes. For this investment, Chrysler bought 30% of the ordinary (voting) and 50% of the A ordinary (non-voting) share capital. At the same time, Chrysler pledged to the British government that it would not seek to gain control against its wishes.

As part of the deal, three Chrysler directors – Irving J. Minett, Louis B. Warren and Robert C. Mitchell – joined the Rootes board, and it soon became clear that Chrysler was now in the driving seat. One of the first corporate moves to be agreed was that the Rootes commercial business (Commer-Karrier) would be merged with Chrysler-Dodge UK truck operations.

It was, of course, easy to be wise after the event. A *Birmingham Post* reaction was that:

'....a powerful backer was rapidly becoming a necessity. A company [Rootes] controlled by a family which wants to keep control never finds it easy to raise extra capital without control passing out of the family's hands....For Rootes it was probably Chrysler or nothing (except perhaps a losing battle with the giants....).

Autocar magazine offered its lofty 'insider's' opinion that:

'The long-expected tie-up between Rootes and the Chrysler Corporation came last week....As America's third largest manufacturer of cars and commercial vehicles, Chrysler have been looking for an outlet in Britain for some time....The agreement will strengthen Rootes' position in Europe as well as providing the company with another chain of distributors throughout the US....'

Motor was very cautious in writing that: 'The commercial implications are far from clear at this stage....'

Although this was never publicly spelt out, much of the financial reshuffling would involve Rootes family holdings. At merger time, the *Coventry Evening Telegraph* noted that there were 15,000 individual Rootes shareholders, but that the Rootes family, or its nominees, held control with the following:

	Ordinary Shares	A Ordinary Shares
General Trust and Securities (of the Bahamas)	2,285,000	2,743,000
Prudential Assurance	474,000	2,650,000
Lady Nancy Rootes	2,000	60,000
Sir Reginald Rootes	179,000	774,000
Sir Reginald Rootes 'and others'	10,000	67,000
Sir Reginald Rootes 'and others'	–	405,000
Sir Reginald Rootes 'and others'	104,000	416,000
Lord Rootes	60,000	518,000
Timothy Rootes 'and another'	–	100,000
The Hon Geoffrey Rootes 'and another'	–	100,000
Field Nominees (of Bermuda)	87,000	1,254,000

Lord Rootes, having secured the future of the business which he and Sir Reginald had founded, let go the reins of the Group and gradually retired to his country home in Wiltshire, near Hungerford. Unhappily, he had little time to enjoy any leisure, for he died on December 12, 1964. He was 70 years old. It was the end of an era. His eldest son, the Hon Geoffrey Rootes, who had already carved out an impressive career in the business, became the second Lord Rootes.

Chrysler, incidentally, had been building up its European operations and influence for some time. It had taken a 35% stake in Simca in 1957 and raised that to a controlling interest of 63% in 1963. Chrysler and Dodge cars had once been assembled at a factory in Kew, in south-west London, but by the early 1960s this factory was building Dodge trucks. Now, with this important stake in Rootes (and everyone assumed that this would become a controlling interest before too long), Chrysler was ready to take its stateside battle with Ford and General Motors into Europe.

To complete the short-term financial reshuffle which followed the arrival of Chrysler, Rootes acquired the British Dodge business in February 1965 by issuing 5,244,557 A ordinary (non-voting) shares to the Chrysler Corporation. This, and other minor moves, helped increase Chrysler's shareholding in Rootes, but it still stopped short of financial control.

In the next few years, Chrysler's influence spread throughout the Rootes Group. Roy Axe recalls that Chrysler's input to the styling department followed almost at once in 1964, though he is adamant that his Sunbeam Rapier fastback style was definitely not influenced by that of the new Plymouth Barracuda! From September 1965, Rootes announced that it was to start displaying the famous Chrysler 'Pentastar' trademark/badge on its cars, and in all the company's literature.

Although the British government tried to persuade Sir Donald Stokes (whose Leyland-Triumph-Rover combine was booming) to take a financial stake in Rootes in 1966, this did not appeal to the entrepreneurial Leyland chairman. Instead, he eventually merged with the BMH (BMC-Jaguar) combine, with altogether disastrous results....

After that, surely a full takeover proposal by Chrysler could not be delayed? It came, in fact, at the beginning of 1967, not without a great deal of ritual whinging from MPs about the control of a 'great British asset' passing into foreign hands. It was, in fact, inevitable. Rootes had lost £3.4 million in the financial year ending July 31, 1966 and was on the way to losing a further £4.7 million

Once Chrysler took a stake in Rootes, it dabbled with restyling the Tiger. One mock-up was produced in 1966 (opposite), and various renderings were also evolved, but the project went no further.

In 1965, Chrysler encouraged Rootes to consider a completely new style of Tiger. Like all such projects, it was abandoned at an early stage.

If Chrysler had produced a Sunbeam Tiger like this, would you have bought it . . .?

in the first half of the current year. By that time, Chrysler had invested £27 million in Rootes and already held 62% of the equity, though only 45% of the voting shares. For a further £20 million they were to tip the balance and take control. At the time, too, it was suggested that another £40 million in capital expenditure would have to follow in the next five years.

As a result, there was a major board reshuffle in March 1967. Sir Reginald Rootes (who was 70 years old and had been Rootes' chairman since his brother had died) retired; his place as chairman was taken by the second Lord Rootes. Brian Rootes (Lord Rootes' brother) and Timothy Rootes (Sir Reginald's son) both left the board, while Messrs B. Boxall (a government IRC nominee), E.H. Graham, Georges Hereil (of Simca), Sir Eric Roll and W.J. Tate joined it.

There was also to be a new managing director – Gilbert Hunt, who was currently managing director of Massey Ferguson UK, the tractor manufacturers with premises in Coventry. He was to stay with the company until the late 1970s, becoming chairman in 1973 when Lord Rootes retired.

Surprisingly, there was no immediate injection of American management staff at top level, for day-to-day management of the company was left in the hands of British nationals. Nor was there any attempt to bring Rootes and Simca closer together.

In the meantime, the British Motor Corporation (BMC) had taken over Pressed Steel, which prompted Rootes to promote all manner of corporate changes. Clearly it was not wise to leave the long-term supply of mass-production bodyshells in the hands of a rival company (which, by definition, Pressed Steel had now become). Fortunately, both BMC and Rootes could see the dangers of this, and both had good reasons to unscramble the commercial arrangement.

Although it was not all that simple to arrange, this is what finally emerged:

BMC/Pressed Steel agreed to sell its Linwood premises to Rootes, complete with its existing contracts. For a time, therefore, Rootes continued to build cars for Rover and Volvo, plus railway rolling stock – the work which Pressed Steel had developed so strongly during the 1950s.

This gave rise to the foundation of Rootes Pressings (Scotland) Ltd, made the Linwood complex an integrated business, and gave Rootes a massive facility and a lot of spare capacity in Scotland. Rootes paid BMC £14,250,000 (and took on Board of Trade liabilities of £8,625,000), and the new company came into operation on January 1, 1966.

For the time being, however, nothing could be done about Pressed Steel supplies from Cowley, particularly as the newly-designed Arrow range of models (Hunter/Minx/Sceptre/Vogue/Rapier) was almost ready for production.

At the end of 1966, though, Rootes announced that all assembly of large Humbers (Hawks/Super Snipes/Imperials) was soon to end, and that when this happened the British Light Steel Pressings factory in Acton would close down and be sold off.

Then, in March 1967 (*after* the launch of the Arrow range) came the announcement that made a lot of manufacturing sense. Rootes (or perhaps I should now write Rootes/Chrysler) was to end its dependence on Pressed Steel (which was currently supplying 2,600 bodies a week) and to expand its own body structure building facilities at Linwood. By the end of 1968 it would take over most of the Arrow range tooling from Pressed Steel, install it at Linwood and start producing bodies of its own.

These were then to be transported 300 miles to Coventry by special liner trains to a dead-end siding at Gosford Green, close to the Humber Road factory. On the return trip, engines, transmissions and other hardware for Imps would take a ride from the Midlands to Scotland. This (see below) was to be a short-lived arrangement.

'Spartan' was a styling study for a rear-engined 1.1-litre car, which might have followed up as a new Minx, if the original Imp project had been a success. We all know, now, that it was not.

Sunbeam Rapier and the estate car shells would continue to be built at Cowley for a time, but would eventually be resourced from Linwood.

A few weeks later it was announced that the famous Thrupp & Maberly plant in Cricklewood was also to close down in August 1967. By that time, after all, there would be nothing for this plant to do – for Humber assembly was already over and the paint/trim work on old-style Humber Sceptres and Sunbeam Rapiers was shortly to end.

Soon afterwards, Rootes also leased an ex-aircraft assembly factory at Coventry's Baginton airport for conversion into a trim and seating centre, and in the same period the ex-Singer factory in Canterbury Street, Coventry, was expensively re-equipped to produce plastics components.

In and around all this upheaval, Rootes/Chrysler

Early work on styling models like this led up to the Arrow project, and to the Hunter of 1966. Note the Imp-like sculpturing along the sides of the upper. example.

The design which finally emerged was neat and restrained, one reason why it was able to continue without substantial change for more than a decade. The original Hillman Hunter of 1966 had circular headlamps, distinguishing it from the Singer Vogue, which had rectangular lamps.

eliminated no fewer than 30 separate operating companies, replacing them by just two – Rootes Motors Ltd and Rootes Pressings (Scotland) Ltd.

Nor was this the end of the transformation. At the end of the 1960s it became clear that final assembly of Arrow models was to be concentrated on Linwood, and that Ryton was to be retooled for the assembly of a new car. Even though Ryton sometimes built 2,900 cars a week at that time, for the first time ever it was to be given its own body assembly facility (pressings and sub-assemblies would come from Linwood) along with a modernized paint shop.

The Hillman Hunter, first appearing in October 1966, had a completely new four-door structure, with MacPherson strut front suspension. The engine was tilted towards the offside to give adequate clearance for manifolds and carburettor on the other side of the engine bay.

In the meantime, there had been a real breakthrough when Rootes (*not* Chrysler) concluded a deal with Iran National Industrial Manufacturing to cover the assembly of Rootes cars in Teheran from kits supplied from the UK. This deal was extended in October 1968 when the Iranian government decreed that only three types of car – one small, one medium and one large – should be built in its country. Rootes/Chrysler clinched the 'medium-sized' deal, supplying Hillman Hunter kits. Over the years, the Iranians produced more and more of the car themselves, but to the end, in the mid-1980s, there was a healthy outflow of parts from Ryton to Teheran.

The first Chrysler influence on new products resulted in the partial development of several Rootes/Chrysler hybrids. Not only was an attempt made to squeeze the 4.5-litre Chrysler V8 engine into the Sunbeam Tiger (in place of the existing Ford V8), a few prototype V8 Humber Sceptres were also produced, and there was a determined attempt to produce a V8-engined Humber Super Snipe/Imperial model as a top-of-the-range option to existing six-cylinder cars.

The V8 Humber project was born in November 1964 and the first prototype ran in 1965, with a view to launching the production car during 1966. In the end the project was abandoned after 10 cars had been produced, though a few survive to this day. In its place, Rootes agreed to import Australian-assembled Chrysler Valiants to the UK from the end of 1966, but these were a complete flop in the market place.

In the meantime, Rootes had been pressing ahead with the design of two new mass-production projects – the Arrow and the B-Car, both of which were to be the mainstay of Rootes/Chrysler production throughout the 1970s.

As I have already made clear, in the early 1960s, the design team led by Peter Ware (with engine design work by ex-Vanwall designer Leo Kuzmicki) had started out on the Swallow project for a medium-sized rear-engined

The new-generation Hillman estate car, launched in April 1967, was really half-Minx, half-Hunter – but before long it officially got the title of Hunter Estate. Those tail lamps were shared with the Sunbeam Rapier Coupe.

saloon, but this was dropped in 1963 in favour of a more conventional car – the Arrow project.

Arrow was a conventional range of cars – saloon, estate car and fastback coupe – intended to take over from every existing Minx, Super Minx, Rapier and Sceptre model. It was, in every way, a pure Rootes design, styled by Rex Fleming (the Rapier was styled by Roy Axe) and virtually unaffected by Chrysler input; a whole range of cars was progressively introduced in 1966 and 1967. By any standards this was a great and lasting success, not only as built in the UK, but as supplied in kit form for assembly in Iran as the Peykan.

At about the time that Arrow went into production, Peter Ware left the company, his place as technical director being taken by Cyril Weighell. By that time, Harry Sheron had become head of design, and he succeeded Weighell at the end of the 1960s.

The B-Car project, first discussed in 1963, styled in 1965–66 with input from both Roy Axe and Tim Fry (who had been seconded to Chrysler-Detroit for some time to get a feel for USA design methods), was still a Rootes design, but rather less 'pure' in that there was a great deal of Chrysler influence once the takeover was complete.

After the trouble caused by the all-new Imp project, one would have thought that Rootes would fight shy of producing another ground-up all-new design, but the B-Car was again completely new from end to end. Not only did it have a new engine, gearbox, rear axle, bodyshell and suspensions, it was to be produced in a completely modernized factory at Ryton, with engines, gearboxes and axles coming from the Stoke works. It did not help, surely, that the design, development and styling departments were all progressively moved out of Humber Road in 1969–70 to a separate factory a couple of miles away at Whitley, an ex-missile design/development facility recently bought from Hawker Siddeley Dynamics. (That factory, by the way, was eventually vacated in the 1980s, and is now the design/development headquarters of Jaguar Cars.)

This time, however, there were no mistakes, because the Avenger was a conventional car (technically too conventional, according to some of its critics) and its birth and early life was almost entirely troublefree.

The new Hillman Minx of 1967 looked virtually identical to the Hunter of the period, only the lack of bumper overriders, and different wheeltrims, signalling the difference. This particular example has 'Sunbeam' on the bonnet, a designation used in preference to the Hillman marque for some export markets but not in the UK.

Full-size styling studies which eventually led to the Avenger: early, square-cut version, above, is badged 'Sunbeam'. By 1967, right, something much closer to the final shape had emerged, Hillman badged and with number plate indicating that it was due for launch two years later.

The Hillman Avenger, although launched under Chrysler ownership, was really a complete Rootes design. It was all new – structure, engine, gearbox, axle, front suspension and steering, a huge investment only made possible by Chrysler capital.

The Hillman Avenger had a deliberately modest style, originally as a four-door saloon like this, with other versions to follow . . .

. . . but not this one, which remained an intriguing 'might-have-been'. Rootes/Chrysler were impressed by the Ford Capri and thought deeply about producing this competitor, based on the underpan of the new Avenger. It never got beyond the full-size mock-up stage.

Unfortunately, a promising Ford Capri-competitor coupe version of the Avenger (R429) was cancelled at the mock-up stage.

This burst of new-model activity took place against the background of a bumpy financial period. The 1966–67 loss shot up to £10.8 million (a record that Chrysler did not want to see beaten, but which would be matched in 1970 and vastly exceeded in 1974), while annual production hovered around 180,000 cars a year (which was only about half of what Rootes could have built if all its factories were at full stretch).

By this time it was plain that Chrysler's USA representatives, though staying strictly at arm's length from the routine operation, were losing patience with the existing organization and doubted its ability ever to start producing regular and sizable profits.

The last straw, really, was the ambitious C-Car project. This was the very first Rootes-Simca joint

The C-Car project emerged as the French-built, Simca-engined Chrysler 180. A British, V6-powered Humber version was cancelled by Chrysler at a very late stage.

project, started in 1967–68, intended not only to replace the large Humbers, but to allow Simca to produce a larger car for the first time in many years. Styled in the UK, but heavily influenced by Chrysler-Detroit (and with a very unmemorable shape....), it was a sizable four-door saloon, to have been built in France with a new Simca engine and in the UK with a newly-designed 60-degree V6 engine.

Design was complete, and development well on the way, with dozens of prototypes running when, suddenly, at the beginning of 1970, the British end of the project was cancelled. Tooling already being installed at Humber Road for production of the V6 engine was ripped out. The Simca-engined car was launched later in 1970 as the Chrysler 180; cynically advertised in France as 'An American, from Paris', it was *not* a success.

A measure of the staff's unease at this situation is beautifully indicated by this anonymous poem which appeared in the *Coventry Evening Telegraph* at the time:

'Lord God Chrysler from afar,
Said we'll build a motor car.
To follow 'Arrow' and the 'B'
Until it's born we'll call it 'C'.
We'll raise a super Power Train crew,
And use some new procedures too.
We'll pay a little over par,
And adorn them with a "Pentastar".
The game is played to Chrysler rules,
Machines a'plenty and all the tools,
Until at last there dawns a day,
And doubt arises, will it pay?
Rumour says the project's dead,
The future's viewed with obvious dread;
Lord God Chrysler pray for me,
And those in peril on the 'C'.

It was, in fact, the end of Rootes as an independent company, and effectively the end of this story. As a manufacturing group, Rootes had been in existence for nearly 40 years.

Chrysler, which owned 73% of the equity capital, was already rationalizing fast (the Singer marque name had already been laid to rest), and in April 1970 the remaining Rootes shareholders were informed that from July 1, 1970 the name of the two principal companies would be changed – to Chrysler United Kingdom Ltd and Chrysler Linwood Ltd.

For the time being Lord Rootes stayed on as chairman and Gilbert Hunt as managing director. The last Rootes connection, however, was lost in June 1973 when Lord Rootes retired in favour of Gilbert Hunt; he had served Rootes for 37 years, having joined Humber Ltd in 1937.

Rootes personalities to the fore of this shot, grouped around the Chrysler-UK designed Alpine of the mid-1970s, were Harry Sheron (technical director, left, with hand in pocket), Roy Axe (styling director, sitting on the bonnet) and Marc Honore (production planning chief, arms folded).

Four years later, Sir Reginald Rootes, who had enjoyed 10 years of retirement, died.

Aftermath

Chrysler never succeeded in restoring the fortunes of the one-time Rootes Group. They were not helped by extremely fragile labour relations, nor by their reluctance to develop new models to freshen-up the model range.

The Avenger range was expanded, with GT, GLS and Tiger versions introduced to add interest, the Arrows were facelifted but not restyled, and the Imp family was cut back, then allowed to die. Avengers were sold in the USA as Plymouth Crickets, and built in Brazil and Argentina in much-modified form. Hillmans eventually became Chryslers, and all individuality was lost. Chrysler-Europe became a reality, which meant that the ex-Rootes Whitley design centre was responsible for the styling and concept of cars like the Chrysler Alpine, the Simca/Chrysler Horizon, and even the Talbot Tagora and Samba which followed.

The UK end of Chrysler-Europe, however, lost so much money that Chrysler threatened to pull out at the end of 1975. Much government aid, and the slimming down of Linwood, followed, but assembly of Alpines in the UK from French-built kits and the rushed development of the Sunbeam hatchback were all to no avail. The companies were only profitable from 1971 to 1973 inclusive, and the peak Rootes figure of £6.8 million in 1959–60 was never even approached.

In 1978, Chrysler, by that time as deep in trouble in the USA as it was in Europe, sold out completely – to Peugeot of France. Within a year the Chrysler name itself had vanished, and Talbot had appeared in its place.

Three years later, the Linwood complex had been closed, the Whitley design/development facility had been disbanded, and the Coventry factories contracted in upon themselves. By the mid-1980s, Ryton was nothing more than an assembly plant for Peugeots, with Humber Road supplying components for those cars.

In its heyday, Rootes held about 15% of the UK market. By the mid-1980s the British-built Peugeot contribution had dropped to a mere 1.5%. Only in the late 1980s, since the highly successful Peugeot 405 was put on sale, has the situation improved significantly.

Rootes-designed models built under Chrysler ownership

Hillman Hunter (1966 to 1977)

(Note: This model family was rebadged Chrysler in September 1977 and finally dropped in 1979.)

The Arrow project covered an entire family of cars – Hillmans Minx and Hunter, Singers Gazelle and Vogue, Humber Sceptre, Sunbeams Rapier and Alpine – which was intended to replace every existing car in the old Hillman Minx and Super Minx families.

Individual Singer, Humber and Sunbeam models have already been described in the appropriate marque chapters. This section traces the birth and general career of the Hillmans and the range itself. As with so many other Rootes cars, those badged as Hillmans in the UK were often rebadged as Sunbeams for sale in export territories.

Compared with the Super Minx range, the car later called Hillman Hunter (the name, of course, comes from that used by Singer between 1954 and 1956), was slimmer, sleeker, more delicately engineered and weighed about 300lb less. The style, by Rex Fleming under Ted White's direction, was neat and modern, but undistinguished, and the chassis layout was much like that of the then-new Ford Cortina. It was, after all, the first Rootes car to use MacPherson-strut independent front suspension. Like the Cortina, the Hunter was eventually sold with a variety of engine sizes, tunes, power outputs and model badges.

All types shared the same basic running gear and the same 8ft 2.5in wheelbase floorpan with 4ft 4in wheel tracks, but in addition to the four-door saloon there was to be a five-door estate car and (styled by Roy Axe) a two-door fastback coupe derivative. Cars badged as

Hunter noses, clockwise from top left: 1970 GT, 1970 GL, 1972 De Luxe and 1972 GLS.

Hillman Hunters were built as saloons or estates, with the coupe always carrying a Sunbeam badge.

In every case the cars used modified versions of the late-model Minx/Super Minx engines and transmissions. The overhead-valve engine range was thoroughly revised, to have a five-main-bearing crankshaft, and for packaging reasons it was mounted at a slight cant in the engine bay. The all-synchromesh gearbox introduced in 1964 was retained, along with the well-established corporate medium-duty hypoid-bevel back axle.

The original Hunter took over from the Super Minx in 1966, but a Hunter-badged estate did not arrive for another four years. The Hunter GT took over from the Hillman (Minx) GT at the same time, a facelift followed in 1972 when the Rapier H120-engined Hunter GLS (with Sceptre-type nose) was also launched. For clarity, I have quoted all power outputs in 'DIN' measure, as adopted for the 1970s.

After the facelift, Chrysler seemed to lose interest in the Hunter, though it continued to produce as many sub-models as possible. The last Hillmans, as such, were produced in 1977, though Chrysler-badged cars were built until 1979, and the much-modified Iranian Peykan derivative until the mid-1980s.

Hillman Hunter family specification

Produced: Ryton-on-Dunsmore, 1966–69, Linwood 1969–77, approx 470,000 Minx/Hunters of all types built.
General layout: Combined (unit-construction) body-chassis structure, 4-cylinder engine and choice of saloon and estate car bodies. Front-mounted engine driving rear wheels.
Engine and transmission: Hillman engine, 4-cylinder, ohv, in-line. Various versions: 1,496cc, 81.5 x 71.6mm, 54bhp (DIN) at 4,600rpm; 73lb ft at 2,500rpm; 1,725cc, 81.5 x 82.55mm, 61bhp (DIN) at 4,700rpm; 85lb ft at 2,600rpm; or 72bhp (DIN) at 5,000rpm; 90lb ft at 3,000rpm; or (GT version) 79bhp (DIN) at 5,100rpm; 90lb ft at 3,000rpm; or (GLS version) 93bhp (DIN) at 5,200rpm; 106lb ft at 4,000rpm; 4-speed all-synchromesh gearbox, optional Laycock overdrive; centre-floor gear-change; optional Borg-Warner automatic transmission; live (beam) rear axle with hypoid-bevel final drive.
Chassis: Independent front suspension, coil springs, MacPherson struts. Recirculating-ball steering. Live (beam) rear axle, half-elliptic leaf springs. Front disc and rear drum brakes. 5.60-13in, 155-13in/165-13in tyres.
Dimensions: Wheelbase 8ft 2.5in; front track 4ft 4in (GLS 4ft 4.5in); rear track 4ft 4in (GLS 4ft 4.5in); length 14ft 0in; width 5ft 3.5in; height 4ft 8in. Unladen weight approx 2,035-2,200lb, depending on model.
Distinguishing features from previous models: Completely new style of Hillman compared with previous models.
Typical performance: (Hunter 1500) Maximum speed 83mph; 0–60mph 17.8sec; standing ¼-mile 20.9; typical fuel consumption 30mpg; (Hunter GL 1,725cc) maximum speed 90mph; 0–60mph 14.6sec; standing ¼-mile 19.6sec; typical fuel consumption 28mpg; (Hunter GT 1,725cc) maximum speed 96mph; 0–60mph 13.9sec; standing ¼-mile 19.4sec; typical fuel consumption 24mpg; (Hunter GLS) maximum speed 108mph; 0–60mph 10.5sec; standing ¼-mile 17.4sec; typical fuel consumption 24mpg.
Derivatives: Arrow-type Minx (1967–70) was same basic car with minor styling and equipment changes and less powerful engine.
Fate: Discontinued in Autumn 1977 in favour of rebadged Chrysler Hunter.

Hillman Minx (Arrow-type – 1967 to 1970)

To replace the long-running Audax type of Hillman Minx (which was in production from 1956 to 1967) Rootes produced a down-market version of the Hunter called simply the Minx. Compared with the Hunter this had a smaller-capacity, 1,496cc iron-headed version of the engine and rather simpler equipment, though automatic-transmission cars always received an iron-headed 1,725cc engine, and from late 1968 that engine was also offered as a manual-transmission option.

What was really a Minx estate car was simply called the Hillman Estate.

In the interests of rationalization (but to the fury of traditionalists) the Minx name was dropped in 1970, the same car henceforth being sold as a Hunter DL. It was the end of an unbroken 38-year run.

Hillman Minx (Arrow-type) specification

As for Hillman Hunter except for:
Produced: Ryton-on-Dunsmore, 1967–69, Linwood 1969–70. For production figures, see Hunter.
Engine and transmission: 1,496cc engine, 54bhp (DIN) and 1,725cc engine, 61bhp (DIN) version only; automatic transmissions only with 61bhp 1,725cc engine.
Dimensions: Unladen weight (saloon) approx 2,000lb.
Distinguishing features from previous models: Completely new style of Hillman compared with previous Minx models, almost identical in style and equipment to 1966 Hillman Hunter.
Typical performance: (Minx 1500) Maximum speed 83mph; 0–60mph 17.8sec; standing ¼-mile 20.9sec; typical fuel consumption 30mpg.
Derivatives: 1967–70 Singer Gazelle was same basic car with styling and equipment changes.
Fate: Discontinued in 1970 in favour of Hillman Hunter DL.

A famous picture of a famous occasion – Andrew Cowan, Brian Coyle and Colin Malkin on their way to winning the London–Sydney Marathon of 1968.

As a result of the Marathon success, Rootes hurriedly pushed through the development of the Hillman GT, really a Minx with the Rapier engine and Rostyle wheels.

The Hillman Hunter GT of the early 1970s was a more completely and thoughtfully specified derivative of the Hillman GT, which it replaced.

The interior of the Hillman Hunter GT displayed simple circular instruments (a far cry from the transatlantic style of some earlier Rootes facias) and a sporty steering wheel.

The most basic Avengers had rectangular headlamps and very little brightwork, emphasizing the sound, practical nature of the design. Other versions were more highly decorated.

Avenger facia styles, left to right: original strip-speedometer version; round dials in a 1973 GT; and hooded display for a Chrysler-badged GLS in 1976.

Hillman Avenger (1970 to 1976)
(Note, this range was rebadged Chrysler in September 1976 and again rebadged Talbot for the 1980 model-year. Production ended in spring 1981.)

The Avenger, or B-Car as it was coded for so long, was entirely designed by Rootes, even though it was not launched until February 1970, three years after Chrysler took control. It was intended to fill a large marketing gap, in both size and price, between the small rear-engined Imps and the larger front-engine/rear-drive Arrow family of cars. It was a direct competitor for the Ford Escort, Morris Marina and Vauxhall Viva. However, unlike previous Rootes cars, it was only intended to be badged as a Hillman in the UK, or as a Sunbeam overseas.

This policy was changed soon after Chrysler took control, because a federalized version of the Avenger was sold in the USA in the early 1970s, badged as a Plymouth Cricket.

The B-Car was a completely new design, and no component, however small, was carried over from other Rootes Group products. Even so, except for the use of a coil spring/radius arm location of the rear axle, it was really another Arrow, but rather smaller, with a slightly shorter wheelbase and narrower tracks.

Like the Arrow which preceded it, the new car, soon named Hillman Avenger, had many derivatives, all using the same basic floorpan, chassis components and running gear, but built as a two-door or four-door saloon, or as a five-door estate car. The four-door came first, the two-door and estate car types followed, with GT, GLS and Tiger versions all following later in the 1970s. Like the Arrow range, too, the Avengers were sold in several engine sizes and states of tune.

Again like the Arrow range, there was nothing exciting – technically, in style or in behaviour – about the Avenger, but it was a thoroughly practical, usable little car which Rootes dealers found very saleable. The 50,000th example was built in August 1970, and at its peak more than 78,000 Avengers were sold in the UK in a year. In seven years no fewer than 638,631 of all Avenger types (whatever their badging) were built.

Rebadged as Chrysler in 1976, then rebadged again as Talbot in 1979, the last Avenger was produced in 1981. The Chrysler/Talbot Sunbeam hatchback of 1977–81 used the same (shortened) floorpan, chassis and running gear as the Avenger.

Avenger variations, top to bottom: two-door Super, 1973; two-door GT, 1973; estate car (De Luxe, 1972); Tiger, 1972; and GL with Talbot badges in the last year.

Hillman Avenger family specification

Produced: Ryton-on-Dunsmore, 1970–76, 638,631 cars built.
General layout: Combined (unit-construction) body-chassis structure, 4-cylinder engine and choice of 2-door or 4-door saloon and estate car bodies. Front-mounted engine driving rear wheels.
Engine and transmission: Hillman engine, 4-cylinder, ohv, in-line. Various versions: 1,248cc, 78.6 x 64.3mm, 53bhp (DIN) at 5,000rpm; 66lb ft at 3,000rpm; 1,295cc, 78.6 x 66.7mm, 57bhp (DIN) at 5,000rpm; 69lb ft at 2,800rpm; 1,295cc (GT) 69bhp (DIN) at 5,800rpm; 68lb ft at 4,000rpm; 1,498cc, 86.1 x 64.3mm, 63bhp (DIN) at 5,000rpm; 80lb ft at 3,000rpm; 1,498cc (GT) 75bhp (DIN) at 5,400rpm; 81lb ft at 3,750rpm; 1,599cc, 87.3 x 66.7mm, 69bhp (DIN) at 5,000rpm; 87lb ft at 2,900rpm; 1,599cc (GT/GLS) 81bhp (DIN) at 5,500rpm; 86lb ft at 3,400rpm. 1,599cc (Tiger) 100bhp (DIN) at 6,000rpm; 96lb ft at 4,600rpm;
4-speed gearbox, synchromesh on all forward gears; optional Borg-Warner 3-speed (later 4-speed) automatic transmission. Centre-floor gear-change; live (beam) rear axle with hypoid-bevel final drive.
Chassis: Independent front suspension, coil springs, MacPherson struts and anti-roll bar. Rack-and-pinion steering. Live (beam) rear axle with coil springs and radius arm location; Panhard rod on estate car. Front disc and rear drum brakes (front drum brakes on some economy versions). 5.60-13in, 155-13in/175SR13in tyres.
Dimensions: Wheelbase 8ft 2in; front track 4ft 3in; rear track 4ft 3.5in; length 13ft 5.4in; width 5ft 2.5in; height 4ft 7.3in. Unladen weight (saloon) approx 1,895 to 1,985lb, depending on model.
Distinguishing features from previous models: Completely new style of Hillman compared with previous models.
Typical performance: (1,248cc) Maximum speed 81mph; 0–60mph 19.8sec; standing ¼-mile 21.4sec; typical fuel consumption 25mpg; (1,498cc, 63bhp) maximum speed 91mph; 0–60mph 15.6sec; standing ¼-mile 20.1sec; typical fuel consumption 28mpg; (1,498cc GT) maximum speed 96mph; 0–60mph 12.5sec; standing ¼-mile 18.5sec; typical fuel consumption 28mpg; (1,295cc 57bhp) maximum speed 85mph; 0–60mph 17.5sec; standing ¼-mile 20.9sec; typical fuel consumption 30mpg; (1,599cc 69bhp) maximum speed 92mph; 0–60mph 14.5sec; standing ¼-mile 19.8sec; typical fuel consumption 27mpg; (1,599cc GT/GLS) maximum speed 100mph; 0–60mph 12.2sec; standing ¼-mile 19.0sec; typical fuel consumption 29mpg.
Derivatives: 1976 Chrysler Avenger was same car, rebadged. Also built as Plymouth Cricket for USA market. Also built under different names, with modifications, by Chrysler-Argentina and Chrysler-Brazil.
Fate: Discontinued in 1976 in favour of rebadged Chrysler Avenger range.

Appendix A

Building the bodies

Pressed Steel, Thrupp & Maberly, Darracq, British Light Steel Pressings and other sources

Until the end of the 1920s, most of Britain's car makers used bodies built by traditional methods, which meant that the panels were assembled around a series of wooden skeletons and frames. The companies which eventually became the core of the Rootes Group in the 1930s – Hillman, Humber, Sunbeam and Talbot – sometimes made their own bodies, but often bought them in from specialist coachbuilders.

Such bodies could not be built in large quantities, so during the 1930s, when Rootes made its move to become one of the British Big Six car makers, a change became necessary. As Rootes production surged upwards towards 50,000 cars a year, the latest technology, featuring all-steel shells with pressed panels spot-welded together, was required, at least for the best-selling family cars.

In the next four decades, Rootes gradually developed and expanded its choice of body sources. In the beginning it was heavily dependent for mass-production shells on the Pressed Steel Company of Cowley, but for rather smaller quantities it took on alternative sources of supply, sometimes favouring specific coachbuilding concerns, sometimes buying up established companies, and later by establishing its own new bodybuilding plants. In 1945, the Group still took the majority of its saloon car shells from Pressed Steel, and for years this company also provided shells, sections or just panels to other companies for completion on Rootes' behalf; it was not until the end of the 1960s, when Rootes had absorbed the Scottish body plant from Pressed Steel and it was finally submerged into the Chrysler Corporation that it became self-sufficient.

Body supplies throughout the 1930s

Once the first series of true Rootes models had been launched, the pattern became clear. The Group would get its quantity-production saloon shells from Pressed Steel at Cowley, and its limited-production shells from a variety of other sources:

Pressed Steel Company

Until the 1960s, Pressed Steel was far and away the most important supplier of bodies to Rootes. The Pressed Steel Company of Great Britain Ltd (this was its first official title) had been founded in 1926 with factory premises at Cowley, a few miles east of the city of Oxford. William Morris (later Lord Nuffield), the owner of Morris Motors, had visited the USA in 1925 and had been very impressed by the welded all-steel bodies being produced by the Edward G. Budd Manufacturing Company of Philadelphia. As a result, he got together with Budd to establish Pressed Steel, a company in which Budd retained a controlling interest and whose premises were literally next door to those of Morris.

Although Pressed Steel immediately started looking around for business, it had big problems at first because other companies were suspicious of Morris' financial interest; as a result, Morris had to surrender its shareholding in 1930. As Lord Nuffield's biographers later wrote:

'....two directors of Morris Motors were on the board of the Pressed Steel Company and the latter found it practically impossible to get business from other car firms, who were reluctant to place orders with a supplier who was so closely tied to their major competitor....'

As soon as Pressed Steel became truly independent, it began to pick up business from the rest of the industry, such that by the end of the decade it was supplying either bodies or pressings to all the major manufacturers.

The first important order from Rootes was for saloon bodies for the 1931 Hillman Wizard, and within a year Pressed Steel also had the contract to build saloon shells for the first-generation Hillman Minx. In those days, Pressed Steel made a limited number of standard cabins which they were prepared to modify to a particular customer's requirements. This is why there was a close similarity between the original types of Wizard and Minx, and one or two other British cars of the period.

Pressed Steel gained so much business from Rootes throughout the 1930s that it erected a new factory block at Cowley, which was actually dubbed the Rootes Building by management. Pressed Steel had only been building 100 bodies a day in 1930, but by 1939 this had risen to 700 bodies a day.

In 1935, it began delivering a new four-door six-window fastback shell to Rootes, in Coventry, for use in a new rationalized range of large Hillmans and Humbers, like the Hawks and Snipes. Two years later, a similar style appeared on the Hillman 14hp, and with a facelift in the autumn of 1939, which included the addition of a boot bustle and the deletion of running-boards, this shell was also used on early-postwar Humbers.

There was also a Pressed Steel saloon shell for the Humber 12 in the early 1930s, and from 1935 there was the second-generation Hillman Minx, later dubbed the Minx Magnificent because of the wording on its radiator badge. Then, in September 1939, the third-generation Minx was launched, with very similar external styling to the previous type (and some shared panels), but built on a monocoque, or chassisless, base.

Bill Hancock remembers this car well: 'The unit-construction Minx was introduced after we made a visit to Opel, the General Motors plant in Germany, to study their methods of production, and this entirely new method of assembly of the Minx was all proved and in production when war started....' This car was re-introduced in 1945, immediately after the fighting was over.

bodies for Rootes Group cars, though it was still building excellent bespoke shells for mounting on Rolls-Royce, Bentley, Alvis and Lagonda chassis.

In 1928–29, the company produced the body for Sir Henry Segrave's *Golden Arrow* Land Speed Record car. This, incidentally, is where the connection with Capt J.S. Irving (who had designed *Golden Arrow*) was established, for he joined Humber Ltd immediately after this magnificent car had proved its point.

For a short period in the late 1930s, Thrupp & Maberly's name was also applied to the factory in Warple Way, Acton, though this was really only a corporate cosmetic device to link the old Darracq facilities (see below) with the new Rootes Group.

Before 1939, Thrupp & Maberly was beginning to concentrate on building the largest and most expensive 'mayoral' Humbers – cars like the late-model Pullmans –

When Rootes designed the first Minx of the early 1930s the main four-door body style was built by Pressed Steel, in Cowley.

Thrupp & Maberly

This distinguished coachbuilding concern was established in 1760 when Joseph Thrupp set up in London as a maker of horse-drawn carriages. Ninety years later, a Mr Maberly joined forces with him, and by the early 1900s the company was in the forefront of bodybuilding for high-class motor cars. Before the First World War, the company had already started buying up many of its smaller rivals.

Between the wars, Thrupp & Maberly built many special styles on Rolls-Royce and other noble chassis, and moved to a modern factory on London's Edgware Road (the London end of A5) in 1924, not far from Vanden Plas. The company was finally taken over by Rootes Ltd (the first of its major acquisitions in the 1919–39 period) in 1925, well before William or Reginald had any direct interest in car manufacture.

From 1926, its head offices were situated at Devonshire House, the new Rootes headquarters, by which time its modern factory on the Edgware Road was well established. By then, it was devoting much of its time to building batches of

along with coachwork for some Rootes Talbots and some of the new-fangled Sunbeam-Talbot models. Rootes had bigger schemes for this concern, but they would not mature until after the Second World War.

Darracq

For some years, the independent (pre-Rootes) Talbot concern took a number of its coachbuilt bodyshells from Darracq, a once-famous French car marque, which at one time assembled cars in the UK, but was now one of STD's coachbuilding subsidiaries based at Warple Way, in Acton, West London. After Rootes took over Talbot from the Receiver, Darracq was eventually made part of the deal. For a time it carried on making bodies for Talbot, but in the next three years these progressively became 'Rootesified' (with different wings and other cheap pressed panels), and the Darracq name was soon abandoned.

By chance, Darracq was next door to a metalworking company called British Light Steel Pressings, with which it was merged in the late 1930s.

Almost a cottage industry, but used for thirty years – this was British Light Steel Pressings, in Acton, where many bodies including the Sunbeam-Talbot 90s of 1948–1956 and the Humber Hawk/Super Snipes of 1957–1967 were manufactured.

British Light Steel Pressings

BLSP later became notorious as the Rootes factory with the most militant labour force, which probably did as much as any other factor to ruin the Group's cash flow capability in the early 1960s.

BLSP, however, had only been founded in 1930, initially to produce any metal product or pressing *except* car bodies. Rootes took over the business in 1937, gaining not only extra floor space in the London area, but also the company's expertise in making steel pressings in large quantities.

After a short period of rationalization with Darracq, BLSP was set up to build a quantity-production series of shells for the new Sunbeam-Talbot Ten, 2-Litre, 3-Litre and 4-Litre sports saloons, as well as to provide petrol tanks, various pressings, including floorpans and sub-assemblies to other parts of the Rootes Group, notably the Commer commercial vehicle sector .

As with Thrupp & Maberly, BLSP's massive expansion would follow in the 1945–65 period.

Other suppliers

Between 1930 and 1939, several other specialist builders also supplied bodies to Rootes. Because supplies were sometimes sporadic (they depended on which models were in production, on fashion, and on which company was in or out of favour with Rootes' designers at any one time!), I have gathered them together:

Carbodies, of Coventry, is now noted for producing the famous London Taxicabs, but in the 1930s it had a thriving business supplying bodies to the motor industry. Whereas companies like Hooper and Park Ward dealt with individual designs at high prices, Carbodies went in for series (if not large-scale) production. Rootes often turned to this company to build special open-top versions of its cars, such as a variety of Hillman Minx tourers and drop-head coupes and Aero Minx models. In addition, Carbodies also produced sports-saloon shells for the Humber 12s and larger Hillmans.

Mulliners, of Birmingham (not to be confused with either

Thrupp & Maberly's factory in north-west London, years after it had been sold off by Rootes/Chrysler in 1967. This is another Humber Road, not to be confused with the one in Coventry.

The combined Humber-Hillman businesses became Rootes, and the Stoke works in the 1930s. This 1960s shot, taken from the south, shows how the complex had developed, with the main administrative offices, and the design/development departments at the top of the picture. The railway line on the left was to be used for the shuttle of components and complete bodyshells, to and from Linwood, in the late 1960s/early 1970s. The Stoke Aldermoor shadow factory later used to make gearboxes is on the lower right.

A view of the Stoke works from the west (City) side, as further developed by Peugeot-Talbot in the early 1980s.

H.J. Mulliner, or Arthur Mulliner), were in the same type of business and supplied sports-saloon shells for cars as various as the Hillman Minx, the Wizard, the Humber Snipe, the Hillman Hawk and 80 and Humber Imperial models.

Salmons, of Newport Pagnell (now better known as Tickford), specialized in convertible coachwork, producing shells for the Aero Minx and some of the larger Hillmans and Humbers.

Whittingham & Mitchell, of London, produced bodies for the Talbot Ten (later the Sunbeam-Talbot Ten) and some of the larger-bodied Sunbeam-Talbots.

All these bodybuilding concerns had an extremely busy time during the Second World War (some producing military-style coachwork for Rootes chassis and some becoming involved in aircraft projects), but by mid-1945 it was time to settle down again, re-group and prepare for postwar private car building.

The bodybuilding supply situation in 1945

The war changed everything. It was impractical and unwise for a company like Rootes to try to put *all* its cars back into production, not only because some body jigs had been destroyed, but because there was a new emphasis on export (rather than home sales), rationalization and social change. The cars of the late 1940s would be based on prewar designs, but would be a more conventional bunch than before.

Once the company had introduced its postwar range, suitably updated from the 1940 cars, it had 12 different models on offer:

Hillman Minx (the new third-generation type)	Saloon
	Drop-head coupe
Humber Hawk	Saloon
Humber Snipe	Saloon
Humber Super Snipe	Saloon
Humber Pullman	Limousine
Sunbeam-Talbot Ten	Saloon
	Coupe
	Tourer
Sunbeam-Talbot 2-Litre	Saloon
	Coupe
	Tourer

(There was also a Hillman Minx estate car, which was effectively a Commer light commercial vehicle with modifications, and for tax purposes was classified as a commercial vehicle. It used the old-style, 1935–39 type of Minx chassis-frame.)

The vast majority of this range was produced by the **Pressed Steel Company**, of Cowley, which built the monocoque Hillman Minx saloon shells and all the Humber Hawk, Snipe and Super Snipe saloon car shells. Pressed Steel also supplied the underpan of the Hillman Minx coupe to **Carbodies** for completion.

Rootes' own subsidiary companies, **British Light Steel Pressings** (who built Sunbeam-Talbot Ten and 2-Litre saloon shells) and **Thrupp & Maberly** (who built the shell of the Humber Pullman limousine and carried out completion work on other models) were also important parts of the jigsaw.

To seasoned Rootes-watchers there was a well-defined body-supply strategy, even at this stage, though this was almost certainly a short-term solution to 'get the show on the road'. It was only in 1948, when three major new models appeared – the next-generation Hillman Minx and Humber Hawk ranges and the Sunbeam-Talbot 80/90 models – that a settled pattern began to develop. For the next few years, it seemed, **Pressed Steel** would build mass-production shells, Rootes' own company, **British Light Steel Pressings**, would gradually become the second-division producer (it was to be responsible for the Sunbeam-Talbot 80 and 90 saloon shells and the 1950s–60s big Humbers), while **Thrupp & Maberly** would tackle all the special jobs and most of the open-top cars. A few jobs would continue to be farmed out – notably to the **Carbodies** concern, in Coventry.

This, then, was the way that Rootes bodies were supplied in postwar years, and we can look in detail at how each plant contributed its piece of the jigsaw.

The Ryton factory in the early 1960s, becalmed due to a shortage of components, but showing the way that Hillman, Singer and Sunbeam bodies were all fed towards the same final assembly lines at this time.

Pressed Steel Company

For 20 years after the Second World War, Pressed Steel was in the enviable position of having something approaching a seller's market. Except on brief occasions when there was a recession in the industry, Pressed Steel could always have picked up more business than it could properly deal with, and it had to expand mightily to keep up with demand. Not only did it establish a factory at Swindon in the 1950s, but in 1947 it had also taken over an ex-Government factory at Linwood, which was a few miles west of Glasgow, in a most unfashionable position for a motor industry concern. That factory was central to the birth of the Imp project, as has already been explained.

In the 1945–65 period (after which Pressed Steel was absorbed by the British Motor Corporation), the company had many large customers. Many thousands of bodies were supplied not only to Rootes, but also to Morris, BMC, Daimler, Jaguar, Standard and Triumph, Rover, Volvo and Rolls-Royce into the bargain.

A few statistics tell their own story:

In 1926, the factories covered 533,000sq ft, but this rose to 2,250,000sq ft in 1950 and 4,750,000sq ft by 1960. An extension of 500,000sq ft was started in 1960 to look after the Hillman Imp project.

Pressed Steel employed 546 people in 1926, 9,000 by 1950 and 16,000 by 1958.

In 1939, the company was producing 700 bodies a day, but this had risen to 1,100 a day by 1950 and it doubled again in the next decade.

Until the late 1960s, Pressed Steel supplied all the Rootes mass-production saloon/FHC coupe shells in these families:

Hillman Minx (1945–48 type)
Hillman Minx (1948–56 type)
Hillman Husky (1954–57)
Hillman Husky II (1958–65)
Hillman Minx/Singer Gazelle (1956–66 type)
Hillman Super Minx/Singer Vogue (1961–66 type)
Hillman Hunter/new Singer Vogue/Humber Sceptre type (1966–69)
Humber Hawk/Super Snipe (1945–57)
Sunbeam Alpine/Tiger (1959–68)
Sunbeam Rapier (1968–69)

– and, from Linwood, 'across the bridge':

Hillman Imp family, all types (1963–65)

It also supplied unpainted, or incomplete bodies of many types (for completion as convertibles, sports cars, or estate cars) to **Bristol Siddeley**, **Carbodies**, **Tickford** and **Thrupp & Maberly**, especially for:

Minx/Super Minx family estate cars
Sunbeam Rapier (1955–67)
Sunbeam Alpine (1959–62)
Humber Hawk/Super Snipe (1945–57)
Humber Sceptre (1963–66)

The Pressed Steel/Rootes situation, however, changed from time to time. From 1959 to 1962, for instance, Pressed Steel supplied Husky-type underframes to Bristol Siddeley, in Coventry, where the Alpine sports car took shape, but from

An aerial view of the Ryton factory in 1982. This is taken from the south, and the Coventry city centre is at the top of the shot. The Coventry–London road crosses from left to right along the edge of the factory, the Coventry–Oxford road runs straight down underneath the aeroplane from which the picture is being taken.

Here's an intriguing picture – an Imp body shell, at the Pressed Steel factory in Cowley, when it still had a short tail, and engine cooling vents in the top of the rear deck. The lengthening would soon follow. In other respects, though, the body style was 'ready to go'.

The Linwood factory, near Paisley, Scotland, with the Rootes factory (closest to the camera) literally 'across the road' from the Pressed Steel body plant.

1962 the complete Alpine shells were built, painted *and* trimmed at Cowley before being dispatched to Ryton; the amount of work on what might be called fringe models varied considerably over the years that such a car was in production.

After BMC took over Pressed Steel in 1965, there was a shake-up and rationalization of its business:

a) On January 1, 1966, the Linwood end of the business was sold to Rootes and became known as Rootes Pressings (Scotland). Production of shells for Rover (the P5), Volvo (the 1800S) and commercial work for Ford and BMC was soon hived off.

b) Starting in 1968–69 and completed within a year or so, all the Cowley assembly operations were closed down, the pressing, jigging, framing and assembly operations for ranges such as the Hunter/Minx/Gazelle/Sceptre and the new Sunbeam Rapier being sold to Rootes and transferred to Linwood.

Rootes Pressings (Scotland)

Historically, this company grew out of the Pressed Steel facility developed at Linwood, years before Rootes was forced to build cars in Scotland. The Pressed Steel building, having started life producing railway wagons, diesel multiple units and other such hardware, began building car bodies in 1959, notably the Rover 3-Litre (P5) and then the Volvo P1800/1800S sports coupe shells.

To accommodate the Imp project across the road, an extra 500,000sq ft of factory building was laid down between 1960 and 1963. By this time, railway industry activity was in decline.

Once BMC had bought Pressed Steel, it decided to rationalize its own body-supply facilities and to progressively squeeze out the non-BMC business. Accordingly, at the end of

With the Imp in full production, the new Linwood factory was full of bodies . . .

. . . the car having been inspected carefully by HRH The Duke of Edinburgh when he opened the plant in May 1963.

1965, the entire Scottish operation was sold to Rootes, who renamed it Rootes Pressings (Scotland).

Right from the start, this operation was merged administratively with the mainstream Linwood factory, and for the first three years it supplied all the Imp structures.

Then, following Chrysler's takeover of Rootes, it was decided to make this the centre of all Rootes bodybuilding operations. Not only were other plants (such as British Light Steel Pressings and Thrupp & Maberly) closed down, but all the production plant previously based at Pressed Steel Cowley (for Hillman Hunters, Sunbeam Rapiers and the like) was purchased, relocated and progressively brought back into use at Linwood. Eventually, special company trains began to shuttle back and forth between sidings at Linwood and a facility a short distance from the Stoke plant in Coventry, bringing complete bodies south and taking back a variety of mechanical items on the return journeys.

In the 1970s, the Linwood factory went on to produce all the shells for the Avenger and Chrysler Sunbeam families. It closed down when the car plant did likewise in 1981.

British Light Steel Pressings

By 1945, with massive postwar expansion planned, BLSP had been earmarked as an important feeder to the rest of the Rootes Group of Sunbeam-Talbot shells, Commer shells for the commercial vehicle division and pressings for Thrupp & Maberly. For the time being, though, it carried on where it had left off in 1939, building Sunbeam-Talbot Ten and 2-Litre shells and supplying incomplete shells and pressings to other Rootes companies.

In 1948, the cramped workshops in Worple Way, Acton, were re-equipped to build Sunbeam-Talbot 80 and 90 saloon shells, and in due course they also provided incomplete shells to Thrupp & Maberly, who completed the convertible versions of the same car, and part-complete shells to Mulliner, who built the Alpine sports car (1953–55).

Then, in 1957, the last of this line, the Sunbeam Mk III, was dropped. In a frantic burst of activity, assembly lines previously devoted to Sunbeams were stripped (even the roof of the building was removed for a time) and new machinery, press-tools and jigging facilities were installed – in 14 days!

BLSP then concentrated on building complete shells for the 1957–67 variety of Humber Hawk/Super Snipe/ Imperial. The Acton plant was also the scene of the long and costly strike of 1961, which has already been described.

When the last of the large Humber range was dropped in 1967, the BLSP business was closed down. By that time, Chrysler had taken complete control of the Rootes Group. Future policy dictated that body production was to be concentrated at the Linwood plant, in Scotland. The Acton complex was eventually sold off and now it has nothing to do with the British motor industry.

Thrupp & Maberly

After the Second World War, Thrupp & Maberly abandoned the traditional side of its coachbuilding business – no more special bodies were produced for Rolls-Royce or other such patrician cars – and the Cricklewood-based company was set to supplying fully painted and trimmed bodyshells for the Rootes Group.

At first, T & M concentrated on building the large Humbers – Imperial and Pullman – but it soon began completing Sunbeam-Talbot 80 and 90 convertibles as well from primer-coated shells supplied by BLSP. During the 1950s, it became the centre of all Rootes convertible body completion (Hillman Minx, Super Minx and Rapier, for instance), starting from nearly-completed primer-coat shells provided by Pressed Steel, finishing off the bodies, painting and trimming them, then delivering them to Ryton for completion. Equally successful, but less glamorous, estate car shells were produced in some numbers.

From 1953, too, T & M also began completing and painting a series of 'speciality' coupe shells, originally for the Minx Californian, and from 1955 for the Sunbeam Rapier, and it did the same job on the Humber Sceptre of 1963–66.

T & M always retained its paint-and-trim work on the big Humbers, which included converting ordinary saloons into limousines by adding divisions. From 1964 to 1967, of course, there was the satisfaction of working on the last generation of Humber Imperials.

Thrupp & Maberly's activities ran down rapidly in 1966–67. The Minx/Gazelle convertibles had disappeared in 1962, the Super Minx convertible faded away in 1964, the last of the original-type Sceptres followed in 1966, and in 1967 the large Humbers and the graceful old Rapier Mk V both died out.

The decision to close Cricklewood was announced in June 1967, with the note that paint and trim work on the new Arrow generation of Minx/Hunter/Vogue estate car shells would shortly be transferred to Ryton. The factory closed its doors in August 1967 and was sold off.

Mulliners

This long-established Birmingham firm, which had produced several series of bodies for Rootes in the 1930s, only picked up one major supply contract in postwar years. This was to complete the building of the two-seater Sunbeam Alpine sports car, which was in production between 1953 and 1955.

BLSP supplied partly finished Sunbeam-Talbot 90 shells, and Mulliners did the rest, painting and trimming them, and sending them to Ryton for completion.

From June 1954, however, Mulliners signed an exclusive supply agreement with Standard-Triumph for its future body supplies, which meant that it could not entertain any fresh contracts with Rootes. Mulliners, in fact, was taken over by Standard-Triumph in 1958.

Bristol Siddeley

In the late 1950s, part of the deal worked out by Rootes with Bristol Siddeley was that this company should assemble the Alpine bodyshell at the Burlington works, in Coventry, before being painted and trimmed and the whole car then completed.

Pressed Steel supplied Husky-type underframes, while Joseph Sankey supplied superstructures, all the sub-assemblies being welded together at the Burlington works.

From 1962, when the original Bristol Siddeley assembly contract was terminated, Pressed Steel took the complete assembly, paint and trim job back in-house.

The end of the Rootes dream – Linwood in the mid-1980s, derelict, and ripe for redevelopment.

Appendix B

Combined operations

The Armstrong Siddeley and Jensen connections

As many sports car enthusiasts surely know, the second-generation Sunbeam Alpine (launched in 1959) was originally assembled by Bristol Siddeley, of Coventry, and the Sunbeam Tiger was always assembled by Jensen, of West Bromwich. That much is simple and straightforward enough, but how and why these two projects came to be farmed-out is a fascinating story:

Bristol Siddeley and the Alpine project

Armstrong Siddeley came into existence in 1919, the fusion of Armstrong Whitworth and Siddeley Deasy. Throughout its existence this marque was really the prestige arm of the aero-engine company of the same name, and the cars were always built at the rambling complex of factories at Parkside, to the south of the city centre of Coventry.

Armstrong Siddeley started up again after the Second World War by building a series of six-cylinder engined cars (Lancasters, Whitleys, Hurricanes and the like), using what was known as the Burlington works, situated towards the southern tip of the factory site.

In 1952, the company announced the smart new Sapphire, a Jaguar Mk VII-sized car which had a brand-new 3.4-litre six-cylinder engine whose cylinder head featured a cross-pushrod layout with twin rocker shafts and part-spherical combustion chambers.

The original Rootes connection was forged here, at first with the transmission, and eventually with the engine design. For the Sapphire there was a choice of manual or electric-preselector gearbox, and although it was never publicized at the time, the manual gearbox option (a four-speed all-synchromesh design with steering-column gear-change) was that of the latest Humber Super Snipe.

The Sapphire was only a little more expensive than the Super Snipe when released – £1,728 vs £1,627 – but since Rootes did not see the Sapphire as direct competition, and the Rootes family was friendly with the Siddeley family, there does not seem to have been a problem....

Unfortunately, the Sapphire did not sell very well. Worse, the *next* new model, the strangely-styled 234/236 type, was a complete flop; it went into production in January 1956, but disappeared during 1958. In the early 1950s, Armstrong Siddeley had entertained hopes of competing for sales with Jaguar, but by 1957 it was struggling to keep the Burlington plant busy, and workers were being laid off regularly.

An approach from Rootes, offering greater co-operation, swap deals and a great deal of contract work, must have been a real life-saver to the hard-pressed car division. On the one hand, Rootes decided to design and develop its new six-cylinder Super Snipe/Imperial engine on the same lines as that already being used in the Sapphire range (for further details, see **Appendix D**) – but on the other hand, it offered Armstrong Siddeley the chance to develop, then manufacture, the new Sunbeam Alpine sports car.

For Armstrong Siddeley, in 1957, this was a real windfall, for it offered the chance of revitalising the Burlington works, which was equipped to produce many more cars than it was actually building. Rootes, on the other hand, really had no space left at Ryton to build the Alpine, for the assembly lines were full of profitable family cars like the Minx, Rapier and Gazelle. Nor did the relatively small Rootes development department have time to look after work on the new sports car, for it was already fully committed on major projects such as the new Super Snipe and the new generation of medium-sized cars eventually badged as Hillman Super Minx and Singer Vogue.

Armstrong Siddeley also arranged to manufacture the 'cloned' six-cylinder engine on Rootes' behalf, and continued to do so until 1967.

By 1957–58, when the author first went to live in Coventry and work in the motor industry, the existence of the 'RAS' (Rootes-Armstrong Siddeley) sports car was well-known. Between then and the middle of 1959, not only the Burlington works, but the Armstrong Siddeley company itself, witnessed upheaval. Out went the unsuccessful 234/236 saloons and the original Sapphires and in came the Star Sapphire and construction of the Sunbeam Alpine sports car.

Parts of the Sunbeam Alpine bodyshells were built by Pressed Steel in Cowley, and part by Joseph Sankey, in the West Midlands. All parts were then transported to Coventry, where they were welded together, painted and trimmed by Armstrong Siddeley. All the car's running gear – engine, transmission, suspension and other chassis components – was supplied from the Rootes Stoke works, or by Rootes' contracted suppliers. After completion, the Alpines were smoothly fed into the usual Rootes distribution system.

In the meantime, Armstrong Siddeley's parent company, Hawker Siddeley, merged with the Bristol Aeroplane Company in 1959. The Coventry-based company, thereafter, was known as Bristol Siddeley Engines (for the main production was concentrated on gas turbine aero engines and rockets), and for a short time there were even some wistful thoughts of bringing the Bristol car production facility to Coventry.

However, in March 1960, the directors decided to wind-down production of Armstrong Siddeley cars, and at the end of July the last Star Sapphire rolled out of the building. After that the Burlington Works only built Sunbeam Alpines.

After the long and damaging strike at British Light Steel Pressings, Rootes had to rationalize and concentrate its businesses as much as possible in an effort to regain profitability. Accordingly, it soon arranged to close down the sub-contracted assembly of Alpines and build the cars in-house at Ryton.

As the *Coventry Evening Telegraph* stated on March 23, 1962:

'Production of Sunbeam Alpine sports cars at the Coventry factory of Bristol Siddeley Engines came to an end today....Bristol Siddeley have now fulfilled the terms of the original contract and the car division has been closed....'

About 350 workers were laid off as a result, but such was the boom in motor manufacture in Coventry that all soon found other work.

Under the new scheme of things, Pressed Steel assembled Alpine bodies, painted and trimmed them, then transported

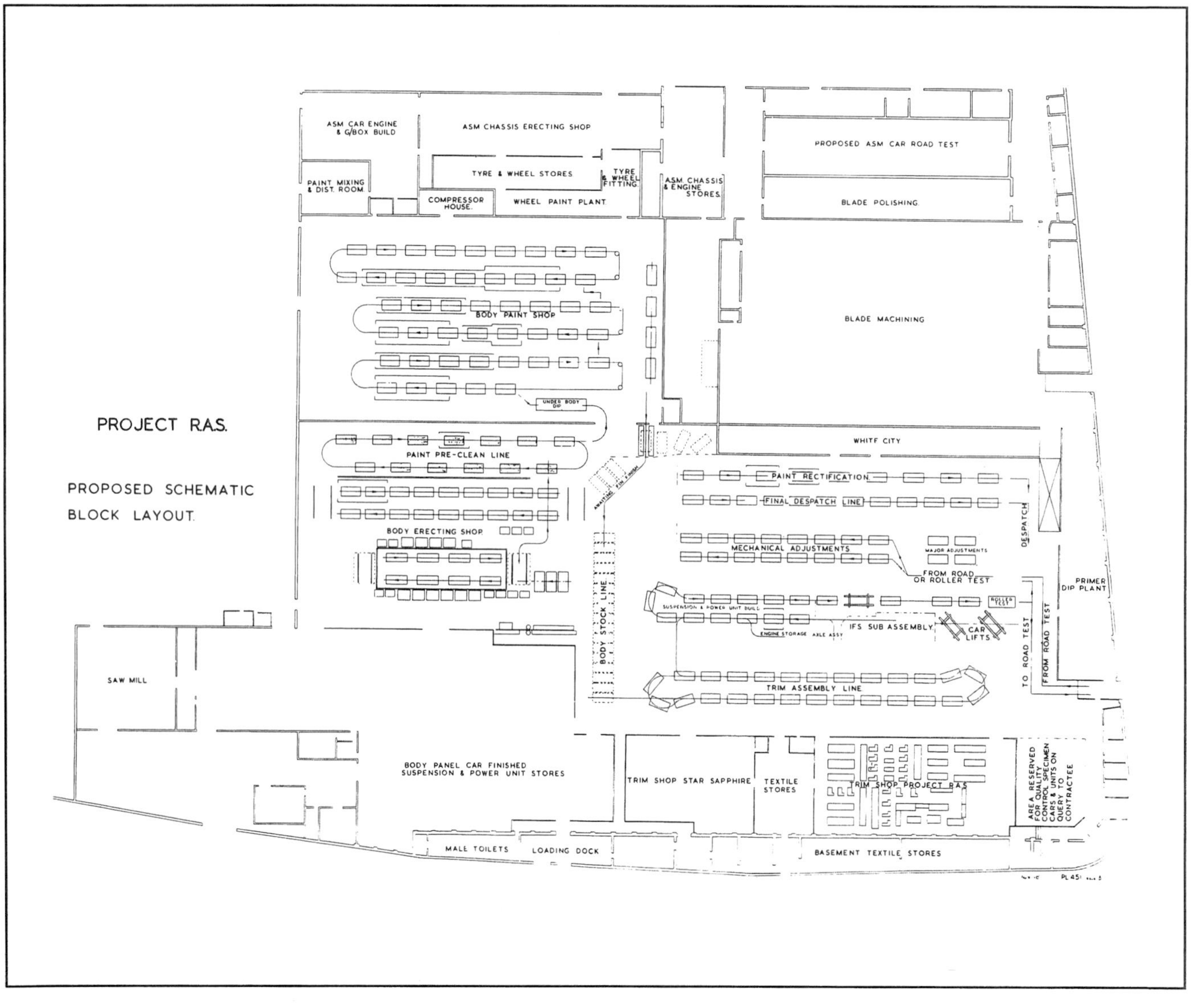

A rarely-seen Bristol Siddeley site plan of the Burlington works, showing how the Sunbeam Alpine ('RAS') assembly facility was closely integrated into other facilities such as the Armstrong Siddeley Star Sapphire trim shop, and gas-turbine engine blade machining shops.

The original Rootes mock-up of the Alpine sports car, at this stage with a scollop in its rear tail fin, and looking rather bald without hoods over its headlamps.

One of the very first prototype Alpines, built in 1957/1958, with a proposed hardtop style which was eventually abandoned.

them up the road to Ryton for completion. There was actually a small overlap (in February and March 1962) when Alpines were being built at Ryton *and* at Bristol Siddeley.

The car-building facility at Parkside was rapidly dismantled, and aerospace work soon filled up the vacant space. In due course, Bristol Siddeley was merged with Rolls-Royce, and the Parkside complex became just one part of the Rolls-Royce aero-engines business. It is now used as a design centre, and the Burlington works is involved in many secret military projects.

Jensen and the Sunbeam Tiger

Jensen Motors, of West Bromwich, started life in the 1930s as a small coachbuilding concern. After the Second World War, the company expanded rapidly, not only by building more and more of its own Grand Touring cars, but by contracting to build large quantities of body/chassis assemblies for Austin and, later, BMC.

After producing the Austin A40 shell, and taking on a long-term commitment to build Austin-Healey bodies, in 1960 Jensen took on the job of assembling the new Volvo P1800

The body assembly shops for the Alpine were located at Bristol Siddeley from 1959 to 1962. Parts came in from Pressed Steel and Joseph Sankey.

Completed Alpines receive a final inspection at the Bristol Siddeley plant.

In September 1959 the Bristol Siddeley factory in Coventry was full of Rootes Alpines. Visible on the upturned car in the foreground is the extra cruciform bracing added to the basic Husky floorpan.

sports coupe for the Swedish company, starting from bodies provided by Pressed Steel at Linwood. A 70,000sq ft factory extension was erected to look after this work, for which build rates of 100 to 150 cars a week were forecast.

In 1963, however, Volvo grew tired of customer complaints about production quality, and took back P1800 assembly in-house in Gothenburg. The last Jensen-built Volvo coupe was produced in March 1963. Jensen historian Peter Browning later wrote:

'It was an amicable agreement, and Jensen was paid a considerable sum in compensation for the lost work, although it continued to supply components and make a number of small items for Volvo for a considerable period afterwards.'

The fact, however, was that Jensen suddenly had a large empty section of its factory for which it needed work as soon as possible. Some good, of course, usually comes after misfortune, and Rootes was delighted to find readily available factory space when the Tiger sports car project came to maturity in 1963. As engineer Peter Wilson once stated in an interview:

'At that time Rootes had neither the space nor the experienced manpower to take on the project, so it was decided to sub-contract the work to Jensen at West Bromwich. Several factors influenced this decision, possibly the most important being the experience the Jensen engineers had with prototype development work and their capacity for being able to produce the cars in sufficient number. Also, Kevin Beattie, who was Jensen's chief engineer, and his assistant, Mike Jones, had both worked for Rootes in the past so they knew our team and how we worked.'

By 1964, when the Tiger was due to go into production, Alpine bodies were being delivered to Ryton by Pressed Steel in the painted and trimmed condition. Starting in June, therefore, the same type of assemblies were supplied to West Bromwich, where Jensen carried out the necessary modifications and finished the assembly of the cars in what had been the Volvo shop.

The original Tiger was developed into the more specialized Mk 2, which went into production at the end of 1966. By this time, however, Chrysler was about to take complete control of Rootes, and as there was an obvious clash of interests because the Tiger was using a Ford engine, the continuation of the project was in doubt.

The last Tigers were built in June 1967, the last Alpines followed at the beginning of 1968, and plans to produce a new Chrysler-engined sports car came to nothing.

Since production of Austin-Healey 3000 body-chassis units at Jensen also ceased in the autumn of 1967, this left Jensen in considerable financial difficulties, and it was not until production of the large and prestigious Interceptors and FFs could be expanded that the company became stable once again.

Appendix C

Rootes model families

A summary of their production life

Even though Rootes built millions of cars, this was achieved with a very limited number of totally different designs. According to my definition, between 1931 (when the first Hillman Wizard was announced) and 1970 (when the last Rootes-designed car, the Hillman Avenger, was revealed), there were only 16 completely different model families. No fewer than seven of these were Hillman Minx types (I count the Super Minx and the Hunter in this way).

Here, for the record, is the list of those families, with start-up and close-down dates of the entire range of passenger car models in each case. I have defined each one by the first (or most important) model and mentioned the obvious derivatives.

Hillman Wizard: Announced in 1931, discontinued in 1935. Hillman 16hp and 20-70 models were descendants. This was the original Rootes Hillman.

Hillman Minx (original): Announced in 1931, discontinued in 1935. The Aero Minx, Talbot Ten and Sunbeam-Talbot Ten were all descendants; the Sunbeam-Talbot 2-Litre was a derivative of the Sunbeam-Talbot Ten. This was the first-ever Minx, which founded the dynasty.

Hillman Minx (second type, Magnificent): Announced in 1935, discontinued in 1939. Still with a separate chassis, but different in almost every way.

Hillman Minx Phase I (monocoque) family: Introduced in 1939, discontinued in 1948. The trendsetting monocoque type.

Hillman Minx Phase III (Loewy-style) family: Introduced 1948, discontinued 1957. Included Hillman Husky (original type). The first of the mass-produced American-influenced Rootes cars.

Hillman Minx Series family: Introduced 1955, discontinued 1967. Also included second-generation Husky, Singer Gazelle, Sunbeam Rapier, plus Sunbeam Alpine (1959–68 type) and Tiger sports cars. The very versatile Minx which underpinned Rootes for 10 years.

Hillman Super Minx family: Introduced 1961, discontinued 1967. Also included Singer Vogue, Humber Sceptre of 1963-67 type and Sunbeam Venezia. Should have been a Minx, pure and simple, but ran in parallel with the previous type.

Hillman Imp family: Introduced 1963, discontinued 1976. Also included Hillman Husky, Californian, Singer Chamois and Sunbeam Imp Sport/Stiletto. The rear-engined project which helped bring Rootes to its knees.

Hillman Hunter Arrow family: Introduced 1966, discontinued 1985. Also included new-model Minx, Singer Gazelle, Singer Vogue, Sunbeam Rapier and Sunbeam Alpine. The rationalized successor to Minx and Super Minx families, which was built for Iran (in kit form) for years after the British-market Hunter died in 1979.

Hillman Avenger family: Introduced 1970, discontinued 1981. Included Chrysler/Talbot Avenger, Chrysler/Talbot Sunbeam, Talbot Sunbeam-Lotus and Brazilian/Argentinian Avenger derivatives. Schemed out by Rootes, but tooled and manufactured under Chrysler ownership.

Humber 12hp: Introduced 1932, discontinued 1937. The first Rootes Humber, the car which introduced the medium-sized four-cylinder engine which ran in cars until 1967.

Humber 16/60 and 25/80 family: Introduced 1933, discontinued 1935. Only built for two years, but a replacement for the pre-Rootes Humber 16/50 model.

Humber Evenkeel family: Introduced 1935, discontinued 1954. Included Hillman 16hp, Hawk 20, 80, Hillman 14hp, Humber Pullman, Sunbeam-Talbot 3-Litre/4-Litre and postwar Hawk, Snipe, Super Snipe, Pullman and Imperial models. All cars used the same type of transverse-leaf-spring Evenkeel independent front suspension.

Humber Hawk Mark family/Super Snipe family: Introduced 1948, discontinued 1957. Different wheelbases, different engines, but the same design family. The Super Snipe did not arrive until 1952.

Humber Hawk/Super Snipe/Imperial (monocoque) family: Introduced 1957, discontinued 1967. The '4–6' model, with different engines, but the same hull. The last of the big Humbers.

Sunbeam-Talbot 90 family: Introduced 1948, discontinued 1957. Also included 80 model, Sunbeam (-Talbot) Alpine sports car and Sunbeam Mk III. Originally distantly related to the Sunbeam-Talbot 2-Litre.

Some real engineering, some 'badge engineering' and some astute marketing enabled the Rootes Group to put a diverse range of cars before the public on the basis of just a few 'building blocks'. These sporty Sunbeams, Series IV Rapiers and Series III Alpines, on display at an early 1960s Earls Court Motor Show, were more or less closely related to the much more mundane Hillman MInx of the period.

Sunbeam-Talbot 90 family: most of the immediately postwar Sunbeam-Talbot/ Sunbeam range were four-door saloons (this is a 90 from 1948) . . .

. . . but Thrupp & Maberly also built thousands of two-door, four-seater drophead coupes, in this case the late Sunbeam Mk III version, and . . .

. . . a limited number were also built as two-door, two-seater Alpine roadsters (Stirling Moss on the Alpine Rally).

From 1948 to 1957 British Light Steel Pressings Ltd built one basic bodyshell to suit the four-cylinder Humber Hawk seen here and the longer-wheelbase six-cylinder Super Snipe.

Like most postwar Rootes saloons, the Hawk was also made available in estate car form later in the run.

Hillman Minx Series family: apart from providing facelifts almost every year, there were many ways of stirring the pot to get the best out of the 1955–1967 Audax range. The four-door saloon, in Hillman or Singer form, like this 1961 Gazelle, was the mainstay . . .

. . . while a five-door estate car was provided for the Singer and Hillman marques, and there was a two-door four-seater convertible produced with Hillman, Singer or Sunbeam badges, grilles and mechanical variations.

The two-door four-seater hardtop, effectively based on the convertible structure, was produced only in Sunbeam form, as the Rapier, while the Hillman Husky and this van version, the Commer Cob, was a short-wheelbase three-door derivative.

The short-wheelbase Husky underframe was the starting point for the two-seater Sunbeam Alpine of 1959–1968, with Rapier running gear.

From 1964 the four-cylinder Alpine had its fins shorn, and soon there was also this V8-engined version, called the Tiger, assembled for Rootes by Jensen in West Bromwich. By this time the relationship to the original Minx saloon was getting distant, but it was still there!

Hillman Imp family: most numerous of the rear-engined Apex models was the Hillman Imp saloon. Clockwise from below, the sports saloons had twin carbs and were badged as Singers or Sunbeams, some with two, some with four headlamps. The coupe was variously badged, starting as the Hillman Californian: with sport engine and twin headlamps it became the Sunbeam Stiletto. There was also a Husky estate version (and Cob van) with its own roof and rear-end panels.

Hillman Super Minx family: developed as a Minx replacement but then produced alongside the smaller model, the base car from which several early 1960s models were developed was the Hillman Super Minx of 1961 . . .

. . . though marketing reasons dictated that the Singer Vogue, with its different nose style, was actually announced first. Estate car versions, both Hillman and Singer followed.

As with the Minx, there was also a convertible Super Minx, though in this case it remained a Hillman-only model.

The Sunbeam Venezia Superleggera of 1963 might look unique, but in fact it was built on the same underpan and running gear as the Humber Sceptre, which was itself a derivative of the Hillman Super Minx.

Hillman Hunter Arrow family. The starting point for this range was the four-door Hillman Hunter saloon first seen in 1966. Over the next 13 years it appeared with a number of different grille and headlamp arrangements: this GL model dates from late 1974.

The estate car version of the Hunter sometimes had circular headlamps, sometimes rectangular ones. There were Singer Vogue and Humber Sceptre estates with this bodyshell too.

The two-door fastback coupe Sunbeam Rapier had the same floorpan, basic running gear and suspension, but more horsepower and a completely different superstructure. The Rapier H120, distinguished by side stripes and a boot-lid spoiler, had a further uprated engine and different wheels.

The permutations of marque badges, trim levels and equipment in the Arrow range were even more numerous than with the earlier MInx-based cars. This Sceptre for export has Sunbeam badges: for the home market it would have been a Humber.

ROOTES: THE MINX FAMILIES

Year introduced (I) and discontinued (D)

Model/Range	1932	1933	1934	1935	1936	1937	1938	1939	1940	1941	1942	1943	1944	1945	1946	1947	1948	1949	1950	1951	1952	1953	1954	1955	1956	1957
Hillman Minx (original)	I			D																						
Hillman Minx 'Magnificent'				I				D																		
Hillman Minx monocoque								I									D									
Hillman Minx (postwar)																	I									D
Hillman Husky																							I			D
Audax range																										
Hillman Minx I-VI																									I	
Hillman Husky I-III																										
Singer Gazelle I-VI																									I	
Sunbeam Rapier I-V																								I		
Sunbeam Alpine I-V																										
Sunbeam Tiger																										
Super Minx family																										
Hillman Super Minx I-IV																										
Humber Sceptre I-II																										
Singer Vogue I-IV																										
Sunbeam Venezia																										
Arrow family																										
Hillman Hunter																										
Hillman Minx																										
Singer (Sunbeam) Vogue																										
Singer Gazelle																										
Humber Sceptre																										
Sunbeam Rapier																										
Sunbeam H120																										
Sunbeam Alpine																										

1958	1959	1960	1961	1962	1963	1964	1965	1966	1967	1968	1969	1970	1971	1972	1973	1974	1975	1976	1977	*Comments*
																				First 'Full Width' style Hillman.
—	—	—	—	—	—	—	—	—	D											Hillman Minx was 'donor' car to all other types.
I	—	—	—	—	—	—	D													
—	—	—	—	—	—	—	—	—	D											
—	—	—	—	—	—	—	—	—	D											
	I	—	—	—	—	—	—	—	—	D										
						I	—	—	D											
			I	—	—	—	—	—	D											Originally meant to be a replacement for the Audax type, but eventually built in parallel with it.
					I	—	—	—	D											
			I	—	—	—	—	D												
					I	—	D													
								I	—	—	—	—	—	—	—	—	—	—	D →	Arrow design replaced both the Audax and Super Minx shells.
									I	—	—	D								Built to 1979 as Chrysler Hunter, then to late 1980s as the Peykan for Iranian sale.
								I	—	—	—	D								
									I	—	—	D								
									I	—	—	—	—	—	—	—	—	D		
									I	—	—	—	—	—	—	—	—	D		
										I	—	—	—	—	—	—	—	D		
											I	—	—	—	—	—	D			

The Ginetta G21 was a limited-production sports coupe which used the 1,725cc Rapier-type engine in the late 1960s/early 1970s. Ginetta also used Hunter components in the GRS estate car and built a successful small sports car, the G15, using the Imp engine and rear suspension.

Other specialist sports cars using the Imp power unit included the Davrian and, seen here, the Clan Crusader, with a glassfibre monocoque bodyshell.

The Bond 875 three-wheeler also used the Imp engine and gearbox, and was made in saloon form as well as this Ranger van version.

Appendix D

Engine availability

Before, during and after the Rootes years

When the Rootes brothers built up the Rootes Group of car companies, they inherited a real mish-mash of products. The only way in which this Group could become an efficient General Motors type of operation was for it to be thoroughly and ruthlessly rationalized. This process had to include the different marques of cars and the light-duty Commer commercial vehicles.

This meant that the sheer quantity of different car models, engines and transmissions had to be pared down dramatically for the vast business to become respectably profitable. By the early 1930s, the process of merging Hillman with Humber was well under way, and in 1938 – only three years after Sunbeam and Talbot had been annexed – the process was complete.

Hillman and Humber engines available at merger time

Immediately after Hillman and Humber merged in 1928, the following passenger car engines were in use:

	Type	Layout	Used in these models
Hillman			
	Four-cylinder	sv, 1,954cc	Fourteen
	Straight-eight	ohv, 2,620cc	Straight-eight
Humber			
	Four-cylinder	oi/se, 1,057cc	9-28
	Six-cylinder	oi/se, 2,110cc	16-50
	Six-cylinder	oi/se, 3,075cc	20-65

Not one of these units was to be an important building block in Rootes' master plan for the mid-1930s.

The four-cylinder Hillman engine had side valves, and was at the end of a long and successful run, having an ancestry stretching back to 1913, including direct links with the Hillman 11hp model of 1919. It was overdue for retirement and would disappear in 1930.

The overhead-valve straight-eight Hillman engine was launched in October 1928, immediately before the Hillman-Humber merger was announced. Historian Michael Sedgwick described it as 'a complete lemon....It had a reputation, well substantiated, for bearing failure....' It was *not* destined for long life – the last model, the Vortic, being dropped in 1932.

Each of the current Humber engines had overhead inlet and side exhaust valves – a tentative, halfway step to modernity which Humber had embraced in the early 1920s. The sweet little 9-28 unit was derived from the original 8-18 of 1922 and was dropped in 1930.

The six-cylinder 16-50 (2,110cc) and 20-65 (3,075cc) engines were of different types, for the 16-50 unit was brand-new (launched in September 1928), with a combined cylinder block and crankcase, while the 20-65 had a cast-iron block and a separate aluminium crankcase and was a development of that originally introduced in 1926. Both had seven crankshaft main bearings.

The new 16-50 type would be produced until 1933, while the old 20-65 type lived on until 1935, also being enlarged to 3,498cc for the 25-70 introduced in 1929. This engine was fitted to early Snipes and Pullmans and was also used in Commer commercial vehicles of the period.

In 1932, the first price-cutting piece of rationalization took place. The 3,498cc engine previously fitted to Snipes and Pullmans was redesigned. The vintage-style overhead inlet/side exhaust layout was abandoned and a new cylinder block and head gave the unit simple side-valve operation. This might have looked like a retrograde step, but peak power actually rose from 72bhp to 77bhp.

This engine did a good job for Rootes for the next three years, when it was finally displaced by the familiar side-valve 'six' which was to be built until the 1950s.

Sunbeam and Talbot engines available at merger time

None of the engines being used in Sunbeam and Talbot cars at the time of their absorption by Rootes in 1935 figured in the Group's plans for the future, so this is a very simple part of the overall story. For the record, however:

Sunbeam was building a relatively new four-cylinder overhead-valve 1,627cc engine to power the Dawn model, along with several versions of the long-established overhead-valve 'six' (2,762cc, 2,916cc and 3,317cc), which had made its bow in the mid-1920s. All Sunbeam production at Wolverhampton was closed down in 1935 and no trace of that company's engineering ever resurfaced in Rootes Group ownership. A magnificent prototype eight-cylinder engine of 4,500cc, designed for Rootes by Talbot's Georges Roesch in 1936, was lost soon after it had been unveiled when the Sunbeam Thirty project was abandoned. Clement-Talbot Ltd was concentrating on several variations of the famous Georges Roesch overhead-valve 'six', which had been introduced in 1926 and was still being improved. For 1935, there were 1,666cc, 2,276cc, 2,970cc and 3,377cc types, respectively powering the 65, 75, 95, 105 and 3½-litre models. These engines (and the cars) carried on, becoming progressively more 'Humberized', until 1937–38, when the Sunbeam-Talbot marque was invented.

Singer engines available at merger time

When Rootes took over Singer at the end of 1955, the Birmingham-based company was building only one engine family, the 1,497cc overhead-camshaft type. The twin-cam version of this design (redesigned and redeveloped from an H.R.G. layout) was only in pilot production.

Singer's 1½-litre overhead-camshaft four-cylinder design was effectively all-new in 1947 when previewed for the SM1500 saloon, for although there had been another 1½-litre Singer 'four' (introduced for the 1938 Super 12), this was different in many ways.

At first it was a 1,506cc unit, but this was reduced to 1,497cc (with a slightly shorter stroke) in 1951, the size remaining unchanged until it was discontinued in 1958. At takeover time it produced 48bhp (single-carb), 58bhp (optional twin-carb form), or 75bhp (stillborn twin-cam form).

More for sentiment than for practical reasons, Rootes used this engine (but not its matching gearbox) in the first Rootes Singers – the Gazelle I of 1956-57 and the Gazelle II of 1957–58. In its final form it produced 49bhp. It was replaced by the standard Hillman Minx type of engine in the spring of 1958.

The true Rootes engines

Whatever the traditionalists might say, Rootes got its forward planning and approach to producing 'model cocktails' exactly right in the 1930s, and it was to carry this philosophy through into the postwar period.

The Rootes master plan, for which technical director Bernard 'B.B.' Winter takes a lot of credit, and for which engine design specialist Albert Booth (ex-Clyno Motors) was mainly responsible, was that the Group should develop three different engine families to power all its cars and light commercial vehicles:

A small-capacity four-cylinder engine
A medium-capacity four-cylinder engine
A large-capacity six-cylinder engine

Until the rear-engined Hillman Imp family came along in 1963, the Group never deviated from this master plan. The original trio of engines was designed, tooled-up and in production by 1936, all with side valves and simple cast-iron construction, and it was not until the late 1940s that completely new families of engines were developed to take their place. Even in the mid-1960s, the descendant of the medium-sized unit (as fitted to the Humber Hawk) was still being made.

At the beginning of the Rootes period, what looked like an aberration was a very important stepping-stone towards the future. In 1931, the Hillman Wizard was introduced with a choice of new side-valve six-cylinder engines of 2,110cc or 2,810cc, these being four-bearing units completely different from the Humber 16-50 or 20-65 layouts. The Wizard itself was only built for a couple of years, but it eventually donated its engine to the Hillman 20-70 and Humber 16/60 models. This Wizard engine was a direct ancestor of the definitive side-valve Humber 'six' of the late 1930s.

The three original corporate Rootes engine families designed for the 1930s, therefore, were as follows:

a) A small four-cylinder unit, introduced in 1931 for use in the Hillman Minx and cars derived from that design in later years. In the beginning it was of 1,185cc, but it was enlarged to 1,265cc in 1949 and was finally supplanted by a brand-new overhead-valve design in 1954; the last of all were produced in 1957.

Over the years this was to power vehicles as diverse as the Sunbeam-Talbot Ten and 80 and the small Commer commercial vehicles, and overhead-valve versions were also developed.

b) A medium-sized four-cylinder unit, introduced in 1932 for use in the Humber 12 and originally of 1,669cc. It was eventually used in cars such as the Hillman 14, the postwar Humber Hawk and the Sunbeam-Talbot 2-Litre and 90 models. As with the small 'four', its design was eventually converted from side valves to overhead valves.

c) From 1935, a large-capacity six-cylinder unit, the Dynamax, developed from the original Hillman Wizard design, took over as the prime-mover for Humber models and (in the late 1930s) in the Hillman 16, Hawk and 80 models.

Although it shared many basic dimensions with those of the superseded Hillman Wizard unit (the cylinder head gasket of an early-1950s 4.1-litre Super Snipe engine fits the block/head of a 1931 Wizard, which means that the same cylinder bore and holding down stud positions were retained for more than 20 years – a sure sign of commonized production machinery), it was a freshened-up design.

Humber Snipes, Super Snipes, Imperials and Pullmans all used this engine, which also powered thousands of Second World War staff cars, a few 'Humber' Talbots, and the large-engined Sunbeam-Talbots. It was also used in Commer vans of the period.

At this point I must acknowledge the achievement of Rootes and its production planners, who announced and started building *three* new families of quantity-production cars between spring 1931 and the beginning of 1933 – the Wizard being announced in May 1931, the Hillman Minx in October 1931 (though in production from March 1932) and the Humber 12 in October 1932 (with production beginning in spring 1933). That was an amazing feat, quite unmatched by any other British car-maker of the day.

The Minx engine

This all-new unit was revealed in the autumn of 1931 to power the Hillman Minx, though this car did not actually go on sale until March 1932. Like the Humber 12 engine which was to follow it just a few months later, it was a simple and rugged design and it was last used in a private car (the Hillman Husky) in 1957.

Like all the new Rootes family of engines, the Minx was simple, rugged and cheap to build. It had a one-piece cast-iron cylinder block and crankcase, with three crankshaft main bearings, side valves and a cast-iron cylinder head. At first, the big-end bearings were metalled direct to the connecting rods, but this feature would be converted to shells later in the life of the unit. Oil pressure was quoted at 20-25psi, and on the original cars there was a sidedraught Solex carburettor. The 'signature' identifying all engines in this family was the 95mm stroke.

Except that a different carburettor was used on some later models and an aluminium cylinder head was used on some later derivatives (Talbot Ten and Sunbeam-Talbot Ten), it was little changed over the years. Originally rated at 27bhp in 1948 for the new Minx, it was later rated at 35bhp and, in overhead-valve form for the Sunbeam-Talbot 80, at 47bhp. All in all, this was much the most numerous Rootes engine to be produced in the next 25 years:

Size	Bore and stroke	Comment
1,185cc	63 x 95mm (sv)	Original Hillman Minx type, also used in Talbot Ten/ Sunbeam-Talbot Ten
1,185cc	63 x 95mm (ohv)	Used only in Sunbeam-Talbot 80 of 1945-50
1,265cc	65 x 95mm (sv)	Used from late 1949 for Mk IV Minx. 37.5bhp and pump circulation of cooling water

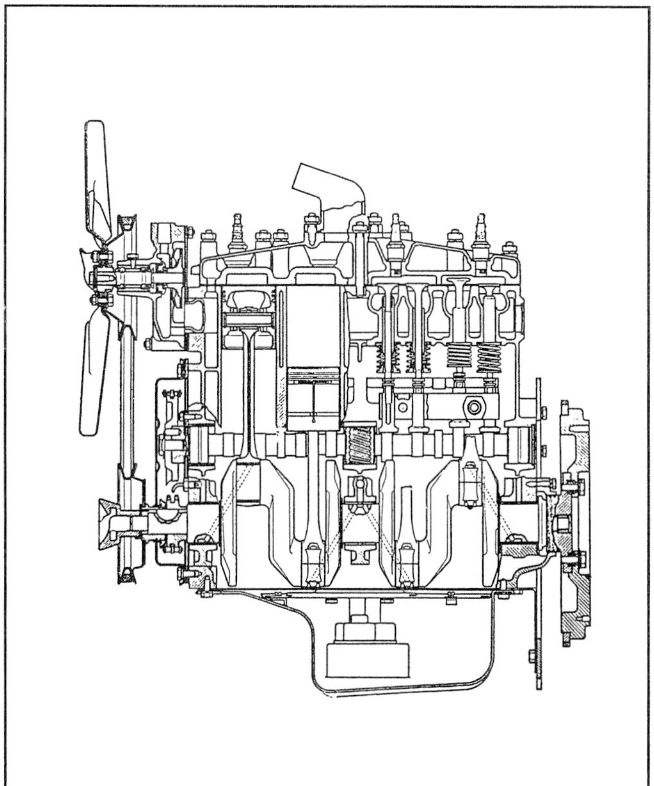

Section of the Minx side-valve engine: this is the postwar version with water pump.

The Humber 12/Humber Hawk engine

This all-new unit was first seen in autumn 1932 for use in the Humber 12hp range. At the time it was a 1,669cc unit, for which 42bhp was claimed. The design – or, more accurately, the descendants and developments of the design – had a phenomenally long life, for after growing to 1,944cc for use in the 1938 Hillman 14, it became a 2,267cc unit in postwar years, eventually being built as an overhead-valve unit. Not only was it used in the last of the large-medium Humbers (the 1967 Hawk Series IV), it was used for several more years in Commer light-duty commercial vehicles. The first 1,944cc units produced 51bhp, the last 2,267cc units 78bhp in Hawk form and 80bhp in Sunbeam Alpine guise.

In its basic design layout, the new 1,669cc engine was like that of the smaller Minx unit in that it was a simple four-cylinder with a three-main-bearing crank layout and a cast-iron block and cylinder head. It's 'signature' dimension was the 110mm stroke, which was unaltered in four decades of production. Like the smaller engine, it started life with a cast-iron head, though the postwar Sunbeam-Talbot 2-Litre had an aluminium cylinder head.

The first overhead-valve version came along in 1948 (Sunbeam-Talbot 90) and the Humber Hawk inherited this in 1954. Although the last such Sunbeam (the Talbot name having been dropped in 1954) was built in 1957, the Hawk continued until 1967.

Size	Bore and stroke	Comment
1,669cc	69.5 x 110mm (sv)	Originally for Humber 12
1,944cc	75 x 110mm (sv)	Originally for Hillman 14, then for postwar Humber Hawk and Sunbeam-Talbot 2-Litre
1,944cc	75 x 110mm (ohv)	For original Sunbeam-Talbot 90
2,267cc	81 x 110mm (sv)	Exclusively for Humber Hawk of 1950–54
2,267cc	81 x 110mm (ohv)	All Sunbeam-Talbots from 1950, all Hawks from 1954

The six-cylinder Dynamax Hillman/Humber engine

Originally launched in two sizes – 2,110cc/2,810cc – for the Hillman Wizard of 1931, this engine was used in many famous and distinguished Hillman and Humber models (including rugged four-wheel-drive Second World War staff cars and scout cars) until the early 1950s.

As with all such Rootes engines of the period, it was simply detailed, sturdy, easy to rebuild and (if properly maintained) very reliable. The base of the engine was a no-nonsense four-bearing combined crankcase and cylinder block, with side valves and a cast-iron head.

In its original form the 'signature' was a stroke of 106mm, but this was increased to 120mm in the autumn of 1935 when the unit was redesigned, rationalized and enlarged; thereafter that dimension remained unchanged. Original Wizard engines had a choice of 65mm and 75mm bore, but other dimensions were used later, the largest being the 85mm of the famous 4,086cc unit.

In the beginning, the engines fitted to Wizards were not given publicly quoted peak power ratings. By the time the 4,086cc derivative came along, in 1935, no less than 100bhp was claimed, this still being the rated figure when the last of this type was built in the early 1950s.

Many versions had an aluminium cylinder head (starting with the Humber 18 and Snipe/Pullman of the late 1930s and related Sunbeam-Talbots of 1938–39), though commercial types and some of the cars had cast-iron cylinder heads.

There was no overhead-valve version of this engine type.

Size	Bore and stroke (all with side valves)	Comment
2,110cc	65 x 106mm	Original for Hillman Wizard 65
2,276cc	67.5 x 106mm	For Humber 16/60 of 1932
2,576cc	67.5 x 120mm	From 1935 for Hillman 16
2,731cc	69.5 x 120mm	From 1935
2,810cc	75 x 106mm	Original for Hillman Wizard 75
3,181cc	75 x 120mm	From 1935
4,086cc	85 x 120mm	Definitive type used 1935–53

Postwar Rootes engine families

In the first postwar decade (1945 to 1955) Rootes worked out its modernization plans carefully. Although it was happy with the medium-sized Hawk/Sunbeam-Talbot engine, the company decided that it would need new small *and* large engines by the early 1950s. The result was the arrival of the new generation of small four-cylinder engines (first used in the Hillman Minx Mk VIII) in 1954, and the new large overhead-valve six-cylinder design (first passenger car usage in the Humber Super Snipe) in 1952.

Later still, the company produced yet another large-capacity 'six', the Armstrong Siddeley-based Super Snipe/Imperial engine, and in the early 1960s the Imp project saw an entirely new type of light-alloy 'four' put on sale.

Our production engines story really ends at that point, though it is also important to mention the completely new generation of small-medium 'fours' which was already being developed for the Avenger project when Chrysler took over the company, and the V6 engine project for the stillborn 1970s-style Humbers which was following closely behind.

Purely for convenience, I describe all these in ascending order of engine size, not in the order in which they were produced.

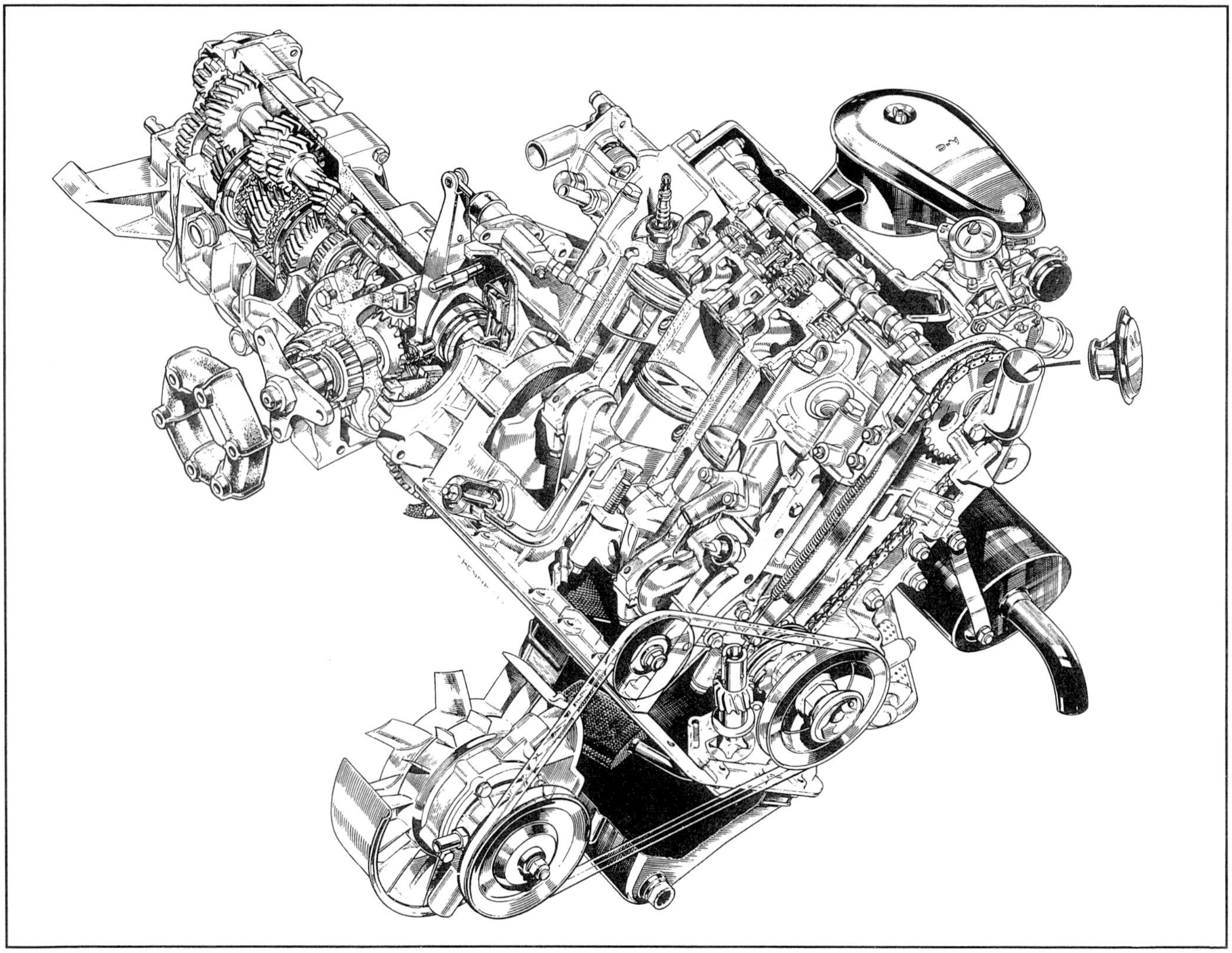

Power unit for the Hillman Imp was a light-alloy overhead-camshaft engine developed from a Coventry Climax design and mated to a new transaxle for rear mounting.

This twin-carburettor version of the Imp engine was used in the Sunbeam Imp Sport, the Stiletto and the Singer Chamois Sport.

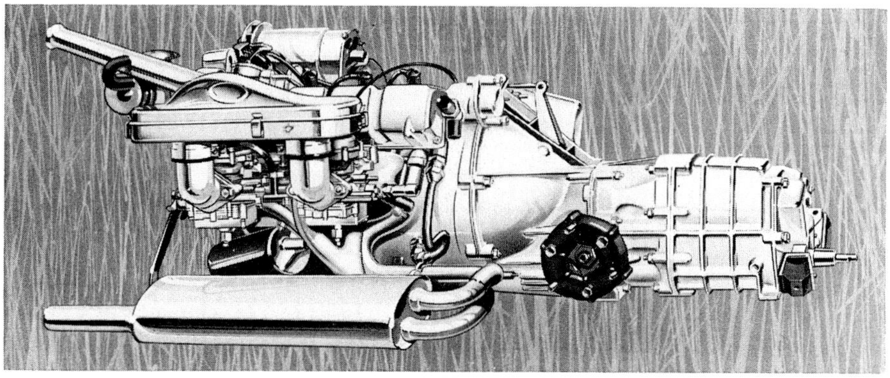

The Hillman Imp family

As it is clear from earlier chapters, the Hillman Imp and all its derivatives were new from end to end and used no common components from earlier Rootes cars.

The engine, in fact, was a much-redesigned version of the Coventry Climax FWMA, which itself was a development of a marine outboard design....

Coventry Climax Engines, with a design team led by Walter Hassan, produced a series of magnificent racing engines in the 1950s and 1960s, some of which started life as entirely different types. The FW (featherweight) series was one which started on water and finished in racing cars!

In the mid-1950s, the first type, the FWM (featherweight marine) of 653cc was built, this eventually growing to 745cc. At first it was a marine engine, but was later adopted for fire pump use. For 1958, Colin Chapman of Lotus persuaded Coventry Climax to produce a motor racing version of the engine, this being the FWMA type, which he used at Le Mans.

[Later still, Coventry Climax produced a twin-carb derivative which produced 83bhp, and from there it was but a short step to developing a V8 engine based on the same head, which of course was the legendary 1½-litre V8 FMWV Formula 1 engine of the 1961–66 period. Tenuously, therefore, you could say that the Hillman Imp engine was related to Formula 1 engines....]

Rootes originally took up the Coventry Climax FWMA engine design 'through the back door' when development engineer Mike Parkes (who was also an accomplished racing driver) bought one to power a small-car prototype. That car – 'Apex' – eventually grew up into the Hillman Imp and spawned a whole series of derivatives.

The racing/marine outboard heritage was almost completely lost when, with the agreement of Coventry Climax, the engine was substantially redesigned so that it could go into mass production. Along the way it was enlarged to 875cc, but the cylinder block dimensions were such that it was nearly impossible to enlarge it any further without spending a fortune in new tooling facilities.

Every Imp derivative had a rear-mounted engine, with the engine canted over 45 degrees to lower its overall height. The engines had a light-alloy block with bonded-in 'dry' cast-iron cylinder liners, light-alloy head and single-overhead-camshaft valve gear. Every quantity-production type measured 875cc, though a 998cc version was made available in small numbers in the Rallye Imp 'homologation specials'. Depending on the application, single or twin-carburettor installations were used, and engine power varied from 37bhp (DIN) to 50bhp (DIN).

Years after Rootes had disappeared, this engine was totally redeveloped, enlarged to 928cc, mounted vertically and used in the front-engined/rear-drive Chrysler Sunbeam hatchback. That car was built until 1981, being renamed Talbot Sunbeam along the way.

Size	Bore and stroke	Comment
875cc	68 x 60.35mm	As used for all Imp family derivatives
928cc	70 x 60.35mm	42bhp vertical engine used in Chrysler Sunbeam
998cc	72.5 x 60.35mm	Offered as conversion to produce Rallye Imp, badged as Hillman or Sunbeam

The Imp's engine was canted over at 45 degrees to reduce its height and lower the centre of gravity. Engine bay access was by no means ideal.

The overhead-valve Minx/Rapier/Arrow engine

The original side-valve Minx engine had been in production for more than 20 years before Rootes replaced it by an all-new design. This was the famous four-cylinder unit used in so many and varied Rootes models from 1954 on. Indeed, the final derivative of this design, the 1,725cc unit, was still being built in the early 1980s for the Peykan car, which was sold, in kits, by Peugeot-Talbot for assembly in Iran.

Rather than redesign the venerable 1930s-style side-valve Minx engine, Rootes started again and installed new machinery at the Stoke plant. The new engine, though still a sturdy cast-iron unit (head and block) with a three-main-bearing crankshaft, was altogether more squat and robust than before, and had overhead valves running in conventional bathtub combustion chambers. In its original form, it had a 'square' bore/stroke ratio – each being 76.2mm/3.0in – and a swept volume of 1,390cc. At first, there was a downdraught Zenith carburettor, but in the next 20 years a whole variety of vertical, horizontal, single and twin-choke instruments would be used. The final stretch, to 1,725cc, came in the autumn of 1965, when the stroke was lengthened and a five-bearing crankshaft rather than the original three-bearing unit was specified. The most sporty of all, as seen in the Chrysler-inspired Rapier H120 of 1968, was the 105bhp (DIN) 1,725cc version, which came complete with twin horizontal dual-choke Weber carburettors.

Size	Bore and stroke	Comment
1,390cc	76.2 x 76.2mm	Introduced in 1954
1,494cc	79 x 76.2mm	From 1958
1,592cc	81.5 x 76.2mm	From 1961
1,725cc	81.5 x 82.55mm	Long-stroke type with five crankshaft bearings, from 1965

The overhead-valve Minx engine first appeared in 1954 and it was produced, in more and more developed forms, until the early 1980s. This is an example of the original 1,390cc version, partially sectioned and much polished up for exhibition.

The Minx ohv engine was progressively increased in capacity, first to 1,494cc, then to 1,592cc. This a 1961 example, still with a single downdraught carburettor.

Above: for the Rapier and Sceptre from 1963, the engine had an aluminium alloy cylinder head and compound-choke carburettor. Above right: when fitted to the Arrow range the engine was canted over to provide more room for carburettors, as in this twin-Stromberg equipped Rapier . . .

. . . and the extra space was even more necessary in the Rapier H120 and Hunter GLS models, where two twin-choke Weber carbs were used to feed the Holbay-tuned unit.

The 1958–67 Super Snipe/Imperial six-cylinder engine

The final engine fitted to Super Snipes and Imperials between 1958 and 1967 was a clone of the Armstrong Siddeley Sapphire engine of the period.

There were straightforward commercial reasons for this – in the 1950s, Rootes wanted somewhere to develop and build the new Sunbeam Alpine sports car, and picked Armstrong Siddeley to use its Burlington works at the Parkside factory, in Coventry, for the purpose.

At the same time, Rootes needed a new engine for its next-generation Super Snipe, for the old Blue Riband six-cylinder unit was too heavy, too large and not efficient enough. The answer, fairly well camouflaged at the time, but very obvious indeed when a side-by-side comparison was made, was to gain the rights to build a design around the layout of the Armstrong Siddeley engine, which had been revealed in 1953.

In those days, British motoring magazines went to great lengths to be discreet, so the most that *The Autocar* could bring itself to do was to show cross-sections of the two engines, side by side, with a caption stating: 'There is a striking similarity in the conception of the Humber Snipe and Armstrong Siddeley Sapphire engines, each of which has a single side camshaft and opposed valves in hemispherical combustion chambers.'

The new Rootes engine, like the Sapphire unit, had 'square' bore and stroke dimensions at first – 82.55 x 82.55mm, giving 2,651cc – and featured a cast-iron cylinder block with four main bearings, and with a high-mounted side camshaft. The cylinder head had part-spherical combustion chambers, with the lines of valves opposed at 63 degrees, operation being via two lines of rocker shafts and (in the case of the inlet valves) by the use of reversed rockers.

At first, the nominal peak power output was 105bhp at 5,000rpm. However, only a year after it had been launched, the engine was enlarged to 2,965cc, with a larger cylinder bore, and peak power rose to 121bhp at 4,800rpm. A little more power was squeezed out in the years which followed (124bhp from late 1962, 128.5bhp from late 1964), but there were no other major changes.

Size	Bore and stroke	Comment
2,651cc	82.55 x 82.55mm	Announced in 1958, built for one year
2,965cc	87.3 x 82.55mm	Announced in 1959, built until 1967

The overhead-valve Blue Riband 'six', Super Snipe variety

As with the Minx engine, Rootes decided to replace the big side-valve 'six' by a completely up-to-date, overhead-valve design after the end of the Second World War.

Surprisingly enough, this was first used in Commer commercial vehicle chassis rather than in a private car. First used in 1948 in the Commer Superpoise van, it was a lay-down design, with a bore and stroke of 95.2 x 111.1mm and a swept volume of 4,750cc.

This, of course, was too large for use in Rootes private cars, so for launch in 1952 in the Super Snipe family, its bore was slightly reduced to 88.9mm, its swept volume to 4,139cc, and it was mounted vertically. Except for the use of a different block to suit the different cylinder bores, the two engines were virtually identical.

The Blue Riband, as it was known, was a solid, heavy, cast-iron engine, with seven crankshaft main bearings, and was originally fitted with a downdraught Stromberg carburettor. In 1952, when new, it was rated at 113bhp, but a year later it was uprated to 116bhp, and from late 1955 it was modified once more to produce 122bhp.

Size	Bore and stroke	Comment
4,139cc	88.9 x 111.1mm	Introduced in 1952 for Super Snipe

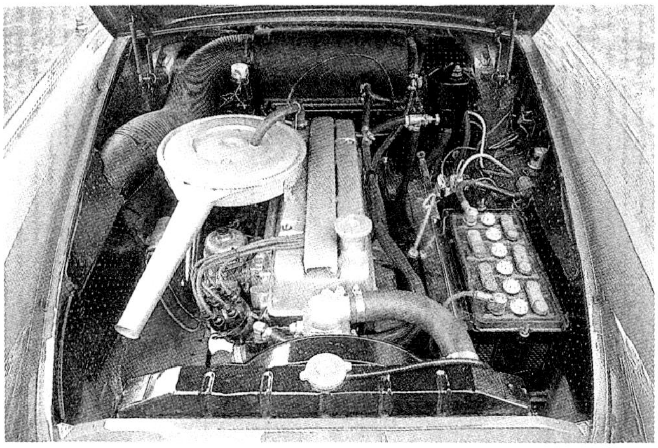

Aftermath – engines designed by Rootes under Chrysler control

Although they fall outside the scope of this book, two other families of engines should now be noted, for both were designed in the mid to late 1960s while the Rootes name still existed, but after Chrysler had taken complete control. One was the **Avenger** unit, which went on to have a long and illustrious career, and the other was the stillborn **Humber** V6 design. In Rootes project-speak, these were the B-Car and C-Car projects.

The Avenger – the B-Car – was one of those rare cars, all-new from stem to stern, featuring a new engine, gearbox and rear axle. The engine was a simple, reliable, but ultimately unexciting four-cylinder design, with a cast-iron cylinder block, cast-iron head, pushrod overhead valve gear and the ability to be 'stretched' from 1.25 litres all the way to 2 litres.

Initially it went into production in 1,248cc and 1,498cc guises, but soon it was slightly stretched to 1,295cc and 1,599cc. For production in Brazil and Argentina it was eventually pushed out to 1,799cc, though the so-called Brazilian 2-litre engine used by the works motorsport department was very much a 'homologation special'.

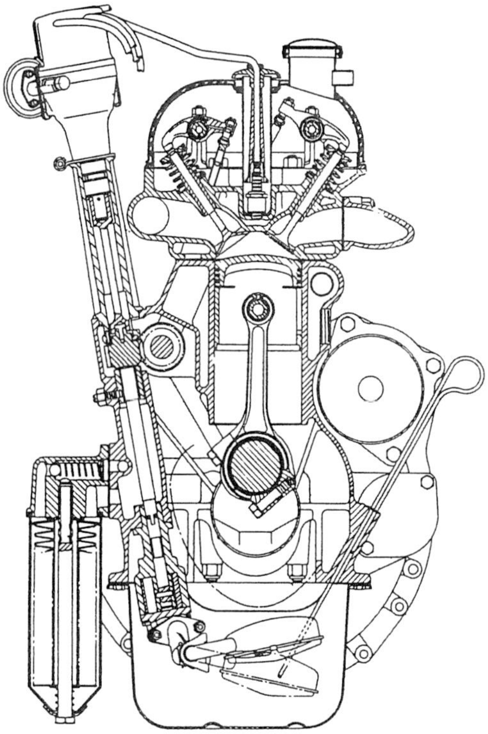

The new Humber six-cylinder engine introduced in 1958, and seen, left, under the bonnet of a 1966 Imperial, had close affinities with the contemporary Armstrong Siddeley design, above, sharing its twin-rocker-shaft head layout.

Display Super Snipe engine of 1958, coupled to a Borg-Warner automatic transmission, reveals the details of its Armstrong Siddeley-derived valve gear and combustion chamber design.

At one time, Rootes planned to fit various versions of the Minx/Hunter/Gazelle cars with this engine, but in the event, the only such marriage was with the final derivative of the 'kits for Iran' Peykans, where the conventional 1,599cc unit was used.

The most interesting series-production version of this engine was fitted to the Avenger Tiger and later to the Chrysler Sunbeam 1600ti, in which two twin-choke Weber carburettors helped the 1.6-litre engine to produce 100bhp.

There was also another 'homologation special' which did not live up to its promise. By 1968, Rootes had noticed the rapturous greeting given to the Ford Escort Twin-Cam, decided it could do just as well, and commissioned a 16-valve twin-cam engine from BRM, in Lincolnshire. This engine, always known as the Avenger-BRM unit, frankly never performed as well as hoped, and even in fully-stretched 2-litre form it was underpowered and no match for the various Ford Escort units. According to the homologation form, at least 100 Avenger-BRMs were produced, but in fact it is doubtful if more than a handful were ever completed.

Whereas the Avenger and its later-life derivative the Chrysler/Talbot Sunbeam had a long life, the C-Car had a more chequered history. In the late 1960s, when Chrysler was pushing for expansion and co-ordination with Simca, it encouraged the design of a big C-Car with an 8ft 9in wheelbase.

This was to be built both in France, as a Simca with a new four-cylinder engine, and at Ryton, as a Humber with a new British-designed V6 engine. By 1970, this cast-iron engine had been built in 2-litre and 2.5-litre prototype forms, and tooling was already being installed at Stoke, but the British end of the project was soon cancelled, the V6 engine died with it, and the C-Car was only ever built as a Chrysler, initially in France and later in Spain.

The author had the pleasure of driving a V6-engined Avenger on many occasions in 1969 and 1970 – a very fast car, for sure, but one in which a new meaning was brought to the word 'understeer'.

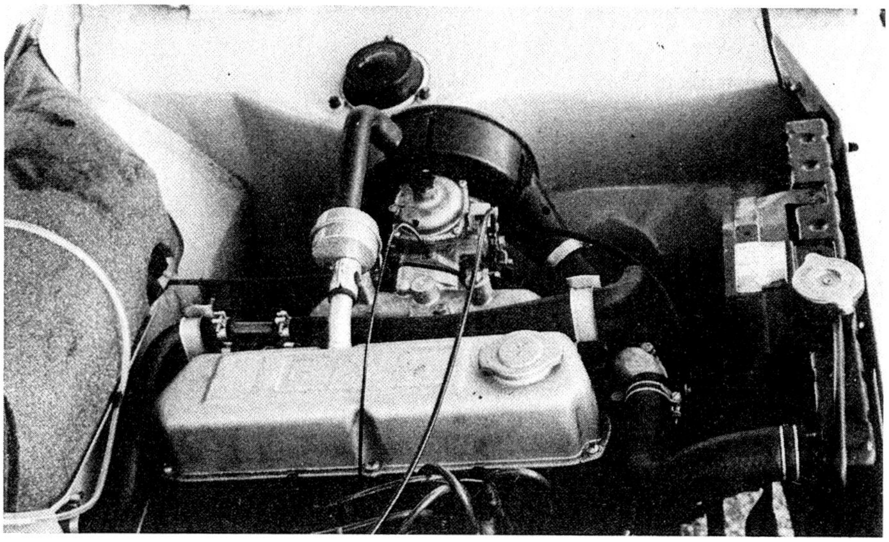

The Avenger's engine, first seen in 1970, was a very simple pushrod ohv unit. It was entirely new, owing nothing to previous Rootes designs.

ROOTES: PRINCIPAL ENGINE FAMILIES

Year introduced (I) and discontinued (D)

	1932	1933	1934	1935	1936	1937	1938	1939	1940	1941	1942	1943	1944	1945	1946	1947	1948	1949	1950	1951	1952	1953	1954	1955	1956	1957
Minx side-valve																										
Hillman Minx	I			D																						
Hillman Minx				I				D																		
Hillman Minx PI-II								I									D									
Hillman Minx PIII-VIII																	I							D		
Husky I																							I			D
Talbot 10				I			D																			
Sunbeam-Talbot 10							I										D									
Sunbeam-Talbot 80																	I		D							

Above: original Hillman Minx engine. 1,185cc at first, 1,265cc (with water pump added) from late 1949. Overhead valves on Sunbeam-Talbot 80, but side valves on all other types.

Below: Humber 12/Hawk engine. Side valves at first, overhead valves on Sunbeam-Talbots from 1948 and on Humbers from 1954.

	1932	1933	1934	1935	1936	1937	1938	1939	1940	1941	1942	1943	1944	1945	1946	1947	1948	1949	1950	1951	1952	1953	1954	1955	1956	1957
Humber 12/Hawk range																										
Humber 12 hp		I				D																				
Hillman 14 hp						I		D																		
Sunbeam-Talbot 2-litre								I									D									
Sunbeam-Talbot 90																	I						D			
Sunbeam MkIII																							I			D
Sunbeam (Talbot) Alpine																						I		D		
Humber Hawk MkI-II														I			D									
Humber Hawk MkIII-VI																	I									D
Humber Hawk SI-IV																										I

	1953	1954	1955	1956	1957	1958	1959	1960	1961	1962	1963	1964	1965	1966	1967	1968	1969	1970	1971	1972	1973	1974	1975	1976	1977
Minx ohv range																									
Hillman Minx PIII-VIII		I			D																				
Hillman Minx SI-VI				I											D										
Hillman Husky SI-III						I							D												
Hillman Super Minx MkI-IV									I						D										
Hillman Hunter														I											D
Hillman Arrow Minx															I			D							
Humber Sceptre MkI-II											I				D										
Humber Arrow Sceptre															I									D	
Singer Gazelle MkIIA-VI						I									D										
Singer Vogue I-IV									I					D											
Singer Arrow Vogue														I				D							
Singer Arrow Gazelle															I			D							
Sunbeam Rapier SI-SV			I												D										
Sunbeam Alpine I-V							I									D									
Sunbeam Venezia											I		D												
Sunbeam Arrow Rapier															I									D	
Sunbeam Rapier H120																I								D	
Sunbeam Arrow Alpine																	I						D		
Sunbeam Vogue																		Only							

1958	1959	1960	1961	1962	1963	1964	1965	1966	1967	1968
									D	

Above: Minx overhead-valve engine. Three-bearing crankshaft at first, five-bearing from 1965. Continued in Chrysler Hunter to 1979 and in Iranian-market Peykan until mid-1980s.

	1932	1933	1934	1935	1936	1937	1938	1939	1940	1941	1942	1943	1944	1945	1946	1947	1948	1949	1950	1951	1952	1953	1954	1955	1956
Humber Big Six range																									
Hillman Wizard		D																							
Hillman 16 and 20-70		I		D																					
Hillman 16/Hawk/80				I			D																		
Humber 18/Snipe/Imperial				I				D																	
Humber Pullman				I				D																	
Humber 16/Snipe						I		D																	
Humber Super Snipe							I	D																	
Humber Snipe/SS/MkIII														I							D				
Humber Pullman I-III														I								D			
Humber Imperial																		I				D			
Sunbeam-Talbot 3-litre (+ Talbot 3-litre)						I		D																	
Sunbeam-Talbot 4-litre							I	D																	

Above: Humber six-cylinder engine. Side-valve layout, all types. Replaced by all-new Blue Riband overhead-valve engine in 1953.

Below: Hillman Imp engine. Overhead camshaft. 875cc, 998cc in Rallye Imp. Also used in modified, front-mounted, 930cc form in Chrysler Sunbeam 1.0 hatchback, 1977-1981.

	1963	1964	1965	1966	1967	1968	1969	1970	1971	1972	1973	1974	1975	1976	1977
Imp range															
Hillman Imp	I													D	
Hillman Californian					I			D							
Hillman Husky					I			D							
Hillman Rallye Imp			I		D										
Singer Chamois		I						D							
Singer Chamois Sport				I				D							
Singer Chamois Coupé					I			D							
Sunbeam Imp Sport				I										D	
Sunbeam Stiletto					I						D				

Appendix E

Rootes production figures

The numbers tell the story

First of all an admission. I have not been able to unearth any detailed Rootes Group production figures covering the 1930s. Although these undoubtedly exist, in private records which have been withheld from me, there appears to be no public source.

On the other hand, I am extremely grateful to John Rowe (a top public relations executive at Rootes in the 1950s and 1960s) for providing accurate figures which cover the period beginning in 1949. These statistics, too, also provide the facts about Rootes' towering export achievements, many of which were made in the form of completely knocked down (CKD) kits to old Empire countries such as Australia, New Zealand and South Africa:

Approximations

Immediately after the Humber-Hillman merger in 1929, cars were built at the rate of 7,500/10,000 per year. The combine's UK production market share was about 4 to 5.5%, a low point on which it was to build in the next decade.

By the late 1930s, when Rootes had become one of Britain's Big Six car manufacturers and the Hillman Minx had become extremely popular, production reached approximately 50,000 cars per year. This represented a UK production share of approximately 16% – the highest ever achieved by the Rootes Group.

Detail production figures

It took time to convert the factories to civilian production immediately after the Second World War, but Rootes car production rapidly built up towards its prewar figure. Here are the accurate statistics which begin from 1949:

Note: Figures prior to 1960 cover the financial year (effectively the model-year) which ends on July 31 – i.e. the 1955 figure covers the period August 1, 1954 to July 31, 1955. From 1960 onwards (*) the figures cover calendar year achievements from January 1 to December 31 inclusive).

Year	Passenger cars produced	Home market	Export market	Share of British motor industry production (%)
1949	39,627	13,938	25,689	9.6
1950	66,262	17,231	49,031	12.7
1951	64,485	15,287	49,198	13.5
1952	56,848	13,048	43,800	12.7
1953	69,017	28,324	40,693	11.6
1954	84,643	39,757	44,886	11.0
1955	104,913	58,729	46,184	11.7
1956	93,516	51,465	42,051	13.2
1957	94,493	41,684	52,809	11.0
1958	120,798	54,584	66,214	11.5
1959	147,529	70,822	76,707	12.4
1960*	149,290	83,213	66,077	11.0
1961	100,337	67,249	33,088	10.0
1962	147,535	97,058	50,477	11.8
1963	177,646	128,973	48,673	11.0
1964	228,562	157,639	70,923	12.2
1965	172,361	121,640	50,721	9.7
1966	170,639	121,103	49,536	10.6
1967	184,243	134,113	50,130	12.1
1968	189,102	123,097	66,005	10.4
1969	172,647	85,589	87,058	10.0
1970	219,235	112,037	107,198	13.4

After the 1970 calendar year, Rootes ceased to exist as a separate entity and became part of the Chrysler Europe organization.

During the two decades covered by the above table, Rootes' share of production by the British motor industry changed very little, usually hovering around the 12% mark. Quite clearly, there was no overall increase following the launch of the Imp in 1963, and in the early 1970s the Avenger also had no lasting effect.

Warning: For the researcher/historian, offering the *exact* figures is almost impossible. Figures differing by several thousands a year have also been provided to me. Some, undoubtedly, refer to 'cars off the assembly lines', some to 'cars leaving the factory', others to 'cars transferred to the Sales Division'....

The above, therefore, are only provided on the 'best guess' basis.

Appendix F

Profits and losses

The financial story of the postwar years

The summary of Rootes profits and losses makes fascinating reading. Although clever accountants can make figures prove almost everything, there seems to be no doubt that Rootes (like BMC) was always a low-profit company. This made it difficult for the company to invest heavily in modernization and new models, and the result was that it struggled to stay in touch with more aggressive companies like Ford.

However, for most of this period, its share stood at about 10% of the British motor industry market, perhaps a quarter of that held by the BMC combine. Using profit/car as a comparison, therefore, BMC was always a more profitable and efficiently run concern than Rootes.

Purely as examples, in 1955, Rootes generated £360,000 for every 1% of its market share, while BMC generated £600,000. In 1960, Rootes generated £680,000 for each percentage point, while BMC generated £820,000. Is it any wonder that *both* companies eventually had to be taken over to ensure their survival?

[Note: Rootes must not be confused with Humber Ltd, for both companies issued sets of financial figures for many years. Humber Ltd did not merely build Humbers, but was actually the manufacturing subsidiary of the Rootes Group.]

Financial year ending July 31	Profit (or loss) in millions of pounds (pre-tax)	Comments
1945	£1.5	Last year of wartime activity
1946	(£0.4)	Includes disruption due to changeover to civiliar production
1947	£0.6	
1948	£1.2	
1949	£1.1	Includes introduction of all-postwar Minx, Humber and Sunbeam-Talbot models
1950	£2.8	
1951	£3.4	
1952	£3.4	
1953	£2.2	
1954	£3.6	
1955	£3.6	
1956	£1.7	Includes loss-making Singer company for first time
1957	(£0.6)	All UK car companies suffered at this time due to general credit squeeze and post-Suez depression
1958	£3.4	
1959	£3.9	
1960	£6.8	
1961	£0.9	Big spending on Linwood/Imp project had begun
1962	(£2.0)	Year of 13-week BLSP strike
1963	(£0.2)	Inauguration of Linwood plant and introduction of Imp
1964	£1.5	Chrysler took financial stake in June 1964
1965	(£2.5)	
1966	(£3.4)	
1967	(£10.8)	Chrysler took financial control in January 1967
1968	£3.7	
1969	£0.7	
1970	(£10.7)	Rootes Motors ceased to exist in June 1970, becoming Chrysler United Kingdom Ltd